Theory of
Commercial Policy

Theory of
Commercial Policy
Trade and Protection

MICHAEL MICHAELY
Hebrew University of Jerusalem

The University of Chicago Press

The University of Chicago Press, Chicago 60637

Philip Allan Publishers Ltd., Deddington, Oxf.

Published 1977

81 80 79 78 77 54321

Printed in Great Britain by The Camelot Press Ltd, Southampton

Library of Congress Cataloging in Publication Data
Michaely, Michael.
     Theory of commercial policy.

     Bibliography: p.
     Includes index.
       1. Tariff.   2.   Free trade and protection.
3.   Commercial policy.   I.   Title.
HF1713.M53   1977   382'.3   77-21657
ISBN 0-226-52285-7

Contents

Acknowledgments

This book was written mostly during my stretches of stay as Visiting Scholar at the Institute for International Economic Studies, University of Stockholm, in 1972 and 1973, with only minor revisions in subsequent years. For the pleasant and inspiring atmosphere at the Institute, and for my opportunity to enjoy it, I am grateful to the Institute's Director, Professor Assar Lindbeck; to its Associate Director, Dr Sven Grassman; and to the secretarial staff, headed by Mrs Birgitta Eliason, whose members provided generously their skilful assistance.

In the course of my work I have been able to draw continuously on the advice of my colleagues at the Institute. In particular, I should like to acknowledge helpful discussions with Brian Hindley, Ephraim Kleiman, and Per Wijkman.

I have been fortunate in having a draft of the study read by Jagdish Bhagwati, W. Max Corden, Assar Lindbeck, Bertil Ohlin, and John Spraos. Their searching criticism and constructive comments have been of the greatest benefit. For remaining flaws in the final product I am, of course, solely responsible.

MICHAEL MICHAELY

To Ora

1
Introduction

1 Scope and method

The subject matter of this book, as its title indicates, is the *theory* of commercial policy. Institutional, historical, descriptive or empirical aspects of the study of commercial policy will be overlooked, with only a few exceptions, although at several points the implications of the theory for empirical work will be obvious.

'Commercial policy' is a set of rules governing the use of available instruments in the government's regulation of the country's international trade. One set, or policy, is simply no interference in foreign trade—the 'free-trade' policy. When interference does take place, it could be handled through various policy instruments. In the greater part of the present discussion, the *tariff* will be assumed to be the instrument chosen for interference. Although many other instruments are commonly in use today, or have been in the past and are sure to reappear in the future, the confinement of most of the analysis to tariffs is not as restrictive as it may seem, since the effects of other instruments could most often be produced identically by the use of tariffs. In several important points in the analysis, however, where alternative policy instruments do differ from tariffs in some significant aspect of their impact, the contrast will be pointed out.

Tariffs may have several functions. One is the protection of a local industry with which imports compete; another is raising of revenue for the government; still another possible purpose is to change the country's balance of trade and, through it, the balance-of-payments position; and, finally, a tariff may be imposed for its effect on total employment in the economy. The subject matter of the present book is confined to the first function: it is a study of the protection aspect of tariffs. Macroeconomic aspects of the tariff will not be discussed. The economy in which commercial policy is contemplated will always be assumed to be in an initial position of full employment. Likewise, a balance-of-payments equilibrium and an equality of the values of exports and imports will be assumed throughout. Since a tariff, whatever its intention, does have an impact on the trade balance, it will always be assumed that counter measures, such as changes in the rate of foreign exchange, are taken to offset this impact and to keep the trade flow balanced. Similarly, a tariff (unless it is prohibitive) cannot fail to have a revenue-raising aspect, even if it is not introduced for this purpose; but this aspect will be overlooked, very often by the device of assuming all revenue to be redistributed among consumers rather than used for financing a government activity.

The study of commercial policy is conventionally described as the normative part of the pure theory of international trade; whereas the analysis of the determinants of patterns of trade and specialization forms the positive part. The classification into 'positive' and 'normative' is not entirely clear-cut. To explain what is 'good' or 'better'—a normative study—one would have first to know the impact of various acts, a knowledge which would probably be characterized as 'positive'; hence, no normative assertions could be provided without relying on some positive aspects of the theory, in which the consequences of various forces and changes are analyzed. The normative study of commercial policy is thus necessarily dependent on the propositions of the positive theory which explains the pattern of trade. Almost no specific, direct reference to this positive part of the theory of international trade will be made here; but a prior acquaintance with it will be assumed throughout.

Once the classification is accepted, most of the present study would definitely qualify as 'normative': it is addressed directly to the question of which policy is better, therefore preferable. The

borderline case, in this respect, is the analysis of effective protection in Chapter 4. Within the generally normative study of commercial policy, this is the positive part, where the question addressed to directly is not whether a policy is good, in relation to
another, but what is its impact on the pattern of specialization
and resource allocation and how it should be measured. But,
again, the justification of this supposedly positive study is the
service it may eventually render to the possibility of evaluating
the desirability of policies.

In the greater part of the analysis of this book—Chapter 4, on
effective protection, is again a major exception—the simplifying
device of assuming a world of two goods will be employed. One
of the consequences of adopting this assumption is the possibility of using relatively simple diagrammatic demonstrations of the
theoretical propositions. Indeed, the same basic technique,
which may probably be characterized as viewing the world from
a transformation curve, will be utilized throughout most of the
study.

In ranking policies as superior or inferior, an object of
reference must be specified: what is better for one may be worse
for another. This object may vary from a given individual, to a
group of individuals within a country, to the country as a whole,
a group of countries or, finally, the world as a whole. The results,
of course, may turn out to be radically different with each viewpoint. In most of the study, we shall adopt the viewpoint of the
whole of a *single* country: policies will be evaluated by their impact on the country whose government is the policy originator.
On a few occasions, some attention will be paid to other units
—part of the country's community on the one hand, and a group
of countries or the world as a whole on the other.

Given the viewpoint, a *yardstick* for the evaluation and
ranking of policies must be provided. We will say that one policy
is 'better' than another, therefore preferable, if it yields a higher
welfare to the community; and the 'best' policy is the one which
yields the highest welfare. But this is only slightly more than
changing the terminology. Before we proceed to the analysis of
our subject matter, we must carefully examine what it is that we
compare and how this is carried out. Since this welfare comparison will be repeated again and again here on many occasions, and in a sense is the cornerstone of a normative study of

the nature of the present one, it will be described here at some length.

2 Welfare comparisons for a community[1]

A device which is most commonly found in international trade theory in deriving both welfare and demand propositions is the community indifference curve. It is used in the same way as an individual's map of indifference curves would be used to derive welfare and demand propositions for the individual. The procedure is simple: if in the comparison of two situations, the community finds itself on a higher community indifference curve in one situation than in the other, the former situation represents a higher welfare level and is thus preferable.

This use of community indifference curves has long been known and recognized to be faulty. To be permitted, such use must assume either that the community consists of a single individual, in which case the 'community' indifference map is simply the individual's; or, alternatively, that all individuals are identical in each and every (economic) sense, such as in their tastes, their ownership of each productive factor, or the size and structure of their families (if, as usual, the economic 'individual' unit is taken to be the family). Both alternative assumptions are highly restrictive, enough to deprive an analysis based on them of much of its value.

Very often in the literature, the indifference curve analysis is carried out without even a hint of any problem which may be involved in applying this device to the community rather than to the individual. Sometimes an awareness of the problem is shown, but the matter is disposed of by a statement like 'we assume the necessary conditions for the existence of a community indifference curve'. On other occasions, authors are more careful, and specify precisely what these necessary conditions are. Recognizing the high degree of restrictiveness of these conditions, or assumptions, the use of community indifference curves is then justified by its convenience in handling the analysis. But welfare theory has equipped us sufficiently with simple tools to make the use of community indifference curves neither essential nor particularly convenient. Thus, in the pre-

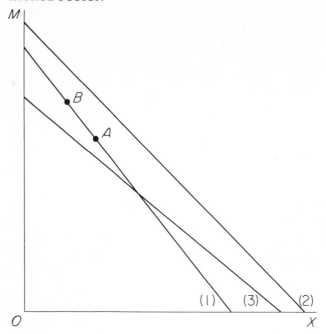

Figure I

sent book this construct will be totally absent. Instead, the principle of revealed preference will be employed. It is not only
superior, by Occam's rule, to the indifference curve analysis for
an individual (requiring fewer assumptions) but, more important, is adaptable for the analysis of the community without
requiring any additional assumptions, and thus avoids any
further restrictions on the analysis. We shall briefly recall the essence of this approach.

Figure 1 represents the situation of an individual who, with an
initial endowment of goods X and M, and facing a market
exchange ratio between the two goods designated by the slope of
line (1), could consume any combination of X and M represented
by line (1) which is the individual's budget restraint. Suppose
the individual is actually found to consume the basket
represented by point B. Having had the possibility of selecting
any other combination on (1), we shall infer that the individual

prefers B to any of the other alternatives; for him, combination B is 'better' than (or at least as good as)[2] any other possibility on (1).

Suppose now that the individual has moved to a situation in which his budget-restraint line is (2), representing another initial endowment and different market prices; and, as depicted in figure 1, the former budget-restraint line (1) is wholly bound within the new line (2). We know that this necessarily represents an improvement for the individual: on line (2) various combinations are available which represent more of both X and M than in B, and—by the assumption that goods are 'goods', hence more of each is better than less—are better than combination B. Since any of these combinations is an open possibility, the consumption basket actually selected by the individual is better than any such combination and thus better than B. This would have been true also had line (2) not been wholly above (1), as it is shown, but had (2) intersected (1) *above* combination B. It would be different, on the other hand, were the individual to move from (1) and B on it to a budget-restraint line such as (3), which intersects (1) *below B*. Here, the consumer would select some consumption combination on (3). Consumption basket B—and, *a fortiori*, any combination representing more of both goods—would no longer be an open possibility. On the other hand, the new consumption basket selected on (3) may not be an open possibility with budget-restraint line (1). Thus, with the information available, we would not be able to rank the welfare levels of the individual in the situations represented by budget-restraint lines (1) and (3).

We shall move now from the individual to a community of many. Suppose the community has an initial endowment of X and M represented by point A, distributed among the community's members in a given way. For each member of the community, thus for the community as a whole, the possibility exists of trading X for M, or vice versa, with members of other communities (call it 'with another country') at the exchange ratio represented by the slope of (1). Line (1) thus becomes a budget restraint for the community as a whole—any aggregate basket of the two goods, consumed by the community as a whole but *selected by individual actions*, will be somewhere on (1). Suppose we find the consumption basket to be actually the combination represented by B. Given the initial endowment of goods of every individual, B must then be the best combination. If it were not, at least some individuals would be wishing to shift to another combination; and since each is free to do so, at the given prices, these individuals would indeed move, and the consumption combination of the community would be not B but some other point on (1). Having in fact found the community at B, this means that no individual can improve his position.

For a community, moreover, we may even go a step further. Suppose a situation in which, as before, the community—by individual actions—trades with the 'outside world' from the initial position A to point B, its consumption combination. But this time there are no constant, given prices at which the outside world is willing to exchange with the community X for M and vice versa: the supply curve of the outside world, for each of these goods, is rising. Yet, each individual member of the community, being a very small unit in the market, feels that he could trade any amount of goods at a given, existing market price. Thus, for the community as a whole, with an initial endowment A, (1) is *not* a budget-restraint line, since trade could not take place with the outside world in *any* amount at the exchange ratio represented by (1). But in equilibrium this price, for the amount of trade represented by the vector AB, is in fact established. And since every individual feels free to exchange any further amount of X for M, or vice versa, at this existing price, and no individual chooses to do it, B is thus revealed to be preferable to any combination other than B on (imaginary) line (1)—just *as if* this line had actually been a budget restraint for the community as a whole.

Suppose now that the community moves to a situation in which its initial endowment and the prices in which it could trade with the outside world make line (2) its budget restraint; and we want to compare this with the former situation. The point selected on (2) must be preferable, given the initial endowments of each individual *in the new situation*, to any other possible combination on this budget-restraint line; and we know that a range exists, on this line, in which total consumption in the community would include more of both X and M than in the original position on (1). Since no assumption is made that the initial endowment of goods is distributed among the community's members in exactly the same way in the two alternative

situations—'income distribution', that is, has changed in the
shift from one situation to the other—we cannot necessarily infer that the position of each and every member of the community
has improved in the shift from (1) to (2). And since we do not
possess any cardinal measure of welfare, and cannot aggregate
the welfare of individuals, the deterioration of the welfare of a
single person would be sufficient to prevent us from making the
unequivocal statement that the 'community's welfare has improved'. All we can do is employ the 'compensation principle',
and derive propositions for 'potential' welfare, or welfare 'in the
situation sense'. Since in the economy as a whole we could have
in the new situation more of both X and M than in the old
one—and could always select such a position—we know that
those who gained from the shift *could* always compensate those
who lose, and still be left with an excess.[3] We should also note
that the opposite would not be possible, as may be easily seen. In
this 'potential' sense, and *only* in this, we may say that the community's welfare has increased in the shift from (1) to (2). Had
the shift been from (1) to (3) instead, we would not be able to
make a similar statement. Welfare levels of the community, even
in the potential sense, in the situations represented by budget-
restraint lines such as (1) (with consumption point B) and (3)
thus cannot be ranked, just as they cannot for the individual.

The criterion utilized for welfare comparisons may be further
clarified by the use of a diagrammatic construct developed by
Samuelson and employed by him and by Kemp for the purpose
on hand.[4] In figure 2, welfare levels of two individuals, I and II,
are represented, respectively, on the horizontal and vertical axes.
Welfare levels are measured only *ordinally*; that is, the further
the point is to the right ('east'), the higher is the welfare level of
I; and the further it is up ('north'), the higher the welfare level of
II. Distances thus have no meaning, but directions do. Any one
point may be selected arbitrarily, but other points have to be
related to it in a specific way—so far as directions are concerned. Thus, for instance, a position in which I is better off but
II is worse off than in the position whose two welfare levels are
represented by point A must be southeast of (to the right of and
down from) A. Or, for instance, if some point C is northeast of
A, it indicates a position in which both I and II enjoy higher
welfare levels than in the position represented by A.

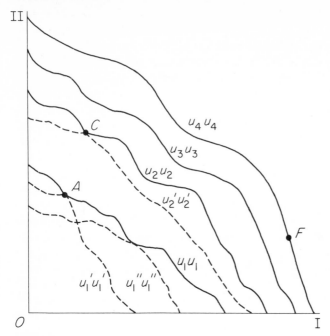

Figure 2

We shall assume that with any distribution of a bundle of goods between two individuals, welfare levels of the two are maximized by trading between them (at given prices) so that the marginal rates of substitution in consumption are equal for the two individuals. Any redistribution of this amount of goods between the two individuals—taking from one and giving to the other—would then necessarily raise the welfare of one and lower the other's. This will be represented by a downward-sloping curve, referring to this specific bundle of goods. Again, since measurement is only ordinal, only the fact that the curve falls from left to right has significance, whereas the actual slope is meaningless. Suppose A represents the welfare positions of one bundle of goods, distributed between the two individuals in a certain way. The curve $u_1' u_1'$—the 'utility possibility curve'—will represent the welfare positions when this bundle is redistributed from one person to another. Suppose now that C represents welfare positions with a *different* bundle of goods, including more of all goods (or at least more of some, and less of none). The curve $u_2'u_2'$ represents, in a similar way, the combinations of welfare levels reached with this new bundle of goods. Now, these two curves cannot intersect each other—$u_2'u_2'$ will be uniformly above $u_1'u_1'$: whatever the welfare level of one of the persons, with a larger bundle of goods, the welfare level of the other person will be higher than with a smaller bundle. When two bundles each containing more of some goods and less of others are compared this is no longer inevitable. Since tastes differ among individuals, with one income distribution (distribution of the bundle of goods) one bundle will be preferable to the other—that is, will show a higher welfare level of one person given the welfare level of the other; whereas with another income distribution, the opposite may be true. This will be represented by an intersection of the curves referring to each bundle—such as $u_1'u_1'$ and $u_2'u_2'$ in figure 2.

Take, now, $u_1'u_1'$ in figure 2 to represent the utility possibility curve of the bundle of goods A on budget-restraint line (1) in figure 1, and $u_1''u_1''$ the utility possibility curve of another bundle of goods on the same budget-restraint line. Similarly, a whole group of such curves could be constructed, each representing the utility possibility of another possible bundle on (1), variously distributed between individuals I and II. The curve u_1u_1, called the 'utility frontier', is the envelope of this family of curves. It does not refer to a *specific bundle* of goods, but to a specific *situation*—to a whole series of bundles possible under the given budget restraint: it shows the highest combinations of welfare levels (of the two individuals) which could be attained with this budget restraint.

In the same way, curve u_2u_2 is the utility envelope frontier of the situation represented by budget-restraint line (2) in figure 1. Just as $u_1'u_1'$ and $u_2'u_2'$ could not intersect, so cannot u_1u_1 and u_2u_2: the latter is uniformly above the former. Whatever the bundle of goods to which a point on u_1u_1 refers, there is always a possible point containing more of both goods, thus making possible a higher welfare for both individuals, on budget-restraint line (2) of which u_2u_2 is the utility frontier. It is in this sense that budget-restraint line (2) represents a higher level of community welfare than budget-restraint (1). Whatever the distribution of goods among individuals I and II with budget-restraint line (1) and utility frontier u_1u_1, both individuals could be made better off, if compensation is carried out, with budget-restraint (2) and utility frontier u_2u_2. This is the welfare criterion which will be used to rank policies.

Suppose, however, that ideal compensation—or any compensation—does *not* take place. It is then possible that although everybody *could* be made better off in one situation, compared with another, some in fact are worse off. In terms of figure 2, suppose one position is A, on u_1u_1, and the other position is F, on the higher utility frontier u_4u_4. I is better off in position F, but II is worse off. What inference could now be made about welfare comparisons of the two positions?

Three alternative answers are possible. One is to say that we just cannot make any welfare ranking of the two positions, since individuals' welfare levels are neither cardinally measurable nor additive. If this approach is adopted, very little remains of all normative aspects of economics: it will be rare, indeed, to find comparisons of situations where it is certain that, either because no compensation is required or because ideal compensations are assured, everybody is in fact better off in one position than in the other. Another possibility, which has been adopted here, is simply to disregard *actual* welfare, and look only at *potential* welfare—that is, to keep analyzing welfare only in the situation sense. This answer avoids the comparison of F with A, and compares just u_4u_4 with u_1u_1: one situation is better than another not because everyone is better off (which is probably not true, and at least not known) but because everyone *could* be made better off, by a proper redistribution of income. The third possibility is to rank F with A by the use of values, or norms, which are the property of the individual making the evaluation—norms about personal or functional income distribution which are contained in this individual's social welfare function. By this criterion it may appear, for instance, that although u_4u_4 is superior to u_1u_1, A is superior to F because person II is relatively poor, and whatever the gain of welfare to I (the rich), it will not offset any welfare loss of II (the poor). Or that, similarly, A is preferable to F because II derives his income from agriculture and I from manufacturing, and a high farm income is an important value by itself, as seen by the 'judge'; and so on. A response along this line would necessarily focus the analysis not only (and perhaps, for some, not at all) on the effect of trade on potential welfare but on the effect on persons, or groups of persons, to whose welfare a particularly high value is attached.

Notes

1 A full presentation of welfare theory is neither necessary on this occasion, assuming familiarity with its basic foundations, nor of course could it be made adequately in the present context. Thus, no survey of welfare literature is intended here, nor will references be suggested. It may only be mentioned that the geometric technique used here for welfare comparisons has been adopted for international trade analyses mainly in the papers of P. A. Samuelson (1962), who is of course the originator of much of the modern welfare theory and of the revealed-preference approach, and of M. C. Kemp (1962).

2 For shorthand, we shall always when saying 'better' include in it the limiting possibility of 'at least as good as'.

3 It should be noted, though, that had compensation been actually carried out, the consumption basket selected on (2), by the actions of the individual community members, would be different from the consumption point selected without compensation.

4 The discussion of this tool in the present context will be brief. For fuller exposition, the original works (P. A. Samuelson, 1962 and M. C. Kemp, 1962) as well as R. Findlay (1970) may be consulted.

2

Free Trade and Restricted Trade

1 The basic argument for free trade

Under certain conditions, free trade is the best commercial policy. It would be convenient to start by stating these conditions, and show why and in what sense free trade is then the best policy. As has been stated, we will look at the issue from the viewpoint of a single country, adding only at the end of the chapter the consideration of commercial policy from the viewpoint of the world as a whole.

Take, as is conventionally done in the pure theory of international trade, a world of two goods—X and M. PQ in figure 3 is the transformation (production possibility) curve, showing the maximum combinations of the two goods which may be produced in the country under consideration by use of the production factors with which it is endowed. The transformation curve is presented here (as in most economic analyses) as convex from the origin. Two attributes of the production functions would be sufficient (though not necessary) to ensure this convexity: constant returns to scale exist in the production of both goods; and factor intensities vary among the two goods.

By definition, the economy cannot produce combinations of goods X and M which are beyond the transformation curve PQ. It is not logically inevitable, however, that the economy will be *on PQ*: it could be found to produce combinations of goods which are *within* the area bounded by the transformation curve.

13

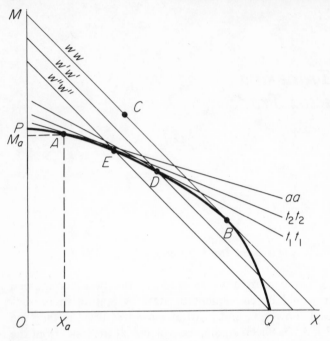

Figure 3

To be on the latter, the economy must fulfil two conditions: substitution ratios among production factors are equal in the production of both goods; and all factors are fully employed. We shall assume indeed that these conditions are maintained, and production is carried out at some point on the transformation curve. We shall also assume that transformation ratios among goods are equal in production and consumption. The fulfilment of all these conditions will be achieved when the economy is in perfect competitive equilibrium.

When no trade with the outside world is possible, the economy will be found at point A, with quantity M_a of M and X_a of X; without trade this is, by definition, the locus of consumption as well as of production. The marginal transformation ratio in production is indicated by the exchange line aa: this represents the price ratio of the two goods, faced by both producers and consumers.[1] We now open the country to the possibility of trade, which is assumed to be free of any restrictions. The country finds that it can trade with the outside world at an exchange ratio which differs from that (aa) maintained in the economy without trade; we shall assume that this price in trade—the 'foreign' or 'world' price—is *fixed*, the trade of the country in question having no influence on it.[2] This is known as the 'small country' assumption. The exchange ratio in trade is indicated by the line ww: M is cheaper and X is dearer abroad. In competitive equilibrium, this must also be the domestic exchange ratio. Producers would then be in equilibrium in producing combination B, at which the marginal transformation ratio in production is equal to the exchange ratio.[3] With trade, however, B will not be the consumption locus: the economy will sell some of the X which it is producing in exchange for some of M, at the given world exchange ratio. Consumption will hence be at some point on ww—such as, for instance, C—left of production point B.

It may now be stated that, *in a situation sense*, the new (free trade) position is better than the old (autarky) position. The two necessary conditions for such assertion exist, namely: those who benefit in the move from the autarky to the free trade position may compensate ('bribe') those who lose, and be themselves at least as well off; whereas, those who gain in the opposite move cannot compensate those who lose and remain as well off. This is self-evident if the free trade position is a point like C, where more of both goods is available to the economy than in the autarky position A. But it must be remembered that in free trade the economy could always be at a point like C. If it is not, the community is evidently at least as well off as at C, since any consumer so willing is free to move, by trade, towards C. Thus, if compensation were applied, everybody would be at least as well off in trade, and some better off, than in the autarky position. This may be summarized by stating that A, the autarky position, is *within* the area bounded by ww, which is the economy's consumption possibility (budget-restraint) curve with free trade.

Suppose the government interferes in the trade process by levying a tariff, at the rate t_1, on the purchase of imports. The home price of M, which includes the tariff, is higher than the world price. The new home exchange line is t_1t_1 in figure 3. At this exchange ratio, producers will be in equilibrium when production is at D. Once more, with trade, this is not the consumption locus: X will be sold and M bought, so that consumption will be to the left of D. But trade with the outside world—the exchange of X for M—is conducted at the *world* exchange ratio, ww. Hence, the consumption locus will be to the left of D on the line $w'w'$, which is parallel to ww, representing the world exchange ratio. It will be immediately apparent that any such consumption locus is inferior, in a situation sense, to the consumption possibilities available to the economy with free trade: the trade-restricted consumption-possibility line, $w'w'$, is fully contained within the free trade line ww. Hence, free trade is superior—it represents a higher potential welfare—than trade restricted by the tariff t_1.

We may proceed, and show that a higher tariff rate, t_2, would lead to a still inferior position. With this rate, the home-exchange ratio, representing a still higher price of M, is t_2t_2. The new production combination is E. Consumption will be to the left of E, on line $w''w''$—again parallel to ww, representing the world exchange ratio between X and M. Since $w''w''$ is wholly contained within $w'w'$, the position when trade is restricted by tariff t_2 must be inferior to the position attained with tariff t_1. In this way it is seen that an unambiguous ranking exists. The best position is that attained under free trade. When trade is restricted by tariff, the higher the tariff the worse the economy's position. The worst restriction is maintained when a tariff raises the home price of the importable good to such an extent that it reaches the autarky price in the economy—the home-exchange ratio becomes again aa in figure 3. The tariff then becomes prohibitive, and the economy is at its autarky position, reaping none of the potential benefits of trade.[4]

In terms of figure 2 in the preceding chapter, take line $u_1'u_1'$ to represent the utility possibility curve of the bundle of the two goods X and M (designated by A in figure 3) which is produced and consumed under autarky. Suppose another point on the transformation curve is selected, in which more of one good and less of the other is produced. The utility possibility curve representing this different bundle of goods is the dotted line $u_1''u_1''$; and so on. The curve u_1u_1 is the utility envelope frontier, showing the highest combinations of welfare levels (of the two individuals) which could be attained in the situation of autarky. In the same way, u_4u_4 is the utility envelope frontier in the situation of free trade: it shows the highest possible welfare combinations under free trade. In the circumstances assumed in the earlier discussion—the 'small country' assumption and fulfilment of optimum conditions—u_4u_4 must be higher than u_1u_1, with no possibility of intersection. One simple way of realizing this is to recall that, with trade, the welfare of each individual is at least as high as in a position in which a bundle of goods is available including more of all goods than in the case of autarky—a case which insures, we have seen, the inclusion of one utility possibility curve within the other.[5] It is in this meaning that free trade is superior to autarky: whatever the welfare levels of the two individuals under autarky, both could be increased by free trade. In the same way, u_2u_2 represents the utility envelope frontier under a high, but non-prohibitive tariff, and u_3u_3 the frontier under a lower tariff. None of these curves intersect, indicating an unequivocal ranking: the lower the restriction, the higher the welfare level, in the situation sense, with autarky being the most inferior and free trade the position of maximum welfare.

This may be summed up by the following statements: free trade is superior to autarky; free trade is superior to restricted trade; and less-restricted trade is superior to more-restricted trade.

Before proceeding with the main line of our analysis, it should be pointed out that while—under the given assumptions—free trade is judged to be best in the 'potential' or the 'situation' sense, we know definitely that in the absence of actual compensation trade will not raise everybody's welfare. It may be established that, under the assumptions used in the analysis (including, it should be emphasized here, the assumption that trade leads only to partial specialization), a shift from autarky to free trade (or from more-restricted to less-restricted trade) would actually make some people worse off. This is a generalization of the well-known Stolper–Samuelson theorem,[6] which in the context of a two-factor model showed trade to lead to the fall of the real income of one of the factors. The proof, by means of an Edgeworth-box diagram, is reproduced in figure 4.

Remaining in the two-good world and admitting, likewise, only two factors, X and M are the two goods, and L (labour) and K (capital)—the two factors. The amounts of factors used in

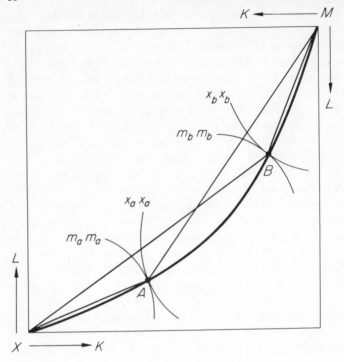

Figure 4

producing each good are measured in X to the right (for K) and upward (for L) from the X-origin, and in M to the left (for K) and downward (for L) from the M-origin. The dimensions of the box are given by the country's total endowment of the two factors. $x_a x_a$ and $x_b x_b$ are examples of the X-isoquants; and $m_a m_a$ and $m_b m_b$ are examples of the M-isoquants. $XABM$ is the contract curve, showing combinations of employment of the two factors in which the transformation ratios between the factors are equal in the two industries and hence, given the production of one good, production of the other will be at its maximum. With perfect competition the economy will indeed always be somewhere on this contract curve. Suppose that under autarky, it is at point A. With free trade, if X is dearer and M cheaper abroad, the country will tend to specialize in X: the production

point will move upward along the contract curve—say, to point
B. With the properties of the two production functions as they
are described in figure 4, this is a shift of production away from
the labour-intensive good (M) to the capital-intensive good (X):
a contract curve below the diagonal shows that, whatever the actual point of production, X is relatively capital intensive and M
labour intensive. The movement from A to B will therefore lead
to an *absolute* fall of the price of labour—the real wage: the L/K
ratio is higher in B than in A in both the production of X and of
M, so that the marginal productivity of labour—equal to its
wages—falls whether it is measured in one good or the other.
Thus free trade has led to an actual fall in the price of one factor—labour—and a decline of real income, or welfare, of owners
of this factor. In the same way, this will happen in the move
from more-restricted to less-restricted trade. In general, trade
will lead to a fall in the real price of factors in which the goods
whose production falls are intensive, and to the loss of welfare of
owners of these factors. In the example on hand, for instance, if
welfare of 'labour' as a group is valued high enough so that any
loss of it would not be offset by any gain of welfare by others,
free trade would be judged to be inferior to autarky; and the less
restricted trade is, the lower would its welfare be ranked.

It should be remarked, at this point, that even if such a social
welfare function is adopted, autarky is *not* the optimum policy if
trade policy could be combined with other policy means (short of
direct, ideal compensation). The optimum policy combination
would be free trade combined with a production subsidy to M
(or a production tax on X) which would leave production at point
A. This will ensure that welfare of labour cannot fall (it will remain fixed in terms of X, and be higher in terms of M), whereas
total welfare (including welfare of owners of other factors) will
rise. This will be proved later in section 4.

From here on we shall revert to welfare rankings strictly in the
situation sense—the sense of *potential* welfare. This brief discussion was meant, however, to draw attention to the fact that
this is not the only possible manner of welfare comparisons—a
qualification which should continuously be borne in mind.

Let us now recount the relevant assumptions made, either
explicitly or implicitly, along the way of the demonstration of
superiority of free trade:

1 The world contains two goods.

2 The economy's factor endowment is given.

3 Production functions are given.

4 Constant returns to scale exist in the production of each good.

5 Goods vary in factor intensities (at given factor substitution ratios).

6 Full employment of all factors prevails.

7 Trade is balanced.

8 The country is 'small'.

9 Perfect competition and Pareto optimum conditions exist in the economy.

In addition, we have defined a position as being 'superior' or 'inferior' in the situation sense—when compensation which leaves everyone as well off and some better off is possible in one direction, and not in the other.

The demonstration of the superiority of free trade is thus dependent on the listed assumptions, as well as on the definition of welfare adopted. In other words, an opposite demonstration, of the superiority of *restrictions*, will necessarily depend on one or more of the assumptions not being fulfilled, or on the use of other welfare criteria. In the rest of this section, we will clear the way for the analysis of such possibilities by discussing the assumptions whose removal does *not* invalidate the conclusions reached thus far; and also by defining those relaxations of assumptions which will remain beyond the scope of the present analysis.

To start with, the assumption of a two-good world (assumption 1) is made only for convenience of the analysis—especially since it allows simple diagrammatic demonstrations. Nothing of substance would change in a model of many goods—a model within which, in fact, Samuelson's classic proof that 'some trade is better than no trade' was first formulated.[7] In essence, the principle which remains true with any number of goods is that trade increases welfare by introducing to the economy further options, beyond those available to a self-contained economy—while closing no existing option.

The assumption that factor intensities vary among goods (assumption 5) was necessary to establish a convex transforma-

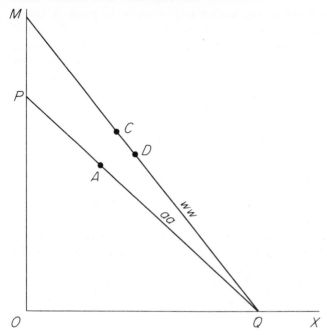

Figure 5

tion curve. Without it—that is, when all goods have the same
factor intensities (and constant returns to scale exist)—the
transformation curve would be a straight line. But this would
not invalidate the conclusions reached in the context of a convex
transformation curve. Since identity of factor intensities among
goods is not a likely event, this situation might have been dismissed. Yet, in view of the importance of this case in the history
of the theory, and in particular of the doctrine of the superiority
of free trade, it may be worthwhile to attend to it.

In figure 5, the transformation curve between X and M is
shown as a straight line. In autarky, production and consumption will be at point A, and the exchange ratio will be aa—the
slope of the transformation curve which, being fixed all along, is
the only possible exchange ratio when both goods are produced.
Now, open the country to trade, at a world exchange ratio
represented by the slope of ww. Since this will by necessity
become the local exchange ratio, all production of M in the

economy will cease: production will move to the point Q, where all the economy's resources are engaged in producing X. Part of the X will be traded for M, so that consumption will be at some point on ww, such as C. The superiority of C, or any other consumption locus chosen by consumers, over A, is established in exactly the same way as before. The only difference between this and the former case, of a convex transformation curve, is the 'corner solution' which is found now for domestic production, namely: the complete specialization of the economy in production of the export good. This is the classical, Ricardian case, by which the principle of comparative advantage and the gains from trade were first demonstrated.

It is interesting to note, however, that comparative advantage and specialization in production, while explaining the superiority of free trade over autarky, do not explain the superiority of free trade over restricted trade. Thus, they do not actually serve the classical case, which probably was designed primarily not to show that free trade is better than autarky but that it is preferable to the existence of tariffs. Suppose a tariff is imposed which leads to a domestic exchange ratio between ww and aa—that is, the tariff is not high enough to be prohibitive. Unlike the analysis applying in the case of a convex transformation curve, we now see that the tariff will have no effect whatsoever on production: this will remain at Q—the economy specializing completely in the production of X, as without the tariff. Comparative advantage and specialization in production thus do not explain any superiority of free trade over trade restricted by a (non-prohibitive) tariff. This superiority is now due to the effect on the pattern of *consumption*—which could not be handled in the classical analysis. With the tariff making M relatively dear and X relatively cheap (in comparison with the free trade position), consumption will move from a point like C to a point like D, with more of X and less of M being consumed. It may be shown that this distortion of consumption patterns—which exists here just as in the case of a convex transformation curve—is a source of welfare loss; that is, it leads to an inferior position, and the higher the tariff the more inferior it is. This will be proven later in this chapter, in a somewhat different context, so that the demonstration will not be offered here.[8]

Relaxation of the assumption of existence of full employment (assumption 6) would indeed change materially the ranking of positions. With less than full employment, production of one good does not come necessarily at the expense of another. The imposition of a tariff on imports when free trade exists (or of a higher tariff when a tariff is already found) would reduce the marginal propensity to import, and raise the propensity to spend on local production; and this, in turn, will increase the aggregate of local production and employment. While this is true, the present analysis, following conventional tradition in this sphere, will abstract from this possibility. It will be assumed all along that instruments of macroeconomic policy are used in order to preserve the existence of full employment, so that tariffs (or other trade restrictions) are not assigned a macroeconomic function. It should be noticed, however, that only unemployment which is due to insufficient aggregate demand is completely ignored, whereas the possibility of unemployment of a structural or frictional nature, which may result from a specific trade policy, will be examined later in this chapter.

In a similar way, unbalanced trade (violation of assumption 7) will not be considered. With an excess of payments abroad over receipts, tariffs will serve to attain balance-of-payments equilibrium. But, again following the conventional division of labour, it will be assumed all along that other means—the foreign-exchange rate, or instruments of demand policy—are used to achieve and maintain balance-of-payments equilibrium, so that the tariffs are free from this assignment. In other words, as has been stated in the previous chapter, throughout the discussion macroeconomic effects of tariffs (or other forms of trade restriction) will be disregarded.

Two assumptions, that factor endowment is given (assumption 2) and that production functions are given (assumption 3), served to confine the discussion to a static analysis. Relaxation of these assumptions will be of relevance if it may be expected that commercial policy itself might have an impact either on the amount of factors or on production functions; that is, in terms of the previous analysis, that commercial policy will not operate within circumstances described by a given transformation curve, but will change the location and slope of the curve itself. The possibilities of such an impact will be discussed in the following chapter, which will be devoted to the impact of commercial policy on growth and its operation in the context of a growing economy. The three remaining assumptions in the aforementioned list—of a 'small country' (assumption 8), constant returns to scale (assumption 4), and the existence of perfect competitive equilibrium (assumption 9)—will be handled respectively in three separate sections of this chapter.

2 Terms-of-trade effect: the optimum tariff

We now relax the 'small country' assumption, and assume instead that the trade of the country in question with the outside world does have an effect on the prices at which it is conducted: the larger the purchases of imports and the sale of exports, the more will the price of the country's imports rise and the price of its exports fall. The price ratio of exports to imports—the country's terms of trade—will thus deteriorate the more it trades with the outside world. In terms of the Marshallian offer curve,[9] this would be represented by a foreign curve which is not a straight line but is convex from below (having the country's exports on the horizontal and imports on the vertical axis). It will be assumed throughout that this offer curve is *given*, and is independent of the home country's action. Specifically, this implies the absence of retaliation by the foreign country to interference of the home country in the trade flows.

It has been long recognized that in this situation, a tariff may raise the country's welfare, just as a monopolist or monopsonist firm raises its profits by limiting its transactions. In an intuitive way, this was described as 'making the foreigner pay the tariff'. Against the improvement in the terms of trade to which the tariff leads, however, was set the loss from trade restriction, in the way described in the former section; and the result seemed to be indeterminate. More modern analysis has shown that it is not so: that when foreign prices are not given, there are definitely *some* tariffs (but *not all* tariffs) which are superior to free trade. The development of this argument is due mainly to the contributions of Kaldor, Scitovsky, de V. Graaff, Baldwin and Samuelson.[10]

We may start by demonstrating that with the terms-of-trade

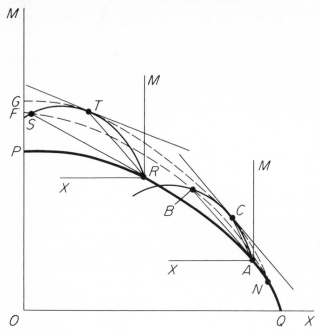

Figure 6

effect present, free trade is still superior to autarky. With the foreign prices no longer fixed, we have to slightly change our earlier demonstration. We shall ask: with any given price ratio, what will production and trade be; in other words, what will be the equilibrium position of local producers and of the outside world? In figure 6 PQ is, as before, the economy's transformation curve. If the exchange ratio between X and M is that shown by the slope of the line AB, local production will be at A. The amount of trade may be seen from the foreign offer curve, which is superimposed on A: with A as the origin, and the amounts of X (demanded by the outside world) read from right to left, line ACB is the Marshallian foreign offer curve (of demand for X and supply of M). The amount of trade will thus be indicated by the ray AB, and B will be the economy's consumption locus. That is, at the exchange ratio indicated by the slope of AB, production at A and trade to B will leave local producers and the outside world in equilibrium. Similarly, with a lower price of X, indicated by the slope of the line RS, local production will be at R, the trade ray will be RS, and the consumption locus will be at point S (RTS being the same foreign offer curve as ACB). Two possible consumption baskets are thus found: B and S. In a similar way, by varying the exchange line (the price ratio between X and M) continuously, a whole set of points like B and S may be found. These are represented by the line $NBSF$. N, the point at which this line departs from the transformation curve, is the production locus at which the marginal transformation ratio in production (the slope of the transformation curve) is equal to the terms of trade when an infinitesimally small amount is traded with the outside world. $NBSF$ is thus the consumption-possibility curve with free trade—replacing the ww curve in figure 3 (which was arrived at with fixed terms of trade).

Suppose now that the autarky position—production and consumption—was at A. Since A is contained within the free trade consumption-possibility curve $NBSF$, it must be inferior—in the same meaning and demonstrated in the same way as in the fixed terms-of-trade case—to the free trade position. And this is true, of course, for any autarky position, since the whole NP section of the transformation curve is contained within the free trade consumption possibility curve $NBSF$.[11] Hence, free trade is superior to autarky.

But this does not prove the superiority of free trade over *restricted* trade. Moreover, it may now be shown that there is always—when the terms of trade are not fixed—some degree of restriction which is superior to free trade. This is done by the use of the 'Baldwin envelope', which is in essence an extension of the transformation (production-possibility) curve. The transformation curve, in its conventional form, incorporates only a limited range of production possibilities: it describes the maximum combinations of the two goods which may be achieved by employing the economy's resources *directly* in the production of these goods. It is reached when one condition (necessary and sufficient, if full employment is postulated) is fulfilled; namely, that substitution ratios among factors of production should be equal in the production of both goods. When an open economy is considered, however, an *indirect* method of producing each good is added: it is possible to produce, through trade with the foreign country, good M by means of good X—and vice versa. Another 'production function'—including trade—is thus added to the relevant data. This extends the production-possibilities limitation; and the new, extended limit is represented by the envelope (which in the small economy case was the straight-line budget-restraint, such as ww in figure 3). Again, the limits are reached only when the marginal conditions are fulfilled. Having added one production function, one marginal condition is added: at the margin, the rate of transformation between goods X and M should be equal whether they are produced directly at home or produced indirectly by trade.

The envelope is constructed in a similar way to the consumption-possibility curve $NBSF$—with the added proviso, now, that the marginal condition just stated is fulfilled. Suppose, again, home production to be at point A. Marginal rates of transformation between X and M will be equal in direct and indirect production if trade is carried to the point C, where the slope of the foreign offer curve is equal to the slope of the domestic transformation curve. C will, therefore, be a point on the extended production possibility curve, or the envelope. Similarly, if home production is at point R, the marginal condition will be fulfilled if trade is carried to the point T, in which the slope of the foreign offer curve is equal to the slope of the transformation curve at R. The curve $NCTG$, which combines all points like C and T, is the envelope looked for: it represents the maximum baskets of the two goods which may be acquired by the combined process of home production and trade.

At a point like C, two different exchange ratios exist. One, represented by AB, is the home price faced by local producers (as well as local consumers). The other, represented by the slope of AC, is the price in the country's trade with the outside world. Since the two are not equal, some interference must be taking place: the difference between the two relative prices is formed by a tariff duty, which raises the price paid by the importer of M to this good's price in home production. This is *one* optimum tariff. It is equal to:

(1) $\qquad \dfrac{\tan M\hat{A}B}{\tan M\hat{A}C} - 1 \qquad$ or to $\qquad \left(\dfrac{dX}{dM} \Big/ \dfrac{X}{M} \right) - 1$

It is thus determined by the elasticity of the foreign-offer curve at point C. In principle, this elasticity will be different at T from what it is at C, and similarly in other such points. Thus, optimum tariff rates will move along the envelope: to each point on the envelope there is a corresponding separate optimum tariff rate. In other words, the envelope is achieved not by fixing one tariff rate, but by a whole set of tariff duties, each corresponding to a different home (and foreign) price.

It is immediately evident that this set of optimum tariffs is superior to free trade: the free trade consumption-possibility curve, $NBSF$, is wholly contained within the optimum-tariff consumption-possibility curve, the envelope $NCTG$. The reason is, of course, that free trade does *not* fulfil the marginal condition set before, namely that *marginal* rates of transformation should be equal in direct home production and in the indirect 'production' through trade. Only in the case when foreign prices are fixed is this condition fulfilled by free trade. This may be regarded as a special case of (1): fixed foreign prices are represented by a straight-line foreign offer curve—a curve of infinite elasticity; in this case $dX/dM = X/M$, and the optimum tariff is therefore zero. If foreign offer curves are conceived in the Ricardo–Mill–Marshall fashion, they will always have *some* section, starting at the origin, in which the curve is a straight line. Along this section, the optimum tariff will be zero: free trade will be an optimum policy. The free-trade consumption-possibility curve $NBSF$ and the envelope $NCTG$ will have a common section, starting at N, which is a straight line, only after which the two depart. The 'small country' case may thus be said to be the special instance in which this common section is long enough, due to the country's relatively small size of trade, to be the only relevant section of the envelope. If the foreign transformation curve is convex—as should generally be assumed—the foreign offer curve would have, strictly speaking, no straight-line section. But if the home country is small enough, movements in the foreign country on its transformation curve may be said to be taking place along a section of that curve short enough to be considered approximately a straight line.

Beyond the straight-line section of the envelope—if any such section exists—free trade is thus not an optimum policy: it is inferior to the policy which constitutes the set of optimum tariffs.

But this does not imply that free trade is inferior to *any* tariff. As may be gathered from a glance at figure 6—without actually constructing the various consumption-possibility curves—free trade is inferior to any set of tariffs which are lower than the respective optimum tariffs: while such tariffs do not fulfil the condition of equality of marginal rates of transformation in home production and in trade, they get closer than free trade towards this equality. Tariffs that are only slightly higher than the optimum set will still be superior to free trade. However, any further increase in tariffs, once they surpass the optimum level, reduces welfare further until a stage is reached when the tariff is inferior to free trade. At the extreme, the tariff would become prohibitive, leading the economy to the obviously inferior autarky position.

The set of optimum tariffs, derived in constructing the envelope, leaves home producers and foreign trade in equilibrium. Only *one* tariff of this set, however, will also leave home consumers in equilibrium, i.e. will make the quantity demanded of both goods equal to the basket indicated by the appropriate location on the envelope. If any other of the set of possible optimum tariffs is fixed by the government, it will not lead to a point on the envelope; that is, in equilibrium (of consumers, local producers, and foreign trade), the amount traded will not be such that the required marginal condition will be fulfilled. Thus, only one tariff rate will actually be 'the' optimum tariff, leading to the attainment of maximum welfare. The sense in which this is indeed a maximum welfare situation should again be made clear: it is the same sense in which only one point on a transformation curve (in a closed economy) is a position of maximum welfare at a given income distribution. It cannot be argued that one equilibrium point on a transformation curve is superior to another, achieved with a different income distribution. But, whatever the income distribution, if the economy is found within the transformation curve rather than on it, welfare could be increased. In exactly the same way, with any income distribution, only one tariff will lead the economy to the envelope—which is an extended production-possibility curve. It cannot be argued that the position thus attained is superior to any other point on the envelope. But should any other point be deemed superior—on what might be called 'ethical' grounds—it should be attained by redistribution of income (or, rather, of wealth) combined with another specific optimum tariff. If the redistribution is accompanied by any other tariff rate, it will lead to a sub-optimal position, lying within the envelope, from which movement could be made to a superior point on the envelope. Thus, to summarize: with any desired distribution of wealth, one tariff exists which is the optimum tariff.[12]

Before concluding this discussion, it should be pointed out that for the purpose on hand, export taxes are equivalent to import duties, as is indicated in Lerner's classic analysis.[13] The divergence between the home and the international price ratio could be achieved in either way—both serve to make imports relatively dearer and exports relatively cheaper at home than abroad. Moreover, as Lerner has shown, the tax *rate*, whether imposed on imports (a tariff) or on exports, would be the same. The 'optimum tariff' should therefore be interpreted as *optimum restriction* of trade, whether by means of a duty on imports or on exports.

Finally, it should be emphasized that the optimum-tariff discussion—and in particular tariff formulae such as (1)—are not intended to, and in any case do not, possess much operational meaning. This is particularly true once we get out of the two-goods model into a world of many goods: here, the optimum solution is not of one tax rate but of many different rates, one each for each imported (or exported) good. What we may conclude in such a world is, first—as with two goods—that free trade is not an optimal policy; that some tariff schedules are superior to it and that there is one 'optimum' schedule of duties (on imports and exports) which leads to the highest welfare level. In this schedule, higher tax rates would be found for import goods whose foreign supply is relatively inelastic, and for export goods whose foreign elasticity of demand is relatively low; whereas low tax rates would be found for goods whose foreign elasticity of supply (of imports) or demand (for exports) are high.

Moving now to the relaxation of other assumptions we will retain, all along, the two-goods model; and, to separate out each argument, we will restore in the rest of the chapter the 'small country' assumption, which always greatly simplifies the analysis.

3 Increasing returns to scale

A situation in which an industry operates within the range of increasing returns to scale could not be one of competitive equilibrium. Hence, it could be included under the heading of section 5, where deviations from competitive equilibrium—'distortions'—will be analyzed. Yet, in the history of doctrines of commercial policies this situation has occupied a prominent place, which may justify a separate discussion.[14] This place may probably be explained by the intuitive appeal of a tariff when an industry with increasing returns to scale is concerned: trade which happens to lead the country away from such industry will involve increasing costs in the industry or, in other words, will direct the country to specialize in an industry with increasing costs, whereas other countries reap the benefits of specialization in decreasing-cost industries. Sometimes, this argument is broadened to justify protection of the sector of manufacturing as a whole, particularly in underdeveloped countries, where this sector is deemed to be subject to increasing returns to scale, whereas agriculture is subject to decreasing returns. The 'infant industry' argument, which has more than one variant, sometimes also implies this situation and justification for tariff.

The argument on hand may be analyzed with the aid of figure 7, which shows a transformation curve concave along a segment, due to industry X being subject within this range to increasing returns to scale. The world exchange ratio is represented by line ww.

The simplest, but incorrect, justification for protection would run as follows. Suppose the free trade production locus to be at point B, and the consumption locus to be somewhere to its right, such as at point C; that is, the country exports M and imports X. Various points along the transformation curve, such as A, are obviously preferable to C; and the economy could reach such points by protection which would encourage production in the increasing-returns industry X, at the expense of industry M.

But a production locus such as B is a point of unstable equilibrium, where the economy may happen to be only by accident, and from which it would be driven away by any accidental movement. Suppose the autarky position to be indeed at point A

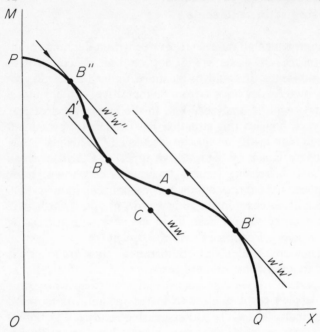

Figure 7

when the economy opens to trade. The production locus would then shift from A not to B but to B', with the country exporting X and importing M. If the autarky position happens to be to the left of B, such as at A', the free trade production point would be B'', and the consumption point to its right; that is, the country would export M and import X. In both alternative situations, a tariff on the import good, which would drive the economy towards the autarky position, would clearly reduce welfare. In other words, with free trade, the economy would be found to operate on segments of the transformation curve where *decreasing* returns prevail, so that the assumed increasing-returns attribute of industry X becomes irrelevant. This version of the argument for protection is thus not valid.

But suppose, indeed, the free trade production position to be at B'', with the consumption combination somewhere to its right on $w''w''$. As figure 7 is drawn, the economy would be better off were production to be at B', rather than at B'', and were the trade pattern to be reversed—with the economy specializing in X rather than in M. Protection of industry X would indeed, in this case, increase welfare. But note that protection by tariff (on import good X) would still be the *wrong* measure: it would only shift the economy from B'' towards autarky (production and consumption) point A', which is inferior to the free trade consumption locus on $w''w''$. The required protection would have to be granted by a measure such as a production subsidy to X, of a size sufficient to expand the production of X beyond point B. Once there, the subsidy could be removed with the economy settling down without protection at the free trade equilibrium production position B'. An initial protection granted in this manner will thus increase welfare.

4 Tariffs vs. production subsidies

We have already encountered on a few occasions in our discussion the proposition that where an intervention is desirable in order to offset, or correct, an existing distortion, a production subsidy would be preferable to a tariff as a means of intervention. In the analysis of optimum policies under distortions, which will be undertaken in the following section, we shall meet this proposition repeatedly. It may be worthwhile, therefore, to precede the analysis of the various situations of distortion by a demonstration of the superiority of a production subsidy over tariffs.

Production subsidies are superior because, while both tariffs and subsidies affect the production pattern similarly, tariffs disrupt consumption patterns whereas production subsidies do not. The formal proof of this superiority is provided in figure 8.[15] In part (a), the relevant segments of figure 3 are reproduced. With a tariff (say t_1) and the domestic exchange line t_1t_1, domestic production is at point D. Trade takes place along the consumption-possibility curve $w'w'$ to, say, consumption point R. Now suppose that a production subsidy is granted *instead* of the tariff, so that it will leave domestic production exactly as it is under the tariff: this will be achieved by a subsidy rate equal to the tariff rate t_1, which will make the price ratio facing local

(a)

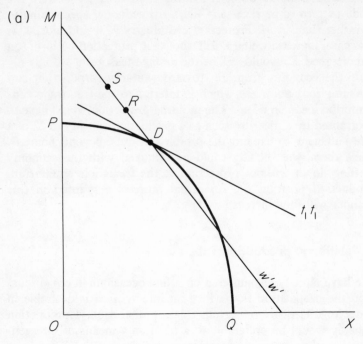

(b)

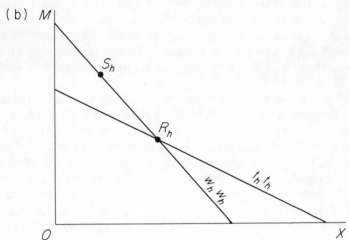

Figure 8

producers $t_1 t_1$, precisely as the tariff does. Prices facing local *consumers*, however, will not be the same as with the tariff: the exchange ratio facing consumers will be the international price, ww. In order to avoid comparisons of different income distributions, suppose that the government, in switching from the tariff to the subsidy, makes by lump-sum transfers everybody's income equal to what it was with the tariff. This leaves the income distribution unaffected by the method of (net) tax collection; but note that it does *not* rule out the income redistribution induced by the change in relative prices in the movement from tariff to subsidy.

With the change from tariff to subsidy, the relative price of M, the import good, falls for domestic consumers. Consumption will hence shift towards the import good: with the same production, D, more trade will take place, so that the consumption point will be S rather than R. It is now possible to see that S is superior to R.

In figure 8(b), a single home consumer, H, is represented. With the tariff, and the economy's consumption locus R, in part (a), the consumption basket of this individual is R_h (scales differ, of course, between parts (a) and (b) of figure 8). This may be viewed as his initial endowment of goods. With the shift to a subsidy, H's budget-restraint line becomes $w_h w_h$. Assuming that the consumer reacts to relative price changes, his consumption basket will move from R_h to S_h (the aggregate of such movements by individuals leading to consumption basket S in figure 8 (a)). But since R_h is still an open possibility, S_h must be superior (or, in the limiting case, equal) to R_h. And since no special properties have been attributed to individual H, the same conclusion must be valid for any other consumer in the economy. The subsidy position is thus superior to the tariff position for each and any consumer, and no attempt to offset consumer losses and gains is required in order to reach the conclusion that, for the economy as a whole, S is superior to R. Hence, the subsidy is preferable to the tariff. If the change in income distribution due to the form of (net) tax collection is not to be abstracted from by assumption, this proof should be understood to have demonstrated the superiority in the situation sense; that is, it demonstrates that subsidies lead to a potential increase of welfare, since some distribution of income exists in which everybody is made better off than with tariffs (at the actual tariff-ridden income distribution).[16]

5 Intervention under domestic distortions

In this section, we shall discuss situations in which efficiency is not maintained (in the autarky position). We shall refer to it as situations where domestic 'distortions' exist, and will discuss a few of the more important possible sources of distortions. The analysis of optimum trade policies in the presence of domestic distortions owes its start primarily to the contributions of Ohlin, Meade and Haberler: these have been made, independently, at various times and at varying levels of detail and precision, yet have reached basically similar conclusions. More recently the analysis has been advanced and formalized mainly by Corden, Hagen, Johnson, Bhagwati and Ramaswami.[17] In stating the principles of this analysis, it would be best to start by defining more precisely the conditions whose fulfilment is required for the attainment of an optimum position. We have referred to the optimum earlier, in a general way, as the existence of 'perfect competitive equilibrium'. More accurately, this would mean the fulfilment of 'Pareto optimality' conditions, which may be spelled out for clarity of further reference:

(a) marginal rates of substitution of goods in consumption should be equal among all consumers;

(b) marginal rates of substitution of factors should be equal among all producers;

(c) marginal rates of transformation of goods in production should be equal among all producers;

(d) marginal rates of transformation in production should be equal to marginal rates of substitution in consumption.

Fulfilment of these conditions ensures the attainment of Pareto optimum, and maximum social welfare in the sense used here, in a closed economy. With trade, we have seen earlier, another condition has to be satisfied, namely:

(e) marginal rates of transformation should be equal in domestic production and in trade.

In our discussion until now, we have first seen that if the four 'closed economy' conditions are fulfilled and foreign prices are given (that is, the marginal rate of transformation in trade is constant), condition (e) will be fulfilled, and maximum welfare attained, with free trade. If foreign prices are not given, and the marginal rate of transformation in trade varies from the average rate, (e) will be fulfilled by a positive optimum tariff. We recall our assumption that foreign prices are given but ask what trade policy should be if any of the closed-economy conditions (a), (b), (c) or (d)—or some combination of them—are not fulfilled.

Perfect competition in all the good and factor markets— including, by definition, perfect mobility and perfect information—ensures the fulfilment of the closed-economy optimum conditions if no external economies exist. 'Distortions' are thus either externalities or lack of perfect competition in any of the goods or factor markets. Externalities, in either production or consumption, may lead directly to the violation of condition (d); whereas absence of perfect competition will also lead to the violation of (d), via (a), (b) or (c).

Whatever the distortion, it thus must be reflected in (d). The analysis may then focus on this condition, distinguishing among various possibilities which prevent the fulfilment of this condition. The question may be summarized as follows: in a situation in which the marginal rate of transformation among goods in production (MRT) is *not* equal to the marginal rate of substitution in consumption (MRC), what would the optimum trade policy be?

This may be answered both in a general way and by discussing specific situations of distortions. First, let us state a number of general theorems applying to the question posed:[18]

1 Situations of varying forms of distortions cannot be ranked.

2 If only one distortion exists, a reduction of the degree of this distortion would increase welfare.

3 If more than one distortion exists, a reduction of the degree of one distortion (including its full elimination) does *not* necessarily increase welfare.

4 The *optimum* policy combination when distortions exist would involve taxes or subsidies designed directly to correct each distortion.

We shall now see how these principles are reflected in their reference to the issue of tariff policy in specific cases of domestic distortions. The discussion will be confined to those examples of distortions which appear frequently in recent analyses of the issue, and which probably include the most important possible violations of the optimum conditions.[19]

(i) **Rigidity of factor allocation.** One possible distortion is lack of mobility of factors of production among industries. Among all distortion cases which are analyzed frequently, this is the only one which does *not* lead to any qualification of the policy rankings established for a distortion-free economy— despite the fact that it does lead to violation of Pareto-optimum conditions (condition (b), and possibly (c), above).[20] This may be easiest to view, without actually having to construct the diagram, in the extreme case in which all factors of production are completely immobile. The transformation curve—if it is allowed at all to use this term and concept in such a situation—is a rectangle, with its northeast corner at the point of actual production. If this is the autarky position, and trade is introduced, trade will have, by definition of this case, no effect on production and specialization. It will, however, have an effect on consumption. From here on, the demonstration of the superiority of trade over autarky would be exactly the one used before to prove the superiority of subsidy over tariff, with a given locus of production. In the same way, free trade will be seen to be superior to restricted trade—just as it is in the Ricardian case, once specialization is complete and tariffs do not have any production effect. Trade cannot, by the assumption of this case, lead to a production gain, production levels being fixed; but it still leads to a consumption gain. In this instance, thus, it remains true that free trade is the optimum policy; and that the less restricted is trade, the higher is the economy's welfare.

(ii) **Rigidity of factor prices.** The next source of distortion is, in a sense, the opposite: we shall assume rigid factor *prices*—whereas the previous case, of rigid factor *allocation*, meant inevitably an extreme flexibility of factor prices. It will be assumed that in autarky, full employment exists, and Pareto-optimum conditions for a closed economy are maintained. Once

there, however, factors of production insist on the prices existing
at this point as their minimum prices.[21] When trade is introduced and the economy tends to specialize in one of the goods
(in a two-good, two-factor model)—expanding its production
and contracting the other's—factor prices would tend to change.
We know, from the Stolper–Samuelson theorem, that with full
price flexibility the price of the factor intensive in the contracting industry would fall in absolute, real terms. Assuming, as we
do here, that such a fall is impossible owing to this factor's in-
sistence on its former (autarky) real price, the inevitable result
would be unemployment of the factor. This outcome may be
explained as follows: call the two factors L and K. With trade,
the L-intensive industry contracts (this is the import good).
With price flexibility, the L to K ratio would have increased
here. With a rigid (real) price of L, however, this ratio cannot increase. Quite the contrary: with a constant ratio and constant
marginal productivities of the factors (and remembering that
constant returns to scale are assumed all along), the real L price
would fall, remaining what it was before in terms of a good (the
import good) whose price is now lower. Hence, the maintenance
of the initial real price of L must imply that the L to K ratio in
the import-competing industry would fall rather than rise. This
means, in turn, that the contracting industry releases L and K in
a higher L to K ratio than with price flexibility. But even with its
releasing smaller relative amounts of L, in the full-flexibility
case, the absorption of the released factors by the expanding
(export) industry would have resulted in a lower real price of
L—as the Stolper–Samuelson theorem tells. Since in this
(export) industry too the price of L could not fall, it must be ab-
sorbing L and K in a *lower* ratio than these factors are released
by the contracting industry. Hence, unemployment of L must
result.

With trade, thus, a distortion exists: at least one optimum
condition—(b)—is not fulfilled.[22] A complete prevention of
trade (say, by a prohibitive tariff) would prevent this distortion,
but would lead to another—the open-economy distortion, namely, the violation of condition (e). Theorem 1 above tells us that
these two situations of distortions cannot be ranked. This may
be demonstrated by means of figure 9, where A is the autarky
position, with aa the exchange line. The world exchange line is

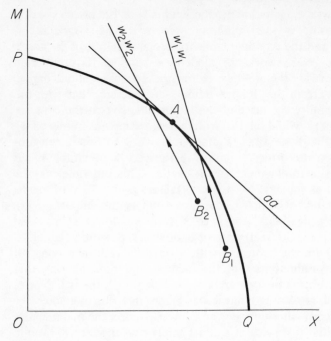

Figure 9

ww, and two alternative prices are shown, represented by w_1w_1 and w_2w_2. X is dearer and M is cheaper in trade, so that the economy tends to specialize in X. With rigid factor prices and unemployment, however, the movement of production in the south-east direction is *not* on the transformation curve, and the free trade production point, B, is *within* the transformation curve. Consumption will be on ww, to the left of B—with X exchanged for M. In the alternative w_1w_1, the free trade situation is superior to A. In the alternative w_2w_2, the two positions cannot be ranked without further information. In general, thus, the autarky and free trade situations cannot be ranked—either may be superior to the other, depending on the circumstances of the situation. It should be pointed out that a free trade consumption location could be superior to the autarky position A even if it is *within* the transformation curve—but only in a very specific sense: by the set of assumptions, A is a closed-economy optimum, hence is superior to any point on the curve, and *a fortiori* to any point within the curve. By these assumptions, however, once A is established as an equilibrium position, a movement from it (due to changes in demand conditions) would *not* be able to take place along the transformation curve: new equilibrium positions must result in some unemployment. Thus, any post-trade position within the transformation curve will be inferior to autarky as long as demand conditions (tastes) are constant; a change in these, on the other hand, may make the free trade position superior to the (new) autarky position.[23]

(iii) **Combined rigidities.** Sometimes a case is analyzed which combines both the present and the earlier sources of distortions, making both factor prices and factor location (as long as they are at all employed) rigid. This reduces welfare, more than when only one of these distortions exists. In the extreme case, of full rigidity of both, the free trade production locus B would be found on the X-axis, exactly below A; that is, the production of X would not expand, whereas the production of M would cease altogether—with all the factors employed in M under autarky becoming unemployed. Whatever the relevance or importance of such a case, it should be noticed that even here, the free trade and autarky positions could not be ranked: a situation such as alternative w_1w_1 would be impossible in this case—it must be the possibility shown by w_2w_2. But we recall that even with w_2w_2, the free trade and autarky positions cannot be ranked without further information.

Using the construct of figure 9, it may be easily verified—this will not be shown here—in exactly the same way, that free trade and restricted trade, or autarky and restricted trade, or more-restricted and less-restricted trade, could not be ranked. This is an example of theorem 3 above: with the existence of a domestic distortion, reductions in the degree of trade restriction—another distortion—do not necessarily lead to an increase of welfare.

Finally, theorem 4 may be easily demonstrated, namely, the optimum policy combination would involve *not* a tariff —creating another distortion—but a subsidy correcting the original distortion combined with free trade. Factor prices may be subsidized so that production expands, until the production locus becomes what it would have been without the factor-price rigidity (subsidies being financed by non-distortive, lump-sum taxes). The consumption locus is then determined, to the left of the production locus, by free trade exchange of X for M, at world prices. This clearly leads to the attainment of the highest possible welfare level, and is unequivocally superior to either autarky (or restricted trade) or to free trade without subsidies.

(iv) **Externalities.** The next distortion to be discussed is the existence of external economies. These may be realized in production, when the operation of an industry brings benefits (or losses) to another industry, or directly to consumers, for which the industry in question cannot charge payments (or cannot be made to pay—in the case of negative economies).[24] Or they may be found in the consumption of a good, when it yields utility for which no charge could be made. We shall confine ourselves here to the probably more frequent case of external economies in production.[25] These benefits rise with the expansion of the industry, and fall with its contraction. Provided such economies are not exactly offset, at each production locus, by external economies in other industries—a case which may be dismissed—the existence of external economies in the industry would thus mean that the marginal social cost is not equal to the marginal private cost in this industry, or that the marginal social benefit is not equal to the marginal private benefit. For producers, marginal rates of transformation will be equal to the market exchange ratios among goods, as also will the marginal rates of substitution in consumption. For the economy, however, the marginal rates of transformation between the good under consideration and others will be different and hence a distortion, by violation of condition (d) of the optimum conditions listed above. We shall assume, for simplicity, that the externalities cannot be attributed to the use of a particular factor of production, but to the process and scale of production as a whole. We shall also confine the discussion, for simplicity, to *positive* external economies: negative economies which may technically be removed (such as the classical example of smoke) would introduce some complications.

The effect of trade in the two-good model is shown in figure 10. Industry M has positive external economies, whereas X has none (alternatively, it could be assumed that external economies

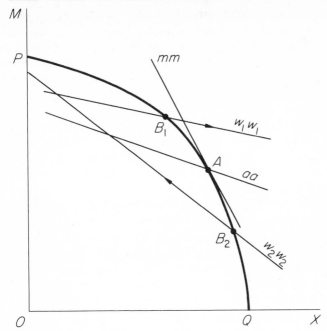

Figure 10

in M outweigh, in the relevant sense, those from X). In autarky, equilibrium is at point A. The exchange ratio facing both producers and consumers is aa. The marginal *social* cost of M, however, is represented by the slope of mm, the tangent to the transformation curve at production point A. With trade, two possibilities are open, leading to specialization in opposite directions. Take, first, the simpler case, where the world exchange ratio is represented by w_1w_1; that is, M is dearer and X is cheaper than the autarky home prices. Production of M will expand, and that of X will contract, and the production locus will shift to a point like B. It should be noticed that home prices with trade will be equal to world prices, but will still not be equal to social marginal costs; that is, w_1w_1 cuts the transformation curve at B_1, rather than being tangent to it. Trade will take place along w_1w_1, and the consumption locus will be somewhere on it to the right of B_1. With the budget restraint w_1w_1, the economy is obviously better off than at A, the autarky position, which is contained within this budget-restraint line. Hence, although with free trade the economy is not at its highest possible welfare level—the domestic distortion having remained—it still reaches a higher welfare level than under autarky. Likewise, as could readily be verified by a similar demonstration, free trade is preferable to restricted trade; and the more restricted the trade policy, the more inferior it is. These conclusions hold because in this case, trade is in the 'right' direction: when the economy is at A—the autarky position—the world price of M is higher not only than the existing home price but also than the social marginal cost of the good. Hence, the economy benefits from specializing in this good.

Take, now, an alternative possibility, in which world prices are represented by w_2w_2. Here, the world price of M is higher than the social marginal cost at home in the autarky position—as before—but it is *lower* than the existing home price of M. Hence production of M will contract, production of X will expand, and the new production locus will be a point like B_2. The economy is specializing, in this case, in the 'wrong' direction—expanding the production of, and exporting, the good (X) which is more expensive (socially) to produce at home than abroad. Yet, it is not inevitable, despite this production loss, that the economy's welfare will be reduced by trade. The economy's budget restraint, or consumption-possibility line, is w_2w_2: the economy will export X and import M, so that the consumption locus will be on w_2w_2 to the left of B_2. If consumption is below the intersection of w_2w_2 with aa, welfare has been reduced from the autarky level; if it is above it, the welfare levels of the two positions—free trade and autarky—cannot be ranked. Once more, it may readily be seen, by a similar analysis, that situations of autarky and of restricted trade, or of a lower and of a higher restriction, cannot be unequivocally ranked.

Since without additional information we do not know whether the case could be described by a situation such as w_1w_1 or w_2w_2 (that is, whether the economy will specialize in the 'right' or in the 'wrong' direction), no general conclusion about the ranking of various policies—free trade, complete restriction (autarky), or different degrees of trade restriction—could be arrived at.[26] This illustrates theorem 3 above: with the existence of one distortion (the external economies), various degrees of the other distortion (gaps between marginal rates of transformation in consumption and in trade, introduced by the tariff), including the situation (free trade) where this distortion is abolished altogether, cannot be ranked.

Again, it would be easy to demonstrate that the optimum policy mix would be free trade combined with the appropriate subsidy. A subsidy to the production of M, equal to the degree of external economies, would make its private marginal cost equal to the social marginal cost. The autarky position will be somewhere to the left of A, and the aa and mm lines will then coincide. Whatever the world prices, specialization must then be in the 'right' direction, and the welfare level will be at its maximum.

(v) **Factor-price differentials.** Let us now take up the distortion, widely discussed in recent years, of non-uniform factor prices among industries: in one industry (or some), one factor (or some) is paid a rent.[27] The difference between this and the former case is, in terms of transformation (production-possibility) curve analysis, that here (just as in a monopoly situation) not only will production be located on the 'wrong' place on the transformation curve, but also the curve itself will shrink and move downward. This may easily be seen from an Edgeworth box analysis: the transformation curve is derived (read off) from the contract curve of this box; but the economy will be found on the contract curve only if factor prices are uniform. With non-uniform factor prices, a distorted contract curve may be constructed, on a point of which the economy will be found. And this distorted curve represents lower combinations of goods (that is, a lower quantity of one good given the other's) at all points—except in the corners of the box, when all factors are allocated to the production of either just one good or the other.[28] In figure 11, $PA'Q$ would have been the economy's transformation curve had factor prices been uniform. With the given distortion, the transformation curve shrinks and becomes PAQ. In autarky, the economy produces (and consumes) at point A. Assuming that the non-uniformity takes the form of one factor being more expensive when employed in M rather than in X, this would mean that at A the marginal social cost of producing M is lower than the marginal private cost: mm,

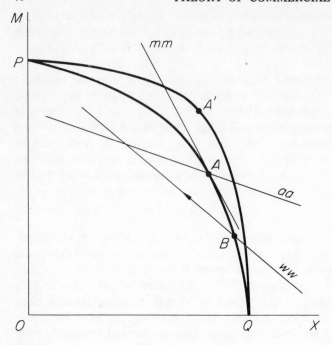

Figure 11

the tangent to the (distorted) transformation curve at A, is steeper than aa, which represents the exchange ratio faced by producers and consumers. From here on, the analysis of the effect of trade restriction runs exactly as in the former case (of external economies), and we shall repeat only the demonstration of the less comfortable possibility; that is, of specialization in the 'wrong' direction. World prices, represented by ww, are between the home-market price ratio (aa) and the 'true' social ratio (mm). The economy thus specializes in X, although it is socially more expensive (at the margin) to produce X than to buy it abroad. The production point becomes B; X is exchanged for M, and consumption will be somewhere on ww to the left of B. Again, although the consumption point may be within the distorted transformation curve PAQ—and *a fortiori* within the non-distorted curve $PA'Q$—the free trade position is not necessarily inferior to autarky: it will be so if the post-trade consumption location is below the intersection of ww with aa, whereas if it is above it the two positions could not be ranked. In general, thus, free trade and autarky cannot be ranked in this case. Similarly, positions of a higher and a lower degree of restriction cannot be ranked.

Once more, as in the earlier cases, the optimum policy combination is that of free trade and subsidy. The subsidy, in this case, should be given to the employment of the specific factor in the specific industry at which it is unduly expensive. If it were given to the factor in general, wherever it is employed, it would not relieve the distortion at all. If it were given to the *good*, rather than the factor, to the extent required to offset the high factor price, this (together with free trade) would ensure indeed that the post-trade situation will be superior to autarky, and, likewise, that lower restriction of trade will be superior to higher restriction. In figure 11, a subsidy to the production of M will shift production towards M, so that marginal social cost will be equal to private cost. In this situation, specialization must be in the 'right' direction, and free trade (or freer trade) must increase welfare. This, however, would not be an optimum policy: it will leave intact the non-uniformity in factor prices, hence will leave the economy on the shrunken transformation curve PAQ. A subsidy to the expensive factor in M—to the extent required to offset its rent—will, on the other hand, restore the transformation curve $PA'Q$. In autarky, the economy will be at a point like A'. Trade must then result in specialization in the 'right' direction, and will lead the economy to the highest welfare level possible with its given production functions and endowment of production factors.

(vi) **Government distortions.** We have analyzed various distortions originating from some flaws in a freely operating economic system. It may be worthwhile to examine also the consequences of trade policies where 'government-made' distortions exist—that is, distortions originating from government interference. The possible forms of such interference are many and varied and we shall examine here only one, namely: production subsidies. These, as we have repeatedly seen, would—if applied correctly—be part of the optimum policy mix where 'private' distortions exist; but we shall now assume that without these

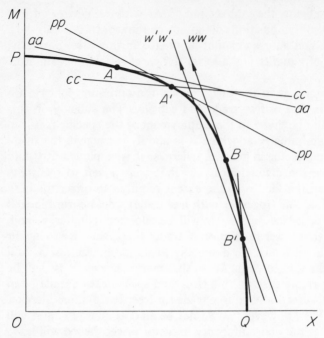

Figure 12(a)

subsidies, all optimum conditions would have been fulfilled, and welfare would have been at its maximum. The introduction of production subsidies thus creates a distortion: it violates condition (d) above.

In figure 12 (a) we assume that the production subsidy is granted to good X which, without the subsidy, would be the export good. In the absence of subsidy, the production and consumption point would be A under autarky; the production point would be B with free trade; and consumption would be at a point on ww, left of B. With the production subsidy to X, the autarky position becomes A': more of X and less of M are produced than without the subsidy. The exchange line of consumers is cc, indicating a lower price of X than at the non-interference exchange ratio aa; whereas the exchange line for producers is pp, indicating a higher X price than at ratio aa. With trade, the *consumers'* price will be equal to the international price; whereas the producers' price of X, equal to its

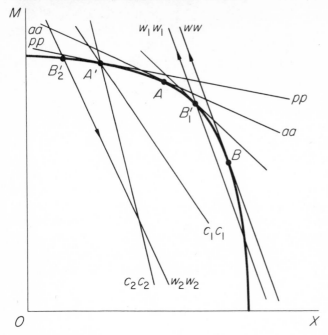

Figure 12(b)

production cost, will be higher by the rate of subsidy. This will be achieved at B', which will be the new production point. X will be sold abroad in exchange for M, and the consumption point will be somewhere on $w'w'$, to the left of B'. As it is shown in the diagram, A' lies to the left of $w'w'$—indicating that welfare at A' must be lower than at the post-trade situation. But A' could also be found to the right of $w'w'$, in which case the two situations could not be ranked. In general, thus, the autarky and free trade situations cannot be ranked, under these circumstances: an over-specialization in the 'right' good may be said to have taken place here, which will be heavier (and the probability of welfare loss from trade higher), the higher the rate of subsidy. In a similar way, it may be shown that situations of higher and lower restrictions of trade cannot be ranked.

Figure 12 (b) presents the case in which production subsidy is granted to good M, which would be the import good under free trade. Again, the non-interference autarky position is A. With the production subsidy, the autarky position becomes A'. The producers' exchange line is pp, which is flatter than aa, indicating a higher producer's price of M. We shall distinguish here two alternative positions. First, assume that A' is reached with a relatively small production subsidy. The consumers' exchange line in this case is c_1c_1. When trade opens, the international price of M (indicated by exchange line ww) is found to be lower than the home price, despite the domestic subsidy. The country will specialize in X, moving to production point B'_1, where the difference between the consumers' exchange ratio (the international ratio) and that of the producers will be equal to the rate of subsidy. X will be traded for M, and consumption will be on w_1w_1, to the left of B'_1. The autarky position A' must, in this case, be contained within w_1w_1. Thus the outcome under these circumstances must be an increase of welfare: the production subsidy leads to under-specialization in the 'right' direction, but trade still yields a welfare gain (which is higher the less trade is restricted).

Next, assume that A' is reached with a high subsidy—high enough to make the consumer's price of M *cheaper* (and of X dearer) in the autarky position than in the international market. This is represented by the exchange line c_2c_2. This would now lead to specialization in M—the otherwise import good. The new production point will be B'_2. M will be sold for X, so that the economy's consumption point will be on w_2w_2, to the *right* of B'_2. This is, thus, a case of specialization in the 'wrong' direction. With no further information, we do not know whether welfare after trade is higher or lower than at the autarky position. Thus, no ranking is possible even if we know that the production subsidy has led to specialization in the 'wrong' good—a knowledge that we do not generally possess. In the way of general conclusions, we are again restricted to a statement of probability: the lower the rate of production subsidy, the more likely it is that specialization would be in the right direction, thus the more likely it is that trade will lead to a welfare gain (though, it should be re-emphasized, even specialization in the 'wrong' direction does not necessarily imply a welfare loss).

We may, at this point, summarize the conclusions arrived at in the discussion of this chapter. With no domestic distortion, and given world prices, free trade is an optimum policy for the country; and the lower the degree of restriction of trade, the higher is the country's welfare. With no domestic distortion but with variable terms of trade, free trade will be superior to autarky; but free trade is not the optimum policy—it is inferior to trade restricted by the optimum tariff. In this situation, no general ranking exists of degrees of restriction: an increase of the tariff raises welfare until the tariff reaches its optimum level, and lowers it beyond this level. With domestic distortions (including the existence of increasing returns to scale), but with fixed terms of trade, autarky and free trade, and positions of higher and lower restriction, cannot generally be ranked. An exception is the case in which the only distortion is immobility of factors, in which lower restriction is superior to higher restriction and free trade is optimum. With domestic distortions, the optimum policy is that of a subsidy to offset the source of distortion, combined with free trade;[29] with such subsidy, the lower the degree of trade restriction the higher the country's welfare.

6 Non-tariff forms of interference in trade: export subsidies

The discussion thus far has referred to trade restrictions by means of a tariff. This is, indeed, the most common and probably the most important instrument used by the government for interference in trade, so that a theory of commercial policy is indeed, to a large extent, a theory of tariffs. Yet, other measures are often involved, sometimes on a large scale and in a persistent manner. As has been pointed out on various occasions in the foregoing discussion, one of these means, a tax on exports, is equivalent to the imposition of tariffs in the context of the present analytical framework: a general-equilibrium analysis in which trade is assumed to be balanced.[30] Other instruments are equivalent to tariffs in another sense: they are in effect tariffs, but may come under the disguise of various other names. Still other forms which affect trade cannot be classified as *commercial* policies. Any policy measure (or any process) which changes the economy's production and consumption must affect trade; as an example, it has just been shown how a production subsidy does it, and how it may change the impact of tariff policy. A discussion of these effects would go beyond commercial policy to a general analysis of the impact of all policy measures on the economy, and *inter alia* on the economy's trade—an analysis which is certainly beyond the scope of the present undertaking.

But even when trade policies alone are regarded, many instruments are still left for discussion. Among these, probably the two most important are direct control of imports (and, to a lesser extent, of exports) and export subsidies. The former policy—control of imports by quotas—is for some purposes and under some circumstances identical with a tariff; for other purposes, and under different circumstances, the two instruments would differ. But a discussion of similarities and differences between tariffs and import quotas, which utilizes partial equilibrium analysis, would require a different frame of reference than the one used here. We would therefore reserve the discussion in the present section merely for the analysis of export subsidies, which fits easily into the analytic model used thus far.[31]

The analysis of export subsidies is carried out with the aid of figure 13. As usual, A is the autarky position; B would be the production point with free trade; and some point on ww, to the left of B, would be the consumption location. Now an export subsidy to X, the export good, is introduced. This expands production of X and contracts production of M until the production locus reaches B'; at this point the home-market exchange ratio (producers' as well as consumers') is $s's'$; and the difference between X's price at home and its (lower) world price—the latter indicated by the exchange line $w'w'$—is just equal to the subsidy. Consumption will be on $w'w'$, to the left of B' (regard the fact that A is located on $w'w'$ as an accident). It may be seen that the export subsidy has led to an *expansion* of trade (whereas a tariff, or an export tax, led to trade contraction). The production of X increases in the shift from B to B', whereas home consumption of the good will fall if the good is normal, since income is lower than with free trade and the relative price of X increases. The amount of exports of X, equal to the difference between home production and home consumption, must therefore increase (and so must the amount of imports of M, the international terms of trade being fixed).[32]

But trade expansion is not synonymous with an increase in welfare. Just as with a tariff, we find here the cum-subsidy

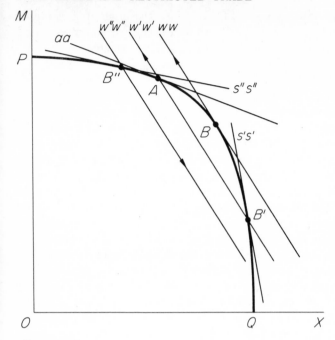

Figure 13

budget-restraint line, $w'w'$, to be below the free trade line ww; hence, subsidy-induced trade is inferior to free trade (assuming, of course, the absence of domestic distortions as well as of a terms-of-trade effect). In the same way, a lower subsidy would be found to be superior to a higher subsidy. Moreover—and here a difference from the analysis of the impact of tariffs does appear—the post-subsidy position may even be inferior to the autarky position (whereas tariffs may only be high enough to become prohibitive, thus restoring the autarky position). The location of B' in figure 13 was chosen so that A, the autarky position, would be found on $w'w'$. In this case, welfare is still *higher* with the subsidy-induced trade than under autarky. This may be seen in the following way. Suppose income is redistributed and everyone is left with the same bale of goods as without trade, so that the economy is left at consumption point A (which is possible in this case, A being on $w'w'$), but now every consumer is free to trade. Since the price of X is higher than under autarky, as indicated by the comparison of exchange line $s's'$ (*not*—it should be emphasized—exchange line $w'w'$) with line aa, consumers will trade X for M, moving the economy's consumption locus to a point on $w'w'$ left of A. But since A (collectively, and appropriately parcelled among individuals) is an open possibility, the new consumption locus must be superior (or, in the limiting case, equal) to it. Thus, an export subsidy which leads to production point B' is superior to autarky; and so would be, needless to say, any lower subsidy. A subsidy beyond that range (that is, at a rate higher than the difference in the prices of X indicated by exchange lines $w'w'$ and $s's'$) would lead, at some point, to a situation *inferior* to the autarky position.

Examine, now, the other possibility: an export subsidy is granted to the free trade *import* good, M. As long as the rate of this subsidy is below that indicated by the difference between aa, the autarky exchange line, and ww, the international exchange line, such a subsidy would have no impact: X would still be exported, and M imported, so that an export subsidy to M would be completely irrelevant. Once the rate of subsidy exceeds this level, however, the pattern of trade will be reversed: M will be exported, and X imported. The new production point will become B'', where the difference between the home price of M (indicated by exchange line $s''s''$) and the international price (indicated by $w''w''$) is equal to the rate of subsidy. Consumption will be somewhere on $w''w''$, to the *right* of B''.[33] Here, the consumption-induced trade is not only inferior to free trade; it is also, necessarily, inferior to the autarky position A. An export subsidy to the free-trade import good would thus, if it is at all effective, reverse the pattern of trade, leading to specialization in the 'wrong' good, and inevitably lead to a deterioration of welfare to below its autarky level—a deterioration which would be larger the higher the rate of subsidy.

To sum up the outcome: an export subsidy, like a tariff, will lead to a welfare loss (in the absence of domestic distortions) in comparison with a policy of free trade. Unlike a tariff, an export subsidy may lead to a welfare loss even in comparison with the autarky position. When the subsidy is granted to the free-trade import good, and is effective, this is a necessary result.

7 The international viewpoint

All the foregoing analysis has been presented from the point of view of a single country. This is in line with the overwhelming part of the literature and analyses of the normative aspects of international trade, and this approach will be retained in most of the rest of the book. It is justified by the simple fact that the policy-making unit is the individual country—and the *raison d'être* of a study of the theory of commercial policy is its implications for policy making. This justification is reinforced when, as we assume in most of the analysis, the country in question is small, so that no foreign repercussions—either by way of foreign policy responses or by way of effects on and of economic performance in the rest of the world—have to be taken into consideration. Yet, both because this is interesting in itself and because some decisions are taken by international concert, or at least with attention to international repercussions, it is worthwhile reviewing briefly the conclusions arrived at in the present analysis from the standpoint of the world as a whole.

The conclusion that free trade is an optimum policy when no domestic distortion exists and the country is small (world prices are given) remains valid when welfare of the world as a whole is concerned—provided no domestic distortion exists in other countries as well.[34] It should be noted, however, that this is not an interesting case from the world's viewpoint. The 'small country' assumption implies that activities, policies or processes in the country have no effect on the outside world; thus, the outcome which is valid in the single-country analysis must also hold for the world as a whole, since the country concerned is the only part of the world affected by its commercial policy.

In the case of a country which does have an effect on its terms of trade, on the other hand, the conclusion of the single-country analysis must be reversed. It was shown that, in this case, free trade cannot be an optimum policy for the country: some non-zero tariff is the optimum. It will be recalled, however, that this non-zero tariff is superior to free trade (or to a lower tariff) because the positive terms-of-trade effect more than offset the negative allocative effect. For the world as a whole, on the other hand, only the negative component exists: the terms of trade effect, which is positive in one country, is equally negative for its trade-partner country. Put differently: we may, in this context, look at the world as a whole as one unit—as if it were a single country. Free trade (in the absence of what was called for a single country 'domestic' distortions) would lead to the fulfil-ment of all Pareto-optimum conditions in this unit, thus yielding maximum welfare; whereas tariffs in one or more countries, the sub-units, would violate conditions (a) and (c)—thus also (d)—and would reduce the unit's welfare.

The conclusion that in the presence of 'domestic' economic distortion free trade and autarky, as well as various levels of restricted trade, could not be ranked, remains valid from the standpoint of the world as a whole. The only qualification that may be added is a probabilistic statement, namely: that trade restriction (and higher levels of it) is more likely to lower rather than raise welfare when the world as a whole is concerned than when only the single country is involved—provided, again, that the 'domestic' distortions under consideration exist only in the single country, whereas other economies are free of distortions.[35] It likewise remains valid—and is perhaps even clearer in this context—that the optimum policy combination is free trade and subsidies (taxes) to correct the source of distortion: such policy would simply leave the world economic 'unit' free of any distor-tions, so that all optimum conditions are fulfilled and welfare is at its maximum.

This review thus leads to the conclusion that all policy rankings established from the single-country's viewpoint are valid also from the standpoint of the world as a whole except one, where variable terms of trade led to the conclusion that for the single country some non-zero tariff is optimum. In other words, from the world's viewpoint there is no exception to the conclusion that under all circumstances, free trade (combined, when appropriate, with subsidies to offset domestic distortions) is the optimum policy. It should be pointed out, however, that once free trade does not exist in other countries, a move in one country from restricted to free trade, or from more to less restriction, does *not* necessarily increase the welfare level. This would be equivalent to the single country situation when, in the face of other distortions, the degree of one distortion is lowered. As we have seen, such a move does not necessarily increase welfare.

Here, as in the single-country analysis, welfare criteria may be questioned. Free trade leads to maximum welfare in the situation sense—potential welfare, that is, or actual welfare of everybody if income-redistribution (ideal compensation) is carried out. When compensation is not made—and income transfers in an international context are probably even less likely than within a nation—actual welfare comparisons cannot be made except by the use of subjective value judgements about various income distributions. Thus, if equality of per capita income levels in the world's various countries is considered good and this target is assigned a heavy weight, one may reach the conclusion that, in the absence of international income transfers, a tariff which raises real income (through its terms-of-trade effect) in poor countries is 'good': it increases welfare, even though it leads to non-optimality and loss of world welfare in the situation sense.[36]

Notes

1 Since the exchange line will appear repeatedly, it may be worthwhile to state precisely its nature at the outset so that it may later be used freely. A line such as aa shows the number of units of one good which are exchanged for a unit of the other good. If aa is extended to meet the M-axis, the tangent of the angle which it thus forms will be the number of units of X exchanged for a unit of M; and this, in turn, will be the *inverse* of the ratio of prices of the two goods: it will be P_m/P_x. In the same way, the tangent of the angle formed by aa and the X-axis will be P_x/P_m. A steeper exchange line means a higher relative price of X (a higher P_x/P_m, or a lower P_m/P_x); and a flatter exchange line—the opposite.

2 For the purpose on hand, it is immaterial—from the viewpoint of the country in question—whether this price is also that maintained in the foreign country (the 'world'); or whether, due to transportation costs, monopolistic pricing abroad, government subsidies to trade in the foreign country, or any other reason, the price ratio between the goods is different abroad from the price ratio with which the country concerned is faced in its trade. The only requirement is that the latter should be fixed.

3 A point like B may not be found if the transformation curve is flatter at all points than the slope of the world exchange line ww. In

this case, a 'corner solution' will be established, by which production will be at Q, with a complete specialization of the country in its export good X. The analysis would then have to be handled by means of figure 5.

4 Once the tariff reaches the level at which it becomes prohibitive, a still higher tariff level would be irrelevant. With a tariff (unlike subsidies), government interference can at most lead the economy back to autarky position.

5 Another way of stating this would be: for each utility possibility curve $u'u'$ under autarky, a curve $u'u'$ under free trade exists which represents a bundle with more of both goods, and thus contains the autarky curve $u'u'$; hence, one envelope frontier will contain the other.

6 W. Stolper and P. A. Samuelson (1941).

7 P. A. Samuelson (1939).

8 See section 4.

9 For the concept, see for instance R. Findlay (1970, pp. 38–42).

10 N. Kaldor (1940); T. de Scitovsky (1942); J. de V. Graaff (1940–50); R. E. Baldwin (1948, 1952); P. A. Samuelson (1938, 1962). See also recent contributions by J. Bhagwati and H. G. Johnson (1961); H. G. Johnson (1968); and J. Bhagwati and M. C. Kemp (1969). The concept of the optimum tariff was first developed by C. F. Bickerdike (1906).

11 It is assumed here that we know in advance that with trade, X will be exported and M imported. But in the reverse case, an exactly symmetrical demonstration would be made by constructing a curve like $NBSF$ to the right of N—using the foreign-offer curve which shows foreign demand for M and supply of X. The demonstration is, hence, entirely general.

12 The present discussion of the optimum tariff has followed what may be described as the Baldwin–de Graaff–Samuelson approach. Another line of analysis is that formulated in Scitovsky's classic article (1942). Scitovsky developed the concept of 'community indifference curves' in an analytic content which does not assume identity of consumers, and does take into account explicitly changes in income distribution. The most significant contribution of this analysis was the statement of what came to be known as Scitovsky's double criterion of welfare comparisons—which has been applied in the present discussion. In comparisons of two positions, A and B, A may be said to be superior to B only if both conditions are fulfilled: that the gainers in a move from B to A may be able to compensate the losers, and still be left with a surplus; whereas the gainers in a move from A to B can *not*

do the same. Scitovsky's community indifference curves are designed to make this comparison possible: if A's community indifference curve is above B, and B's community indifference curve is below A, the double condition for the superiority of A over B is fulfilled. Scitovsky's use of a system of community indifference curves for determining the optimum tariff is, however, unwarranted: in this demonstration Scitovsky employed the indifference-curve system to determine *demand* and equilibrium positions—for which the system, by its definition, is not fit. Scitovsky did recognize some difficulty, which led him to state that there may be many optimum tariffs, whose welfare levels could not be ranked; but this did not remove the inaccuracy in his method of reaching equilibrium positions. In applying the concept of community indifference curves to the optimum tariff issue all that Scitovsky legitimately achieved was a demonstration that when the foreign offer curve is not infinitely elastic, free trade is a sub-optimal policy. But the concept of community indifference curves was not essential for this purpose, and the theorem of sub-optimality of free trade had indeed been stated and proved earlier, by Samuelson (1938), without resort to such concept.

13 A. P. Lerner (1936).

14 See G. Haberler (1936, pp. 198–208).

15 This demonstration partly reproduces my brief note on the topic (M. Michaely, 1967). See also W. M. Corden (1957b); J. Bhagwati and V. K. Ramaswami (1963).

16 This provides the proof, omitted earlier, of the superiority of free trade over restricted trade in the classical, Ricardian setting of straight-line transformation curves (or with corner solutions of convex curves), where full specialization is achieved even by restricted trade. In such models, a (non-prohibitive) tariff would have no effect on production—making the situation equivalent in this sense to the one assumed in the present discussion, in which production was taken as given in the change from tariff to subsidy. A free trade situation in the Ricardian model would thus be similar to the subsidy situation, in which prices facing home consumers are equal to world prices; whereas trade restricted by tariff would, by making price ratios unequal at home and in foreign trade, lead to an inferior position.

17 See B. Ohlin (1931); G. Haberler (1950); J. E. Meade (1955b, ch. 14); W. M. Corden (1957b, 1967a); E. Hagen (1958); H. G. Johnson (1965c); J. Bhagwati and V. K. Ramaswami (1963); and J. Bhagwati (1971a). A survey of the development of the analysis may be found in S. P. Magee (1973).

18 These have been developed mainly in Bhagwati (1971a); see also Bhagwati and Ramaswami (1963) and Johnson (1965c). Basically similar propositions to (1) and (3) have also been offered in the so-called 'theory of the second best', which will be referred to later.

19 These examples have been introduced to the analysis mainly in Haberler's article (1950). Although Haberler did not use the tool of collective indifference curves, and specified his objections to such use, later writers did not commonly share this reluctance: in most demonstrations, community indifference curves are used either without explanation or with some proviso such as: 'the individual tastes and distribution of income that determine the demand for the two commodities are assumed to be summarizable in a set of community indifference curves, such that for any given income and exchange ratio the consumption of the two commodities will be that which places the community on the highest attainable indifference curve' (Johnson, 1965c, p. 12). In fact, the assumptions required are extremely restrictive—and are entirely dispensable for the purpose on hand. All the conclusions arrived at, in this context, by using the tool of community indifference curves, can be reached without it—as will be done in the following discussion.

20 This is a 'violation' in the sense that the equalities of rates of substitution are not maintained. But with a 'corner solution', as we have in the present case, the absence of required equalities does *not* have any welfare consequence. Hence also the following conclusion about optimum policy.

21 This seems to be a somewhat uncomfortably forced set of assumptions. It is adopted here partly because it so appears (either implicitly or explicitly) in the most well-known analyses of this type of distortion; and, more important, because nothing in the conclusions is changed, as could be easily verified, if it is assumed that even in the autarky position the economy is found to produce (and consume) *within* the transformation curve.

The assumptions underlying this case of 'distortion', as well as the following one, would make more sense were they to be regarded as applying to a stage of *transition*; the costs involved in the shift from one position to another being then adjustment costs.

22 We might have listed separately another optimum condition: equality of marginal rates of substitution between time (leisure) in production and consumption. The existence of unemployment *of labour* would be a violation of this condition (which could, however, be regarded as a special case of the general condition (d)).

23 If the international exchange line is w_1w_1, consistency makes it in-

evitable that the consumption point would be *outside* the transformation curve.

24 The case of *internal* economies is simply that of increasing returns to scale, which has been analyzed in section 4. One of the several variants of the 'infant industry' argument is the case of (positive) external economies. It is preferable, however, to confine the interpretation of this argument to the situation of a change in the whole production function. This will be undertaken in the next chapter.

25 This would be in line with most of the literature on this subject. An important instance in which particular attention is paid to externalities in consumption is Meade's work (1955b, ch. 14).

26 Only a probability statement could be made: the less important are external economies, the less likely it is that specialization would be in the 'wrong' direction; hence, the more likely it is that the more free is trade, the higher the welfare level.

27 We specify that the non-uniformity involves a rent payment in order to rule out cases in which apparently non-uniform factor prices are just sufficient to offset non-uniformity in non-pecuniary elements involved in the employment in each industry, or the transition costs involved in moving from one industry to another; in these cases, factor prices *are* uniform in the meaning relevant for economic analysis.

The discussion of this distortion has been focused primarily on wage differentials among industries. Much of the substance of the analysis is already anticipated in B. Ohlin (1931); but the more recent discussion starts with Hagen (1958), who thought that in underdeveloped countries, the price of labour (the wage rate) is generally higher in manufacturing than in agriculture. Although Hagen was not entirely clear in separating out the rent element in this case—this was pointed out by Bhagwati and Ramaswami (1963), as well as others—there seems to be little doubt that long-term non-uniformity of factor prices may exist, so that the question of optimum policies under this distortion does merit serious consideration.

28 J. N. Bhagwati and T. N. Srinivasan (1971) have shown that in this case not only does the transformation curve shrink, it may turn from being convex from the origin to being concave. In the situation marked by this distortion, some of the elementary propositions lose their validity. Thus, for instance, production response to price may become 'perverse'—a lower price calling forth a larger production—and multiple equilibrium positions rather than a unique equilibrium may be found.

29 It should be recalled that such subsidy is assumed to be financed by non-distortive, lump-sum taxes. Alternatively, instead of a subsidy

an opposite *tax* could be levied to correct the distortion (for instance, a tax of X instead of a subsidy to M, or a tax on the use of a factor in X instead of a subsidy to the use of the same factor in M). With this alternative, the tax proceeds would be assumed to be disbursed to consumers in a non-distortive, lump-sum manner.

30 See, again, A. P. Lerner (1936).

31 But see, for both a comprehensive institutional description and an analytic discussion of non-tariff interference, R. E. Baldwin (1970); see also J. Bhagwati (1965) and F. D. Holzman (1969).

32 For this reason—the trade expansion—we switched here from the use of the term 'trade restriction' to 'interference in trade'. The term 'trade barrier', which is frequently found in the literature, also suggests trade contraction and has therefore not been adopted here.

It should be mentioned that, as we shall shortly see, not *any* export subsidy leads to trade expansion!

33 In comparison with free trade, the size of trade may in this case be either smaller or larger: a high enough export subsidy to M would lead to trade expansion—where, of course, the direction of trade is reversed from its free trade pattern.

34 It should be recalled that in the analysis of a single country, the process by which prices are determined in other countries (the 'world') was irrelevant to the outcome; no assumptions had thus to be made about the fulfilment of optimum conditions abroad, or its absence.

35 The conclusion that the world's and the single-country's viewpoints should lead to identical inferences would be clear under the circumstances assumed in the analysis of 'domestic' distortions: the 'small country' assumption was made all along so that, as has just been explained, the rest of the world becomes irrelevant. If the analysis of policy ranking under distortions were conducted under circumstances in which a terms-of-trade effect does exist, any tariff imposed by a single country would have the following additional effects: a positive terms-of-trade effect in the imposing country, a negative terms-of-trade effect in the rest of the world, and a negative allocative effect in the rest of the world. Since the two terms-of-trade effects cancel each other, the world as a whole realizes (in comparison with the single-country viewpoint) the additional negative allocative effect on the rest of the world. This leads to the probabilistic statement in the text, that trade restriction is more likely to be inferior in the world than in the single-country context.

36 M. Fleming (1956) has analyzed an 'optimum tariff' based on such a viewpoint, where income distribution within each country is

assumed to be equal, utility functions of all individuals in the world are identical and income is assumed, in the Marshallian way, to have a diminishing marginal utility. Needless to say, only the poorer countries are found, in such model, to have positive levels of optimum tariffs.

3

Trade Restriction, Change and Growth

In this chapter, two forms of inter-relationship between trade restriction and change and growth will be examined. First, we shall ask how does an exogenously given growth process affect the economy when trade restrictions are maintained—in contrast with a situation of free trade. Second, we shall examine how the existence of restriction itself affects the process of growth and economic change.

1 Effect of growth when trade is restricted

Let us take first the simplest case. Suppose that all the Pareto-optimum conditions are maintained, and the 'small-country' assumption holds. This is, then, the case in which policies may be clearly ranked: free trade is best, less-restricted trade is superior to more-restricted trade, and autarky is the worst possible situation (confining the means of trade restriction to tariff alone). In Chapter 2 this was analyzed using figure 3. We assume, now, that *unbiased* growth takes place, and compare the pre-growth with the post-growth positions. Unbiased growth will be defined as a change which, at given relative prices of goods, will leave unchanged the relative share of each good in an increased total product. It could come about (recalling that we assume throughout constant returns to scale) in either of two ways—or their combination. One is the increase of all factors of production by the same proportion; in a two-good, two-factor model, this will be represented in the Edgeworth box diagram by a shift from one box to another in which both dimensions of the box are increased by the same proportion. The other way is an unbiased increase in productivity: production functions change so that each function is higher than the original by the same given fraction.[1] In both cases, the new transformation curve will simply be a multiple of the former one, this multiple being above unity by the ratio of increase of the productive factors (in the first case) or the production functions (in the second): each point on the new transformation curve will represent a bundle of goods which contains more of both goods, by the same uniform fraction, than the corresponding point on the old transformation curve on the ray from the origin.

The effect of trade restriction can, under these circumstances, be analyzed without using any new construct—by simply referring again to figure 3. In the new situation, the same transformation curve is valid, with a change in scale: each point on it now represents a higher bundle of goods than before, by the given multiplier. Similarly, budget-restraint line ww, reached by free trade, represents now a line higher by the same multiple; and so do autarky point A, budget-restraint line $w'w'$, and so on.

In the new (post-growth) situation, the ratio of ww to A, or of ww to $w'w'$, is thus the same as in the original situation. Had it been possible to say the same about the relationship of *consumption* locations to each other, we would have reached the conclusion that the loss from trade restriction is, *in terms of a bundle of goods*, higher in the post-growth position than in the original position by the uniform growth ratio; or, similarly, that this loss is the same *fraction* of a given bundle of goods (such as the autarky position, or the free trade position, or national income in the latter in terms of one good or another) as it was before growth took place. Within our present use of welfare criteria, however, such a statement would be devoid of meaning: since welfare is not measured cardinally, we cannot tell whether the loss of welfare in our comparison is 'bigger' or 'smaller' in one situation than in the other.[2] Moreover, we do not know whether the locus of consumption does, indeed, change simply by increasing the consumption of both goods by the given growth ratio: usually, we may assume that such an outcome—of unitary income elasticities—will only be an accident. Thus, such quantitative statements may *not* be made in comparisons of consumption positions.[3]

We shall now move to the analysis of situations in which the exogenous growth process is biased towards one good or another. When the bias is in favour of the economy's export good, there is little by way of general principles which may be added to the discussion of the effects of trade restriction under unbiased growth. When growth is biased, on the other hand, in favour of the import good, a new element is introduced, which may lead to 'perverse' results of growth.

As before, we shall distinguish between the two sources of growth: an increase in the economy's endowment of productive factors; and an increase in productivity of these factors—that is, a change in the production functions. We shall start with an analysis in which the growth is due to an increase in factor endowment. A bias towards one good would then be the result of a change in factor proportions. Specifically, the bias will be in favour of the good which is relatively intensive in the factor whose amount has relatively increased. For the purpose of separating out clearly the effect of the bias, we shall assume—using again a two-good, two-factor model—that the amount of one factor, in which the export industry is intensive, remains unchanged; whereas the amount of the other factor, in which the import industry is intensive, increases, thus raising both the economy's total factor endowment and the ratio of the latter factor to the former. The analysis is carried out with the aid of figure 14.[4]

In figure 14, $P_0 Q_0$ is the economy's transformation curve in the original, pre-growth period 0. As usual, A_0 would be the autarky position, B_0 the free trade production point, and $w_0 w_0$ the international exchange line and the economy's free trade budget restraint. A tariff exists, which leads production to the point B_0': $t_0 t_0$ is the domestic exchange line, and consumption is at some point on the budget-restraint line $w_0' w_0'$ to the left of B_0'. Now growth takes place in the form of an increase in the amount of the factor in which M is intensive. This shifts the economy's transformation curve away from the origin, and a new transformation curve $P_1 Q_1$ is established. An important relationship of the new transformation curve to the original one is given by the

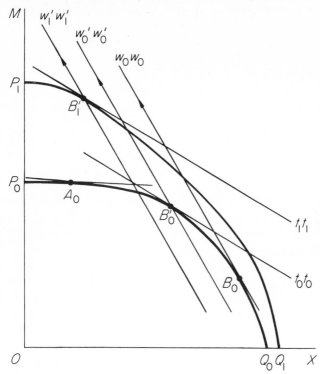

Figure 14

Rybczynski theorem: at any given transformation ratio between the two goods, the production position on the new curve will contain more of the good (M) intensive in the expanding factor and less, *in absolute amount*, of the other good (X).[5] In the case on hand, we do know that the transformation ratio is indeed unchanged from one position to the other: it is equal, in equilibrium, to the exchange ratio facing local producers, which remains unchanged—both the world price ratio and the tariff rate being the same after growth as before it. We thus know that the new home-production point B_1', at which the transformation ratio, indicated by exchange line $t_1 t_1$, is the same as it was at B_0' $(t_0 t_0)$ is to *the left* of B_0' and it contains a smaller production of X. As before, X will be exchanged for M: the economy's consumption point will be on the new budget-restraint line $w_1 w_1$, to the left of B_1'.

If B_1' is contained within $w_0'w_0'$, as it is shown in figure 14, then $w_1'w_1'$ will also be contained within $w_0'w_0'$. Hence, under these circumstances, welfare is *lower* after growth than before it. This is known as a case of 'immiserizing growth': growth has led, due to the existence of trade restrictions, to a decline of the economy's welfare.[6] The intuitive explanation of this 'perverse' outcome is that biased growth has, in these circumstances, two contradicting effects. The impact of *growth* as such is, of course, favourable: it tends to increase welfare. The impact of the *bias*, on the other hand, is in the opposite direction: it serves to attract, to a larger extent than before the change, the economy's resources into the protected (import-substituting) industry, where the social benefit yielded by the employment of resources is lower than in the other, export industry. If the latter factor is strong enough to more than offset the former, immiserizing growth would result.

It is, of course, by no means inevitable that this should be the net outcome of a growth process biased in this way: in terms of figure 14, B_1' and $w_1'w_1'$ may be found to the right of $w_0'w_0'$, indicating a post-growth higher welfare level than before growth has taken place. The probability that this, rather than the 'perverse' result, would be the outcome will be higher the lower is the tariff rate (in terms of figure 14, the smaller the difference between exchange ratios ww and t_0t_0). This is intuitively clear: since the tariff is the source of distortion which gives room to the possibility of immiserization, the lower the tariff the less likely is this possibility to materialize. This probability will also be lower the smaller is the difference in factor intensities among the two goods; the smaller this difference, the smaller is the *bias* in the growth process when one of the factors expands, thus the smaller the (perverse) impact of the bias and the lower the chance of its offsetting the 'normal' impact of growth.

If the expansion of factors is unequal, but *both* factors expand, the probability of an immiserizing growth is, of course, smaller. Suppose that the economy's factor *ratio* changes as in figure 14, but that the factor which was assumed before to remain constant also expands. The new transformation curve (not shown) would be a blow-up of P_1Q_1 with all transformation ratios between X and M found at the same X/M ratios as in P_1Q_1, but with both more of X and M. The point which corresponds to B_1' would thus be further to the right, and the probability that it will be found left of $w_0'w_0'$ will thus be lower; in other words, the probability of a 'normal' outcome will be higher.[7] The impact of such growth may, indeed, be divided into two. First, we may say that part of the expansion of factors, due to an equal proportional increase of all factors, leads to an unbiased growth—with its impact on welfare as analyzed previously. The other part is due to the expansion of only one factor and it is biased, leading to the outcome analyzed under the assumption of such growth. In other words, the analysis of the outcome of a biased growth in which one factor is assumed to be constant serves to separate out the impact of this element in the pattern of expansion. It shows that the more the expansion of factors is biased in favour of the factor in which the protected good is intensive, the more growth is subject to the immiserizing impact of the bias. Thus, for instance, an increase of labour without an accompanying increase of capital in an economy in which the labour-intensive goods are protected would lower per capita income, in its welfare sense, not only because marginal (and average) productivity of labour is falling but also owing to the added effect of drawing resources to the protected (labour-intensive) industries.

We shall turn now to the other source of growth, namely, an increase in productivity. Again, in order to focus the analysis on the part of growth which contains the bias element, we shall assume that the production function of one of the goods—the export good X—remains unchanged; whereas the production function of the other good—import-substituting good M—increases by a given factor.[8] Figure 14 describes adequately this case as well. Again, P_0Q_0 is the original transformation curve. And in this situation too, a given relationship exists between the new transformation curve, P_1Q_1, and the original one: at each transformation ratio between the two goods, more of M and less of X, in *absolute* amounts, will be produced. This may be realized by way of 'verbal geometry'. In an Edgeworth box diagram, the Hicks neutral expansion of the production function of M will leave the contract curve unchanged; but each M isoquant will now stand for a larger amount of M than before the change—larger, that is, by the factor of expansion of the production function.[9] Whatever the point selected on the contract curve, it will show that the specified allocation of factors among the two goods will now produce the same amount of X as before the change, but an amount of M higher by the factor of expansion. Since this is true for all points, we shall find—moving to the transformation curve which is derived from the contract curve—that at any given quantity of X, the transformation ratio between X and M will consist of more units of M per unit of X, in comparison with the original position, by the factor of expansion of M's production function. Thus, if we take, in figure 14, a point on P_1Q_1 vertically above B_0'—the original production locus—we will find at it a transformation ratio higher, in terms of units of M per unit of X, than at B_0'. To find a point with the same transformation ratio, we would have to move to the region of P_1Q_1 *left* of this point—a movement in this direction leading to diminishing rates of transformation of X in terms of M. We have thus found that P_1Q_1 has the same property, in its relationship to P_0Q_0, as it had in the formerly analyzed case of biased growth. All the conclusions derived formerly therefore hold now as well.[10] Thus, we find, again, that this growth may be immiserizing, in the presence of the tariff.[11] Here, too, contradicting tendencies are at work. The change in productivity, leading to a larger product out of a given amount of resources, tends to raise welfare; whereas the increased share of the protected industry, with its lower social yield, tends to reduce welfare—and may do it to an extent which will offset the favourable impact.[12]

We have analyzed, thus far, the possibility of immiserizing growth when trade is restricted—in situations in which free trade would have been an optimum policy: condition (e) of the aforementioned optimum conditions (namely, equality of marginal rates of transformation between goods in home production and in trade) is violated by a tariff. But suppose, now, that the terms of trade are not fixed. Here, the optimum policy would be *not* free trade but some positive tariff—the optimum tariff. Free trade would, in this case, be a violation of the condition just mentioned. It is not surprising, therefore, that under these circumstances *free* trade may lead to immiserizing growth.[13] This is shown with the aid of figure 15.

As before, P_0Q_0 is the original transformation curve. A is the pre-growth autarky position, and B_0 the free trade production point. C_0 is the free trade consumption point. The line B_0C_0

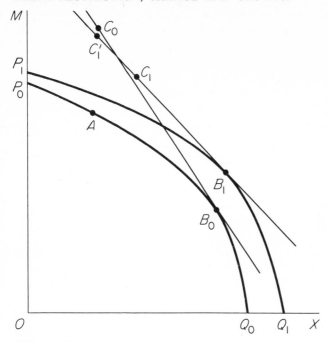

Figure 15

represents the actual exchange ratio in equilibrium; it is *not*, it should be recalled, the economy's budget-restraint line, since the terms of trade are not fixed; yet C_0 is superior, at the actually established income distribution, to any point on the line C_0B_0—or else C_0 could not be an equilibrium position. Suppose now a biased growth to take place—this time in favour of X, the *export* good. We shall assume the growth to originate from changes in factor endowment; but, as we have just seen, an equivalent outcome would follow in the case of growth originating from changes in productivity. We thus assume that the factor of production in which X is intensive expands; whereas the quantity of the other factor remains constant. P_1Q_1 represents the new transformation curve. Again, the Rybczynski theorem tells us that at unchanged prices, the equilibrium production point on P_1Q_1 would contain more of X and less of M, in absolute terms, than the pre-growth production point B_0. But, assuming that both X and M are normal goods, at the original price ratio *more* of M would be demanded by local consumers. That is, if the quantities traded are unchanged—and this is necessarily implied by having no change in prices—an excess demand for M and an excess supply of X would be found. Thus, for a new equilibrium to be achieved, the price of X must fall and the price of M must rise; that is, the country's terms of trade will necessarily deteriorate. The new price at which the economy trades is represented by the exchange line B_1C_1 (which is again, it should be emphasized, *not* a budget-restraint line). If this line cuts the extension of the line B_0C_0 above C_0, the post-growth position is preferable to the original position, regardless of whether the actual post-growth consumption is below or above this intersection point. If, on the other hand, the new exchange line cuts the original line *below* C_0, as it is drawn in figure 15, and the consumption locus is to the left of the intersection—such as C_1'—the new position is inferior to the original one. If, in this case, consumption is to the right of the intersection—such as C_1—the pre-growth and post-growth positions cannot be ranked.

We thus find here too the possibility of immiserizing growth—growth which leads to a welfare loss—due to the violation of the open-economy optimum condition: the violation in this instance is due to the policy of free trade. As before, the probability of such an outcome is a function of the degree of distortion; that is, of the degree of violation of this optimum condition. The higher the optimum level of the tariff—the more, that is, free trade (zero tariff) deviates from the optimum—the more likely is the 'perverse' outcome to materialize. Put differently, free trade is more likely to lead to immiserizing growth the lower is the elasticity of the foreign offer curve. Also, as before, this probability is higher the more the growth process is biased—this time, though, biased towards *exports*. With the distortion now under consideration the export good is the one which attracts an excessive share of the economy's resources; the one, that is, in which resources yield lower social benefit than in the other. The loss in the growth process is due, this time, to the fact that the pattern is biased towards exports, thus increasing further the share of the over-expanded industry.[14] In the present case, a further element—namely, consumption patterns—is introduced in determining the probability of various outcomes. The higher the income elasticity at home of demand for *M*, the import good (and the lower, by the same token, the elasticity of demand for the export good), the more will the terms of trade tend to change against the country; and the more likely, therefore, will be the outcome of immiserizing growth.

We have seen here that a 'perverse' outcome, of welfare loss, may follow from a growth pattern which is biased in a specified direction, when the open-economy optimum condition is violated. But in a similar way, it may be shown that such outcome is also possible when growth occurs in the context of *domestic* distortions.[15] In a general way, then, a welfare-reducing growth may result whenever trade is accompanied by the existence of distortions, be they violations of the domestic or of the open-economy optimum conditions.

2 Effect of trade restriction on growth patterns

In the preceding section, the growth pattern has been taken as an exogenous given development. We shall now turn to the question of how trade restriction affects the growth process and the growth pattern.

Once more, it will be helpful to recall that growth may originate from either of two sets of factors: increases in factor endowments and increases in factor productivity (although, as will be pointed out shortly, the classification into one or the other of these two sets may sometimes be arbitrary). We shall thus ask how trade restriction affects each of these two sets; and what are the welfare implications of these effects. In the present section, we shall explore the impact of trade restriction on specific factor endowment and on productivity. The following two sections will be devoted to the effect of trade policy on the economy's endowment of capital.

The discussion of effects on specific factors and on technological changes is combined here mainly because the distinction between the two is somewhat blurred, and is often a matter of arbitrary definition. This applies, *inter alia*, to the possibility which will form the centre of the present analysis, namely that trade and specialization affect *with time* the production process. It is possible that specialization in a given industry, involving increased production in it, leads in time to cost reduction through the process known as 'learning by doing'.[16] The emphasis on the time element here should be noticed. The cost reduction involved in this process does *not* arise from a production function specifying increasing returns to scale: these may be assumed to be constant. The contention is, rather, that the combination of the scale of production with the length of time of operation of the industry governs the change of conditions in the industry's production; or, in other words, that these conditions are a function of the accumulated production in the industry, throughout the period considered.[17] Now, these 'changed conditions' may be described as either changes in factor endowments or in the industry's production function (its technology). If, in the production function, 'factors of production' are defined in minute detail, so that each 'factor' is strictly homogeneous, we may say that this accumulation of production has led to an increase in specific factors. Productive factors—primarily labour of various shades—have changed in nature, thus changing, by definition, factor quantities. For instance (this is probably one of the most important examples), unskilled labour, or labour of some other skill, can acquire particular skills specific to the industry under consideration. We may then say that the economy's factor endowment has changed: the amount of this specific factor—labour of a particular skill—has increased; whereas the amount of unskilled labour, or of labour of other skills, has diminished. If, on the other hand, we define factors in the production function in a broader way—for instance, in the extreme case, into just 'labour' and 'capital'—we would say that the factor endowment remained constant, but the production function has changed. This would be a technological expansion in this industry: with the same amount of factors, production will now be higher, due to the new knowledge (skill) acquired in the industry.

As we shall see—and as we have already seen, in a slightly different context, in the analysis of the former section—the outcome of the analysis would be the same whether the changes take place in factor endowments or in technology, or whether we chose to define these changes in one way or the other. It is more important, on the other hand, whether the changes in factor endowment, or in technology, are neutral or not. In the case of changes in factor endowments, the difference would be between equiproportional change in the amounts of factors employed by the industry and a change in one (or some) of the factors and not (or in a lesser proportion) in the others. In the case of a technological change, the distinction would be between a neutral expansion and one which is biased towards some of the factors versus the others. In the present discussion, we shall assume consistently the simplest possibility, namely, that the change is neutral.[18] We shall also separate out the impact of the process on hand, by way of assuming that without it no changes would have taken place; this isolates the impact on the growth *pattern*. If, in addition, an exogenously given growth takes place, this could be superimposed on the pattern indicated. We shall also remain in the two-good world. We shall assume throughout a small country, and the absence of distortions—conditions in which free trade was found to be an optimum policy.

In figure 16, P_0Q_0 is the transformation curve at the starting period. As usual, A_0 is the autarky position; B_0 would be the free-trade position, with ww representing the world exchange line and the free-trade budget restraint of the economy, and the consumption locus somewhere on it to the left of B_0. We now assume that the economy's factor endowment is affected by its specialization pattern: an increase in the production of one good tends to raise the available amount of the factor (or factors) in which this good is intensive, and *lower* the amount of the other factor (or factors) in which the other good—whose production contracts—is intensive. We shall also make, for the moment, a specific assumption, namely that these two changes, in opposite directions, precisely offset each other at the original point of production; with the new factor endowment, this production combination is still one of the open possibilities. We shall call this a 'pure-rotation' change. In figure 16, P_0Q_0 should be interpreted as the transformation curve established under the autarky pattern of production, after all the potential dynamic effects have materialized. Switching the economy now to the free trade pattern of specialization, and realizing the dynamic changes involved in the new pattern, a new transformation curve, P_1Q_1, is eventually established. Under the assumption of a pure-rotation change, B_0 will be a common point to the original and the new

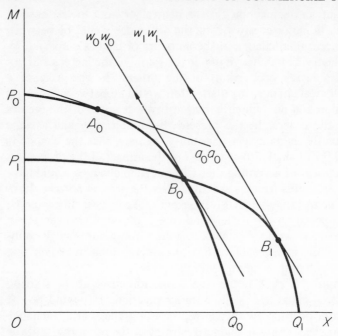

Figure 16

transformation curves. But with the new factor endowment, we know that OQ_1, the maximum possible production of the good (X) in which the country specializes, must be higher than OQ_0, the maximum possible production at the original situation; whereas the opposite is true for M, the import-substituting good from which production turns away: OP_1 must be lower than OP_0.

It is immediately evident that B_1, the eventual equilibrium production point after the dynamic changes are realized, must be to the right of w_0w_0, and so is, hence, the new budget-restraint line w_1w_1. We thus find that the new budget-restraint line contains the original one: welfare has increased. In other words, the welfare loss from following an autarkic policy is *higher* when the dynamic process, following any specialization pattern, is taken into account.[19] It would be easy to see, in a similar way, that the welfare loss involved in autarky (that is, in a prohibitive tariff) in comparison with *restricted* trade (that is, a non-prohibitive tariff) will be higher, when the dynamic change is taken into account—assuming, again, a pure-rotation change. The reason is similar: with restricted trade, some specialization (although not as much as under free trade) takes place, leading to some further gains, due to the dynamic process, which are denied by the autarkic policy. It cannot be stated unequivocally, on the other hand—even adhering consistently to the assumption of pure-rotation changes—what is the relationship between the original and the post-change welfare losses of restricted trade in comparison with free trade. In any case, this comparison could be made only in terms of aggregates of goods; or, in other words, it would require welfare to be cardinally measurable.

While a tariff policy could only retain an autarky position, we have seen that an export subsidy granted to the free-trade *import* good will, if it is at all effective, lower welfare to below its autarky level. In this case the economy will specialize in M and contract the production of X. This situation is represented in figure 17. In this case, under the present assumption of changes in factor endowments, the economy's transformation curve will be skewed towards M, so that OP_1 (the maximum possible production of M) will be *larger* than in the original transformation curve and OQ_1 smaller. In this case, the direction of the added impact of the dynamic process—in the comparison of the export subsidy with the *autarky* position—cannot be predicted unequivocally. In figure 17, the original production point is B_0', the budget-restraint line $w_0'w_0'$, and consumption somewhere on this line to the *right* of B_0' (M becoming, in this case, the exported good). We know that B_1', the new production point after the change, must be to the left of B_0'; that is, it will be a combination including less of X than in the original position. But B_1' could be either to the left or to the right of $w_0'w_0'$, the original budget restraint. In the latter case, which is shown in the diagram, $w_1'w_1'$, the new budget-restraint line will be to the right of $w_0'w_0'$, and welfare will have increased from the original position; that is, the welfare loss (again, in comparison with the autarky position) due to the interference in trade via export subsidy will in this case diminish by the dynamic change. But B_1', and $w_1'w_1'$, could also be found to the left of $w_0'w_0'$—in which case the welfare loss will have increased from the original position. The reason for this equivocal outcome is that two contradicting

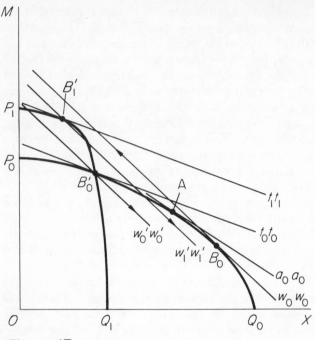

Figure 17

factors are here at work. On the one hand, with the change, the production turns even more than in the original position towards specialization in the 'wrong' good—a factor which tends to lead to a further welfare loss. But on the other hand, the change in factor endowments improves the relative position of that good; that is, it is becoming less of a 'wrong' good than before—a factor which tends to raise welfare, and offset the effect of the former factor.

As has been noted, all this analysis could just as well be conducted by means of specifying as the dynamic process not a change in factor endowments but a change in technology: we might have assumed that with specialization in a given good, the production function of that good changes so that any combination of productive factors would produce more of that good than before the change; whereas in the other good, whose production contracts, an opposite change in the production function takes place. Both the analysis and its conclusions would be exactly the same as in the case of changes in the economy's factor endowment.

Until now, we have discussed what has been termed here the pure-rotation change: the slope of the transformation curve changes, but the original and the new transformation curves both include (that is, they intersect at) the original production position. In this specific sense, this may be understood as a no-growth situation. This, however, would be only one possible case, which may best be regarded as an *aspect*, or a component, of any change. In the general case, the development of factor amounts, or of production functions, would have what may be called a 'pure-growth' effect—either positive or negative—as well as a 'rotation' effect. If one industry realizes the impact of dynamic developments (of factor amounts, or of technological expansion) more than another, and the economy specializes in this good, the result will be a positive growth effect; whereas if the economy happens to specialize in the other good, it will realize a negative growth effect.

The possible resulting positions are numerous and we shall not elaborate upon them. In general, it is obvious that when the 'pure growth' effect is positive in specialization in the export good, and negative in the import-substituting good, this will work in the same way as the impact of the rotational change, and will tend to increase even further the welfare loss involved in following an autarkic versus a free trade policy. When the positive growth potential lies in the import-competing industry, on the other hand, the two impacts will work in opposite directions.

We shall now analyze such a case, assuming for simplicity an extreme situation: when we specialize in the (free trade) import good, this leads to an increase in the endowment of factors which is *not offset* by an opposite change in the other industry whose production contracts; it may be partly offset, but the net effect is still a change in factor endowments which expands the production frontier—the transformation curve—all along. Alternatively, we may assume that in the expanding industry a technological advance—expansion of the production function—is realized, whereas no opposite technological change takes place in the contracting industry.[20]

In figure 18, we start with a free trade pattern of specializa-

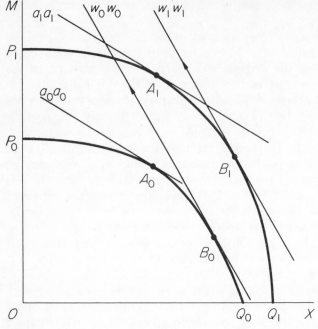

Figure 18

tion. The original transformation curve is P_0Q_0; the free trade production position is B_0; and consumption is somewhere to its left on w_0w_0. The transformation curve is assumed to represent a stationary state; that is, it shows production possibilities after the economy has fully adjusted, in its factor endowment and technological capability, to the free trade production pattern. The autarky position, under these circumstances, is A_0. Suppose, now, that a prohibitive tariff is imposed, leading indeed to production (and consumption) position A_0. The immediate effect is, of course, a welfare loss. But now the dynamic impact starts, leading eventually in the new stationary state to the new transformation curve P_1Q_1. In line with our present assumptions, we see here not merely a rotation of the transformation curve, but an overall expansion, which is extreme in the sense that the new transformation curve fully contains the original.[21]

We do not know precisely where the new autarky position will be, on P_1Q_1: all we know is that, if trade is still restricted by tariff, this position will be left of B_1—the point at which the world exchange line, w_1w_1, is tangent to the country's new transformation curve. It is self-evident that the new consumption locus is superior to the original autarky position. But we can easily see, moreover, that the new autarky position may be superior to the original *free trade* position. If the new autarky locus is left of w_0w_0 the original free trade budget-restraint line, it is obviously still inferior to the free trade situation. When, on the other hand, it is a point such as A_1, the new autarky position *may* be superior to free trade: if the free trade consumption locus were on w_0w_0 at a point below its intersection with a_1a_1 (the new autarky position home exchange ratio), the new autarky position would be superior to the original free trade position; if the latter were above this intersection, the two positions could not be ranked.[22]

It thus appears that, due to the dynamic element being biased in the specified way, the eventual (stationary-state) autarky position may be superior to the free trade position. This is, in essence, the basic content of the most famous—and most respectable—argument for trade restriction; namely, the 'infant-industry' argument. As has been noted on a few earlier occasions, this argument has more than one variant, and is subject to more than one interpretation. Thus, some of its proponents may have had in mind the case of an industry which is *statically* subject to increasing returns to scale; whereas others may have based the argument on the existence of externalities. But at least something resembling the circumstances analyzed in the text has usually appeared in the argument, either explicitly or implicitly; and this is the only solid foundation for the 'infant-industry' argument as a separate one, independent from the general situations of distortions analyzed previously in the static content.[23] Very often, the argument is applied to whole sectors, such as the industrial sector in less-developed economies. Due to the prominent place occupied by this argument, it would be worthwhile to point out in some more detail the conditions and the attributes of this situation.[24]

First, it should be recalled that for this favourable outcome for trade restriction to hold, the dynamic element must indeed be biased in this specified way: the effect of the cumulative scale of production on factor creation and technological expansion must be relatively important in the import good, and unimportant in the country's export good. If the dynamic effects are unbiased, in the sense defined previously—that is, if a changed pattern of specialization only rotates the transformation curve—the outcome, we have seen, would be quite the opposite: the dynamic element would only reinforce the static welfare loss. And this, of course, is *a fortiori* true if the dynamic element is biased in favour of the free trade export good.

Second, it should also be noticed that an outcome which shows a welfare-superior autarky position (over free trade) in the new stationary state does *not* necessarily lead to the conclusion that a welfare gain is involved in the process as a whole. This would have been true only if the social discount rate for delayed consumption were zero: in this case, whatever the length of the transition period (that is, the time from the original period until the static loss turns into a static gain), the process must pay, since the new stationary-state gain would be maintained 'forever'. With a positive discount rate, on the other hand, which assigns continuously diminishing weight the further away is consumption in time, the present and immediate future losses weigh particularly heavily. The higher the discount rate, the lower is the probability that the net balance of losses and gains throughout the years would show a welfare gain.

Third, for the infant-industry argument to be applicable as a claim for restriction of trade, the dynamic benefits must be *external to the firm*. If the accrual of specific factors is strictly at the disposal of the firm which expands production (that is, only this firm enjoys the ensuing relative fall of prices of these factors) or the technological improvement is strictly the domain of this individual firm, then it alone would reap the added benefit of the dynamic process. If, then, this process as a whole results in a net gain to the community, it must also lead to a net gain to the individual firm. In other words: the firm would find it profitable to expand production of the import-substituting good in the present, under *free trade* prices, knowing that future profits (discounted properly) would more than offset present losses. If, under these circumstances, the individual firm finds the process unprofitable, so would it be for society as a whole (assuming, *inter alia*, a perfectly competitive capital market, in which the interest rate on borrowed funds reflects the discount rate, at the margin, of consumption over time). It is only when the dynamic benefits are—partly at least—the domain of other potential firms as well as of the firm which undertakes the expansion of production (without the latter being able to charge others for their access to these benefits), that the process may yield a net welfare gain to the community and yet a net loss to the individual ('pioneering') firm. The existence of such externalities is thus a *necessary* (but, of course, not sufficient) condition for the validity of the 'infant-industry' situation as an argument for trade restriction.[25]

Using figure 18 it is possible to see, on the other hand, that another criterion used often in judging the desirability of protecting an 'infant industry' is unduly severe, and actually represents a misconception of the case. It is stated often that if at the new stationary state, after the expansionary benefits are fully realized, protection is still required, this would be a demonstration of failure, indicating *ex post* that the argument of gains from protection must have been wrong. In terms of figure 18, fulfilment of such indication of success would mean that the new autarky home exchange line, a_1a_1, has to be at least as steep as ww, the international exchange line; or, in other words, that A_1, the new autarky position, would be either to the right of B_1—M turning them into the export good—or at least that the two points should coincide, making the opening of the economy to free trade irrelevant. But, as has just been shown, this situation is not required at all for the demonstration of a (static) gain in the new stationary state: all that is needed is that A_1, the new autarky position, should be superior to C_0—the original consumption locus, somewhere on w_0w_0. This may be fulfilled by any point, such as A_1, which is to the right of w_0w_0, even though it is *left* of B_1; that is, even though the existing production level is maintained only by trade restrictions. Thus, the post-expansion existence of restrictions is *not* an indication of a necessary failure and welfare loss from protection of the infant industry.

It is not clear, moreover, whether in the new stationary state, the removal of trade restriction should be recommended. Moving to free trade in this situation will involve the shift of the production point to B_1, and of consumption to a point left of it on the budget-restraint line w_1w_1; a *static* welfare gain will then be realized. If the preceding expansion—by way of changes in factor endowment, or in technology—is *irreversible*, nothing should be added to this conclusion: the static gain in welfare will remain permanent, through time, and free trade will thus clearly be superior. If, on the other hand, the dynamic process is fully reversible, then the economy will gradually return to its original production frontier, P_0Q_0, with a static welfare loss clearly resulting in this eventual position (assuming, of course, that A_1 is indeed superior to the original free trade consumption locus).[26] If the process is only partly reversible, the magnitude of this reversibility will determine whether in the end result (where the production possibility will be represented by a transformation curve lying between P_1Q_1 and P_0Q_0) a welfare gain or a welfare loss is involved in the post-expansion shift to free trade.

3 Effects on capital endowment: domestic capital formation

Trade policy could affect the economy's capital endowment either by its impact on domestic capital formation or via its effects on capital inflow from abroad. The former channel will be discussed in the present section and the latter in the following one.[27] These discussions can no longer be handled solely, or even primarily, by the analytic method applied consistently until now—the general-equilibrium, microeconomic analysis of a two-good world. Macroeconomic analysis has now to be used. Specifically in the present section reliance will be placed on the neoclassical growth model. The adoption of this model implies, *inter alia*, making the assumption that domestic capital formation is determined by the supply (availability) of savings: market forces (the interest rate) make *ex ante* investment equal to saving. It will be assumed, first, that the saving rate is fixed and constant—it is uniform, at all income levels—and is unchanged by trade and trade policy. Later on, we shall ask whether the saving *rate* itself may be influenced by trade. As in the preceding discussions, a small country will be assumed throughout, with no domestic distortions, so that free trade is an optimum policy on static grounds.

Figure 19 is a familiar presentation of the neo-classical, one-

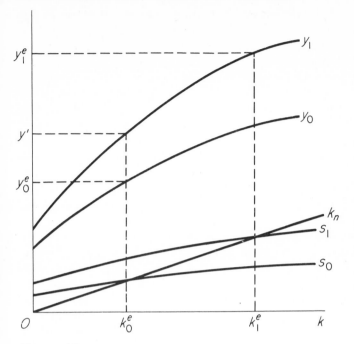

Figure 19

sector growth model.[28] Two factors, labour (L) and capital (K), produce one good, which thus also constitutes income. All scales on the diagram are *per worker*:[29] k, measured on the horizontal axis, is the amount of capital per worker, whereas y and s measured on the vertical axis are, respectively, annual income and saving per worker. With a given production function, y_0 relates the size of y (income per worker) to the size of k (capital per worker). At a given saving ratio, the amount of saving per worker, s_0, is derived from y_0: at any k, the s/y ratio is the same. It is assumed that the labour force (L) grows at a given, fixed annual rate, of n per cent. The line k_n shows the amount of new capital formation per worker that has to be added in order to maintain any given level of the stock of capital per worker in the face of this growth of labour force. This amount is a linear function of the existing size of capital: the larger this size, the larger, by the same proportion, is the addition required in order to maintain the level of capital per worker constant. Thus, k_n is a straight line, starting at the origin, whose angle is determined by the value of n, the assumed rate of growth of the labour force. In this economy k_0^e will be the equilibrium level of the capital stock: when the existing level is below it, the amount of saving (indicated on s_0) is higher than the amount required to maintain the given stock of capital, and the amount of capital per capita will hence increase; whereas when, to the contrary, the existing level of capital is higher than k_0^e, the new savings generated will not be sufficient to maintain per capita capital on this level, which will thus tend to fall. Only if k_0^e is the existing capital level will it remain so from one period to the next: this is, thus, the steady-state equilibrium level of capital. At this level, y_0^e is the income level, which is hence the steady-state equilibrium level of per capita income.

Let us now assume that y_0 represents the income generated in the economy under *autarky*. But when the economy is opened to trade and specialization, this level rises. Trade is the equivalent of a technological expansion—a change in the production function: with any given amount of labour and capital (and the capital/labour ratio specified by it), a higher income is generated with trade than without it.[30] This new income level, with any given amount of capital, is represented by the new curve y_1, which is higher than y_0. Assuming, we recall, that trade does not affect the saving ratio, the saving curve rises—from s_0 to s_1—by the same proportion. We now see that the steady-state equilibrium level of capital rises, from k_0^e to k_1^e. Consequently, the equilibrium level of income rises too, to the new steady-state level y_1^e. Thus, trade has led to a rise of income, from one equilibrium level to another, of the size $y_0^e y_1^e$. This may be divided into two parts. First, we get the rise from y_0^e to y', which is equivalent to the 'static' gain from trade: with unchanged capital, income is now higher than under the autarky position. Next follows the rise of income from y' to y_1^e, which is due to the increase in the size of capital (per worker) in the economy. This is hence an added 'dynamic' element of the gains from opening the economy to trade. The increase in the capital stock is itself, of course, the result of the rise of income at any given level of capital stock: at the former equilibrium position, the increase in income and savings raises the rate of increase of capital; and the process of increasing the capital stock continues until a new, higher level is reached, which the current savings are just sufficient to maintain constant from one period to the next.[31]

We thus reach the conclusion that in a situation in which free trade leads to a 'static' welfare gain, a further, 'dynamic' gain is created, by way of leading to an increase of the equilibrium level of capital stock and thus to a further increase of income. This would hold also for the comparison of free trade with restricted trade; or of restricted trade with autarky. This dynamic process, it should be emphasized, is separate from—hence additive to—the element discussed earlier, of the loss from trade restriction which is involved in biasing the pattern of expansion. On the other hand, the argument would be reversed in circumstances in which free trade is not a static optimum. If the existence of a certain domestic distortion, for instance, leads to a loss from free trade, the impact of this trade on the stock of capital would be the reverse of what it has been shown here; and a dynamic element of loss would be added to the static loss.

We have assumed, in this analysis, a given saving rate. If, however, the opening of the economy to trade could also be shown to raise the saving rate the outcome of the analysis would be reinforced. If, on the other hand, trade leads in the opposite direction—lowering the saving rate—an offsetting factor would be at work. There is no general presumption which may be made about the direction of the effect of trade, and of trade restriction, on the rate of saving in the economy. Two main channels through which such an effect is possible are income distribution and the relative prices of investment goods. Trade may be expected, except by an accident, to change income distribution in one way or another.[32] If, as is often assumed, the propensity to save out of profits is higher than it is out of wages—an assumption whose theoretical ground or empirical justification are not entirely obvious—trade would lead to an increase of the economy's saving rate when the economy is relatively capital abundant and specializes in the capital-intensive good; and to an opposite tendency in a labour-abundant economy. In a similar way, if the marginal propensity to save is rising—another assumption whose validity is questionable—trade would lead to a higher saving rate if it raises income inequality, and would lower the rate if it leads to a greater equality of income.

A somewhat better-founded proposition may be established

with regard to the impact of trade on saving via relative prices. If the price of investment goods falls, in relation to the price of consumption, the substitution effect would lead to an increase in the saving rate.[33] Thus, in an economy which specializes, with trade, in consumption goods, the relative price of investment goods will fall, and trade will lead to a rise of the saving rate; the opposite tendency will be established in an economy in which trade leads to specialization in investment goods.[34]

Still another argument relates trade and trade restriction to the saving rate not via relative prices of certain goods but through their *availability*: it is suggested that if 'conspicuous-consumption' goods are imported and no domestic production of these goods would be forthcoming even if imports are totally prohibited, such complete import prohibition would lead to an increase of the saving rate.[35]

4 Effects on capital endowment: foreign-capital inflow

By its impact on the rate of profit, either in the economy as a whole or in certain segments of it, trade policy may have an effect on the size of capital inflow from abroad. Let us take, first, the rate of profit in the economy, assuming—as we explicitly or implicitly have throughout the analysis—that this rate is uniform. We shall also assume the existence of a positively sloped, but not infinitely elastic, foreign supply curve of capital to the country, in which this uniform profit rate is the relevant price.[36] We recall that, by the Stolper–Samuelson theorem, trade will lead to an absolute increase in the price of the factor (or factors) in which the economy is relatively abundant, and to an absolute decline of the price of the other factor (or factors). Thus, in a capital-abundant country, free trade would lead to an increase in the rate of profit—the price of capital; and this rise, in turn, will result in an increase of capital inflow from abroad. In a labour-abundant economy, free trade will have the opposite impact; and trade restriction would be the policy which leads to a rise of the rate of profit. This is nothing but an illustration of the familiar description of movement of goods and movement of factors as being substitutes for each other: instead of importing capital-intensive goods, the labour-abundant country will import from abroad the capital itself. It should be noted, though, that the rise of profits, and the ensuing capital imports, are one side of an impact the other side of which is the fall of real wages.

Beyond this possible effect, is there any other channel through which trade restriction may influence capital inflow? A traditional argument for trade restriction on this score is applied in a partial-equilibrium context, which may easily yield misleading conclusions. The argument runs approximately as follows:[37] if a tariff is imposed on the import of a certain good, the foreign producer may often be motivated to establish a plant—a so-called 'tariff factory'—in the domestic country, as a possible way of circumventing the obstacle posed by the tariff. The argument obviously rests on imperfections in capital markets. Specifically, two of the assumptions just used in the general-equilibrium analysis are disposed of. First, no uniform rate of profit in the economy is assumed. Instead, the protection of the specific industry in question is assumed to lead, not only as a transitional phenomenon, to an increase of the rate of profit in this industry; a factor which, in turn, gives rise to the foreign capital inflow. Second, it is no longer assumed that *one* supply schedule of foreign capital to the country exists, but that this supply is segmented, each segment being responsive not to the domestic economy's 'profit rate' in general but to profits in a specific industry: potential foreign capital supply is not general, but 'sector specific'.[38] This is believed to be an attribute mainly of capital which flows in the form of direct investment, rather than by acquisition of financial assets.

But even if these two assumptions are granted—as they probably should be, so far as the evidence of empirical studies suggests—the conclusion that trade restriction leads, in this way, to capital imports, does not necessarily follow. Beyond the aforementioned possible impact on the *general* level of profits, the profit rise in one sector is matched by a profit decline in another sector. In the two-good world, the protection of the import-substitute good leads to the contraction of the export good; and this would remain true for an economy with many goods. In the contracting sectors, profits will fall; and capital inflow from abroad will diminish (or capital *outflow*, of a domestic capital specific to these sectors, will increase). In the general case, it is not possible to assert which of these two offsetting tendencies will be stronger, and what will be the net outcome. The result depends on the supply elasticities, in both the foreign and the domestic markets, of the sector-specific capital in the various sectors: if these happen to be particularly high in the protected sectors, the outcome will be a net increase of capital inflow; whereas the conclusion will have to be reversed in the opposite case. It is conceivable that the process will not be random, but biased in favour of capital imports: this will emerge from trade restrictions designed specifically—either in full or in part—to serve the purpose of encouragement of capital imports. Such policy will involve a tendency to impose tariffs (or higher tariffs) on industries in which the supply of sector-specific capital is relatively elastic; whereas industries in which capital supply is comparatively inelastic will be discriminated against.

It is not self-evident that in instances in which a net inflow of capital does result—either owing to a general rise of the level of profits, or owing to protection of sectors which face relatively elastic foreign capital supply—this inflow will indeed lead to an increase of welfare. It must be emphasized that this question refers to any *additional* impact, beside those previously analyzed. We have seen that, under given assumptions, both static and dynamic losses will result from trade restriction; but we ask now whether the net capital inflow from abroad tends in any way to offset—or reinforce—this impact.[39] The answer is that in the absence of distortions of any type, the capital inflow will be immaterial: capital will be paid its marginal product, which is equal—under this assumption—to the private firm and the community as a whole. Since the ownership of the incoming capital is foreign, and the profits will be transferred abroad to the capital owners, the contribution of the foreign capital will be fully appropriated by the outside world.[40] The possibility of a net gain, leading to an increase of the community's welfare, may arise only when a distortion of one kind or another exists. One such possible distortion, often mentioned, emerges from external economies of foreign capital:[41] it is thus argued that foreign direct investment, by introducing and bringing to the fore new (for the domestic country) techniques of production or management, establishing new channels of communication with the outside world, and so on, creates a new 'atmosphere' and leads to the availability of more information—contributions to the community for which the owners of the foreign capital are not rewarded in the market by way of profits. Another likely distortion would be imperfections in other factor markets—particularly in the market for labour in general or for labour of specific categories. If (domestic) labour of such a category whose market price is above equilibrium level (namely, in the market of which excess supply and unemployment are found) is employed in conjunction with the added capital, the social marginal productivity of the incoming capital will be higher than the profits remitted abroad.[42] In such instances, thus, the inducement of capital inflow will, *per se*, tend to increase the community's welfare.

5 Trade policy and development

A few hypotheses are frequently found in the literature on development concerning the impact of trade policy on growth of countries which are at the early, pre-industrial stage of economic development.[43] These are not normally presented within rigorous, self-contained analytical constructs: the hypotheses may more aptly be described as yielded from historical experience—which itself may be and often is subject to quite different interpretations and conclusions. To a large extent, these hypotheses incorporate, either explicitly or implicitly, some of the arguments discussed earlier, in the present and former chapters; but often, they go beyond it. At least a brief mention of some of these hypotheses would be in order, partly because postwar policy patterns in the category of countries under consideration have apparently been materially influenced by these arguments for trade restriction.

The most common contention is that economic growth, in the countries which belong to the category under discussion, must be based on industrialization. These countries are now found, on the other hand, to specialize in primary production—the production of agricultural goods and raw materials. If left to the market forces alone, the argument runs, this pattern of specialization will remain intact. Hence, a protection policy is called for, which would lead to the replacement of imports of industrial goods by domestic production.

To an extent, this conclusion is based on the assumption that the establishment of manufacturing has both a static externality and the dynamic impact discussed earlier under the heading of the 'infant industry' argument—and nothing need be added on it in the present context. But additional arguments are involved. One of the contentions made most frequently, in this connection, is that the import substitution is called for because the terms of trade are expected, as a matter of long-run historical trend, to turn against primary products and in favour of manufactured goods. The historical evidence does not support this contention unambiguously, nor do some *ex ante* predictions based on assumed models. But even if such a trend is granted, the policy implication would not be obvious. The argument may be referring to the need for an optimal tariff system—including taxes on exports as well as on imports—due to the effects of supply of the countries concerned on their terms of trade. An element which is sometimes added is that the impact of the group of countries under consideration, as a whole, on its terms of trade with the world outside the group, is stronger than the impact of each individual country. Hence, an improvement will follow if these countries work in unison, rather than separately, and this would imply, in turn, a system in which the optimal levels of tariffs are higher than when each of the countries operates independently. What is more often understood by the argument is, however, a 'dynamic' projection, in which adverse price movements are to be expected. It must be implied, furthermore, that while this is a correct projection, it is not shared by private entrepreneurs: private considerations based on correct predictions will have taken this trend into account; and if it is still found worthwhile to invest in the primary industries, this must also be true for the community as a whole. No trade restriction would then be called for (beyond that required by the static optimum-tariff considerations). Alternatively, the assumption implied may be that private discount rates are, due to imperfections in the capital market, higher than the social discount rate; hence, the future loss of revenue due to the (expected) deterioration of terms of trade is discounted more heavily by the private entrepreneur, leading him to establish an enterprise which would not have been found profitable had the 'correct' discount rate been used. This, in turn, would again be an argument for protection due to the existence of domestic distortions, which has already been analyzed.

Part of the argument for trade restriction derives from an assumption of a process in which, unlike the mechanism of the neo-classical growth model, the amount of capital in the economy (and the rate of investment) is not determined primarily (or solely) by the available supply of savings but by demand for investment. The latter, in turn, is apparently not dependent so much on the cost of capital (in which case it could easily be affected by monetary–fiscal policy) but by the availability of sufficiently large local markets for the goods in question. The clearest analysis along these lines is probably Nurkse's 'balanced-growth' theory: growth can take place, according to this hypothesis, only if investment is undertaken in many lines simultaneously. The additional income generated, and the demand thus created, justify the undertaking of the various investment projects; whereas investment which is concentrated in one area will produce goods for which no sufficient demand would be found.[44] The next step in the argument (although it is not entirely clear whether Nurkse himself follows this step) is that, in order to be able to diversify investment in this way, imports have to be displaced, thus putting local demand for industrial goods at the disposal of potential local enterprise. A few justifications are, in turn, offered to defend this pattern—of import replacement rather than of specialization, and investment, in export goods. One argument simply falls back on the aforementioned expected deterioration of the terms of trade. But this, even if granted, would only indicate the need to tax exports of primary products, rather than to tax all exports—including exports of manufactures—as the import-replacement policy would imply (in comparison, that is, with a policy of uniform exchange rate and no discrimination in favour of import substitutes). Another argument, more closely related to this basic approach, is that local entrepreneurs are made aware of the availability of local demand by the existence of imports; hence, import restriction (after imports have been in existence) will put at their disposal a market about which they have information, leading them to invest in order to provide for this market. Export markets, on the other hand, are far removed and risky, and are beyond the realm of relevant considerations by local enterprise at the early stages of development. Hence, a discrimination in favour of import substitutes and against exports is called for. Still another hypothesis—concerned this time with policy patterns—is that developed countries will not tolerate to any significant extent the 'encroachment' upon their markets for industrial goods, by exports from newly industrializing countries, and will counteract with their own import restrictions. This would, in turn, lead to a deterioration of the terms of trade of the underdeveloped countries, or will even (by import quotas and administrative prohibitions) close before them altogether their potential export markets—a development indicating again the desirability of discrimination in favour of import replacement.

Notes

1 That is, the increase of productivity is Hicks neutral in each of the goods, and is equal in both goods. In comparison of the functions in the original period (0) and the post-growth period (1), we have, in the two-good, two-factor model:

(1) $f_1^x (L, K) = \lambda_x f_0^x (L, K)$
(2) $f_1^m (L, K) = \lambda_m f_0^m (L, K)$
(3) $\lambda_x = \lambda_m > 1$

where f^x and f^m are, respectively, the production functions for the two goods X and M; and L and K are the two factors of production. Had $\lambda_x \neq \lambda_m$, growth would have been Hicks neutral, but not unbiased. This case will be analyzed later. The case in which growth is biased not just towards one good but towards one factor of production—that is, where the process is not Hicks neutral—will not be discussed here. The basic analysis of this situation has been provided in R. Findlay and H. Grubert (1959).

2 It is only when we give up the purity of the welfare concepts, and measure 'gains' and 'losses' in terms of bundles of goods or some other cardinally specified yardstick, that we may conceivably make quantitative statements and comparisons. This will be undertaken in Chapter 5.

3 It is tempting to say that when growth takes the form specified in the first version—of an increase of all factors of production by the same proportion—consumption of all goods (as well as produc-

tion—and hence also trade) will also increase by the same proportion. In this case, per capita income remains the same, as well as income distribution (all marginal productivities remaining unchanged); hence, per capita consumption of all goods will presumably remain unchanged, and total consumption of each and every good will rise by the rate of increase of the size of labour (which is the same as that of other factors, and as the growth ratio). But this conclusion would be wrong unless we make a specific assumption, namely that the tastes of the added labour are exactly equal to those of the formerly existing labour; one sub-assumption necessary for that to be true is that family structure remains unchanged.

4 A similar analysis may be found in H. G. Johnson (1967); but the conclusion there rests, unnecessarily, on the use of indifference curves for the determination of consumption and welfare.

5 This is proved by means of an Edgeworth box diagram, extending one dimension of the box following the increase in the amount of one factor; see T. M. Rybczynski (1955).

6 The term 'immiserizing growth' was first coined by J. Bhagwati (1958) in reference to a different case, which will be discussed shortly. It has been later extended, however (Bhagwati, 1968b, 1971a), to cover the general possibility of welfare reduction by growth resulting from the existence of distortions.

7 Growth may also take place when one of the factors is actually *contracting*, the expansion of the other factor being more than sufficient to offset this decline. If, in this case, the expanding factor is the one in which the protected industry is intensive, growth is even more likely to be immiserizing. An analysis of a somewhat similar situation will be found later in this chapter.

8 We shall maintain consistently the assumption that in each good, technological expansion is Hicks neutral. Thus, in the good (M) in which the production function changes, substitution ratios between factors at any given factor proportion remain the same in the new production function as in the original. In terms of note 1 above, conditions (1) and (2) remain as they are. But instead of (3), we now have $\lambda_m > \lambda_x$; and, specifically, we assume $\lambda_x = 1$.

9 In terms of the expressions in note 8, each M isoquant will stand for λ_m times the former quantity of M.

10 One difference which may be noted is that in the present case, Q_1 and Q_0 will coincide: when all the economy's resources are employed in producing X, the change in M's production function becomes irrelevant. But this does not change any of the conclusions.

11 Here, as well as in the analysis of growth biased due to changing factor proportions, it is assumed that in the post-growth situation the autarky price of M would still be higher than its international price. Otherwise, the trade pattern is reversed: M becomes the *export* good, and the tariff duty imposed on it becomes irrelevant.

12 There is no complete symmetry between this and the former case, on the other hand, in stating the conditions of likelihood of immiserizing growth. As before, this outcome is more likely the higher is the tariff rate. But we have here no equivalent to the rule which stated, in the former case, that immiserizing growth is more likely the larger the difference in factor intensities between the goods. It should be noted that in both cases, the impact of the factor which leads to growth is not obvious: here the larger the expansion of M's production function, the further left will the new production point, B'_1, be found; at the same time, however, it will be on a *higher* transformation curve. It is thus not possible to state whether it will be more or less likely to be left of $w'_0 w'_0$. The same conclusion holds, in the former case, for a large expansion of the factor of production from which growth originates.

13 This, indeed, is the situation to which Bhagwati first applied the term 'immiserizing growth'. See J. Bhagwati (1958).

14 It might be said, although this would go beyond the conventional use of the term, that in this situation the export industry is 'protected'—measured, that is, in relation to what it would have been under optimal policy.

15 This will not be demonstrated here, lest the topic occupies an unduly large proportion of the discussion, but see J. Bhagwati (1968b, 1971a).

16 The classic analysis of this process is K. J. Arrow's (1962).

17 This has been referred to as 'dynamic economies of scale'. See M. V. Posner (1961).

18 For the case of technological change this is, as before, Hicks' neutrality; that is, it is assumed, using the notation of note 1, that

$$f_1^x (L, K) = \lambda_x f_0^x (L, K)$$
$$f_1^m (L, K) = \lambda_m f_0^m (L, K)$$

19 This could be seen also if the change, and with it the dynamic element, are assumed to take the opposite direction. Suppose that in figure 16 the *initial* position is that of free trade, and $P_1 Q_1$ is the stationary state transformation curve, incorporating all the dynamic movement due to the free trade structure of production. Home

production is at B_1, and the budget-restraint line is w_1w_1. Introduce now a tariff with the (static) production position at B_0, and budget-restraint w_0w_0. From this change in the production structure a change in factor endowment will follow, and (assuming pure rotation) the new stationary state transformation curve will become something like P_0Q_0. Unless the dynamic impact is strong enough to turn, at the original cum-tariff production combination (B_0), the import into an export good, the economy's new budget-restraint line must be to the left of w_0w_0. The welfare loss due to the tariff thus becomes higher when the dynamic process is added.

20 Here, one difference does exist between these two alternative sets of assumptions. If the change takes place in the production functions then at most no technological retrogression would take place in the contracting industry. Hence, when *all* the economy's resources are allocated to this industry (in the *new static* position), production would be the same as before. At this corner, thus, the new transformation curve will coincide with the original one. When factor endowment changes, on the other hand, we may conceivably realize such a substantial factor development in the expanding industry that the new transformation curve will fully contain the original one—including the corners in which only the contracting good is produced.

21 Nothing in the *direction* of the conclusions depends on this extremity: these conclusions might conceivably have been reached with a new transformation curve which intersects the original one to the *right* of the autarky position A_0. But the extreme case is convenient for pointing out clearly the impact of the 'growth' factor.

22 It should be noted that it would only be a coincidence if the slopes of a_0a_0 and a_1a_1 were equal; that is, if autarky home prices are the same in the original and the post-growth positions. In other words, the level at which the tariff just becomes prohibitive would not normally be the same in the new as in the original position.

23 As will be shortly noticed, though, some element of externality is also necessarily involved in the infant-industry argument. For the history of the infant-industry argument, see G. Haberler (1936, 278–285).

24 Aside from the points raised in the following discussion, it should be noted that the dynamic benefits under consideration are due to the process of *production*. If the argument for protection on these grounds is found valid, it would hence always be preferable to grant the protection by means of a production *subsidy*, rather than by a tariff. A subsidy which maintains the same size of production as the tariff would lead to the realization of the same dynamic benefits; whereas, as we

have seen in the former chapter, it would lead at each point of time to a higher welfare, by avoiding the consumption loss.

25 If the dynamic gain is due to an increase in factor endowment, a necessary condition is also that owners of these factors cannot capture the full gain. Thus, for instance, the 'creation' of skilled labour does not call for government intervention when the workers can themselves reap the benefit of acquiring the skill: workers would find it then profitable to forgo some income at the start, expecting a higher income to follow and compensate them for the initial loss; and this, in turn, implies that the firm in which the skill is acquired gets compensated by the market mechanism. Such argument would, in turn, depend on the existence of perfect markets, and in particular of a perfect market for capital borrowed for investment in human capital. On the issues involved here, and the discussion of possible situations in which the dynamic benefits are not privately appropriable, see H. G. Johnson (1970).

26 In this case, thus, the infant-industry protection should be given to the industry even when it is no longer an infant, having reached full maturity.

27 The most comprehensive discussion of the effect of trade on factor endowment—labour as well as capital—is probably still Ohlin's classic *Interregional and International Trade*. See B. Ohlin (1933).

28 See H. G. Johnson (1966a, figure 1). This construct, designed for a closed economy, is sufficient for the present purpose of examining the impact of commercial policy on growth via savings. The positive theory of the growth process of open economies has incorporated dynamic models of trade into the growth model. See H. Oniki and H. Uzawa (1965), or P. K. Bardhan (1965, 1966).

29 It is assumed, for simplicity, that population and labour force are identical; 'per worker' thus means also 'per capita'.

30 This assertion must be made only in this intuitive and somewhat vague manner. There is no simple and rigorous way of translating the results of our former analysis into the framework of the present model. Here, 'income' is measured in terms of one good—and only one good is produced; whereas earlier, the benefit of trade, both in production and in consumption, depended on the shift from one good to another. Moreover, we have refused until now to measure welfare cardinally—whereas here 'income', which stands for welfare, is so measured. One may perhaps best think of the change in the present y as standing for changes in the ww budget-restraint lines of the earlier analysis, in terms of aggregates of goods—although these overlook the consumption gains from trade.

31 For further elaboration, see W. M. Corden (1971b).

32 Even when compensation is carried out, income distribution still changes: compensation only ensures that nobody loses by the move from one position to another—but not that the gains are somehow equally distributed.

33 See on this, again, the analysis in W. M. Corden (1971b).

34 It should be noted that there is no necessary correlation between specialization in *investment* goods and in *capital-intensive* goods: one attribute specifies the use of the good, whereas the other applies to the method by which it is itself produced.

35 See the discussion in J. Bhagwati (1968a, pp. 23–24). As Bhagwati indicates, this argument may be viewed—if correct—as a constraint on the government's ability to determine the saving rate through tax policy. Likewise, any argument for trade restriction as a means of increasing the saving rate through changes in the distribution of income must be a second-best argument, implying constraints or the use of fiscal policy: without such constraints, the optimal policy combination would be free trade joined by an appropriate fiscal policy to determine the saving rate.

36 An assumption that this supply curve is infinitely elastic would have led to 'corner solutions'. See R. Mundell (1957).

37 For a classic survey and critique, see again G. Haberler (1936, pp. 273–278).

38 See W. M. Corden (1967a) for this concept, as well as for the analysis of the argument on hand.

39 In his critical appraisal of the argument, Haberler failed to make this distinction clearly. His major argument is that capital imports of the nature under consideration must lead to a welfare deterioration in the community: the 'tariff factory' means that production has shifted from abroad, where it was carried out at a low cost, to the local country, where costs of production are higher; and this reduces the country's welfare. This, however, confuses the analysis of the problem on hand with the general analysis of a welfare loss from protection, disregarding the added element of the availability of additional capital to the economy. See G. Haberler (1936, pp. 274–275).

40 This assumes perfect divisibility of the foreign capital inflow. Without it, some gain will be appropriated by the local economy: inter-marginal units of the foreign capital invested will yield a higher product than the rate at which they are paid.

It may also be noted that since the foreign supply of the sector-specific capital discussed here is assumed to be of less than infinite elasticity, a set of optimum rates of restriction on these inflows would exist, similar to a set of optimum tariff rates on commodities, which would be superior (from the viewpoint of the receiving country) to a free flow of incoming capital.

41 This should not be confused with external economies of the *industry* to which the capital flows: such economies, we have seen, *may* justify restriction of imports of the industry, if the first-best policy combining free trade with a production subsidy is not followed; but this is entirely separate, and distinct, from the impact of foreign capital which is now being considered.

42 Once more, as we have seen, in the face of such distortion there may be room for the encouragement by trade restriction of an industry which is intensive in such factors (failing the first-best use of subsidies to these factors), regardless of the existence of foreign capital. But the possibility of attracting foreign capital inflow is, in this instance, an *additional* element, which increases the likelihood of a welfare gain resulting from the trade restriction.

43 In a broad way, these hypotheses may be found mostly in what may be referred to as 'U.N. economics', chief proponent of which has been for many years R. Prebisch. For a summary and critical appraisal, see J. Flanders (1964).

44 R. Nurkse (1953).

4

The Theory of Effective Protection

1 Introductory remarks

The theory of effective protection is the most notable recent development within the sphere of the theory of commercial policies. It has been slowly in formation since the mid-1950's, but has reached explicit, full-scale formulation only in the mid-1960's. During the last decade, it has occupied a prominent place in the literature of commercial policies. The fundamental ideas and concepts appear to have been developed simultaneously, in various countries and by various scholars. The major analytical contribution is that of W. M. Corden, who gave the theory its fullest and most thorough exposition.[1] Other basic contributions to the development and application of the tool are those of B. Balassa and H. G. Johnson.[2] The present discussion will draw heavily on Corden's formulation in his book *The Theory of Protection*.[3]

Several attributes distinguish the theory of effective protection from the main line of analyses of other aspects of commercial policies. As has been noted in Chapter 1, it is largely a *positive* theory, analyzing the impact of commercial policies on the structure of production, consumption and distribution—in the order mentioned, with the focus on production, some attention to consumption, and only scant references to distribution—whereas welfare issues, the core of most of the rest of the theory of commercial policy, occupy here only a minor position. A central feature in the theory of effective protection is its multi-commodity aspect. It emphasizes the role played by intermediate inputs in the production process, whereas the rest of the literature tends to abstract from the existence of such inputs and to consider only the contributions of primary factors of production to the productive process in a model of two final goods. As a result, the new theory analyzes the effect of the whole *structure* of the tariff system, rather than the impact of a single tariff. It is concerned with *relative* protection of industries—a problem which needs no separate discussion in a two-good world.

The rise of the new theory may probably be explained primarily by the revival of interest in the role of tariffs which was, in turn, a consequence of the return of the industrial world to a regime of free foreign-exchange system. In the late 1940's and early 1950's, foreign-exchange controls as a means of balancing the country's international transactions were widespread enough to overshadow all traditional measures of commercial policy. Since the middle, and mainly late, 1950's, the resumption of roughly free exchange markets was common enough to bring the role of tariffs again to the fore. Two specific developments which reinforced this interest were the Kennedy Round of tariff negotiations in the GATT, which started towards the mid-1960's and which aroused practical interest in issues such as tariff levels or the impact of various tariffs and of their removal; and the process of formulation and of gradual development of the European Economic Community (the Common Market), essential elements of which were inter-Community and external tariff adjustments by Community members (and by would-be members).

For much the same reasons, probably, a greater receptivity was accorded to issues involving *measurements* of tariff levels and costs—to be discussed in the next chapter—which are to a large extent tied with the new theory. Much like the simultaneous, interrelated developments of macroeconomic theory and national accounting during the 1930's, the theory of effective protection and the measurement of commercial policies seem to a large extent to have relied on and reinforced each other.

While the emergence of the new theory is sometimes connected with problems of developing countries, it is not primarily suited to issues with which the least developed countries would be concerned. This may be seen from some of the theory's major assumptions, which describe an essentially well-developed economy, fully employed (and, specifically, harbouring no significant disguised unemployment of labour). In essence, countries to which the new theory would be most relevant are developed, complex economies, undergoing a substantial further process of industrialization, which do not play a dominant role in the world markets of goods which they buy or sell but in which, on the other hand, foreign trade is substantial in relation to the size of the economy. It is thus not surprising to find the new theory, primarily in its earlier stages, being developed and applied in countries like Canada, Australia, or Israel, which possess these attributes.

2 Basic elements of the theory

The theory of effective protection in its simplest form incorporates a few basic assumptions about the economy. First, it is assumed that a state of perfect competition prevails, the economy is in full employment, balance-of-payments equilibrium is maintained, and no domestic distortions other than those due to government interference exist. In combination, these assumptions ensure the uniformity of factor prices in the economy (and, in the absence of government interference, the equality of the social marginal product for each activity in the economy). Hence they also ensure that a tendency of factor prices to rise in any activity will attract factors of production to that activity. Next, it is assumed that tariffs and other policy measures are non-discriminatory among foreign countries and, most important, that the country is 'small', that is that it faces infinitely elastic world demand for its exports and world supply of its imports. As a corollary, it is also assumed that other countries' policies are given, not responding to policies (or changes in them) of the country under consideration, and that repercussions on the employment or resource allocation in foreign countries are absent. All these are basic assumptions, scarcely removed from the analysis. Other assumptions, of a more technical nature, with which the analysis starts, are the following: imports of any final good under consideration exist both before and after the tariff, if any tariff on this good exists; likewise, one or more *inputs* employed in the production of this final good are imported with or without any tariff which may exist on such inputs; these inputs are required in physically fixed amounts for each unit of output of the final good; with the small-country assumption, this amounts also to fixed proportions of inputs in *value* terms—value being measured in foreign (world) prices. The small-country assumption, signifying fixed foreign prices, also makes it irrelevant whether the tariff is specific or *ad-valorem*: any specific tariff has a unique *ad-valorem* size, and vice versa. Likewise, the aforementioned assumption of perfect competition implies, *inter alia*, a rising price (rising supply curve) of any domestic activity. Some of these assumptions may be relaxed in later stages of the analysis, with qualifications following from this relaxation.

We are now ready to observe the fundamental elements of the theory. In a small country, a tariff imposed on the import good implies an increase in the home price of that good by the proportion of the tariff. In the two final-good world, with no intermediate inputs, this is necessarily also the rate of increase in the price of *value added* in the home production of this good—the value added in this activity being identical with the total ('gross') value of the good. Likewise, since only one good is imported, we know that this price increase must be also *relative* to the price of the other good, hence to the price of value added in the other activity. Hence, we know the *protective* effect of the tariff: it must lead to the attraction of domestic resources into the activity for whose product the tariff is imposed. When we shift to a multi-commodity world, we face a double task. First, with the existence of intermediate inputs, the tariff on a given final product does *not* measure the impact of this tariff alone, and *a fortiori* of the tariff system as a whole, on the price of the value added in the activity producing this product. We have to look, instead, for another measure which will tell us what the impact of the tariff system on this price is. Second, in order to infer from this the impact of the tariff structure on the direction in which domestic resources would tend to shift we have, in a multi-commodity world, to take into account the effect of the

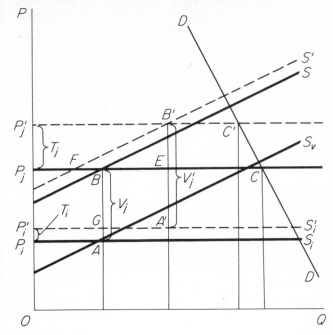

Figure 20

tariff structure on other activities in the economy. The first of these tasks will be performed, in a partial-equilibrium analysis, with the aid of figure 20.[4]

Figure 20 describes the production of and trade in a final good, j, the world's supply of which to the country under consideration is infinitely elastic at the price P_j. For convenience, P_j is normalized at unity: units of the good j are so defined that $P_j = 1$. To avoid confusion, units of foreign currency are defined so that the rate of exchange is also unity; thus, $P_j = 1$ whether prices are quoted in local currency—as is done in figure 20—or in foreign currency.

Production of good j is done by the employment of primary factors and the use of an intermediate input i. The contribution of the primary factors is the value added in the activity of producing good j; whereas the intermediate input is purchased by the industry from others. For convenience of exposition—this assumption could be easily removed—we assume

that within the relevant price range input i is not produced locally at all. It is only imported, and the foreign supply of it—S_i—is
infinitely elastic at the price per unit of P_i, where units of i are so
defined that one unit of i is required to produce one unit of j. We
recall that one assumed attribute of the production function is
that this physical proportion is fixed—whatever the levels of
output and of relative prices.[5] Designate this proportion as a_{ij}.
By the selection of units we have

(1) $$a_{ij} = \frac{P_i}{P_j} = P_i$$

S_v is the supply schedule of the domestic value added in the
activity of producing j. Supply of final output j by the domestic
industry is the combination of S_v, the supply of value added, and
the cost of input i. In free trade, the domestic supply curve of j
would thus be S—the vertical combination of S_v and S_i. The
free trade price of j is, of course, the foreign offer price P_j. At
this price, domestic consumption of j is P_jC, of which P_jB is
produced locally and the remainder, BC, is imported. V_j, the
domestic value added per unit of output, is AB ($=P_iP_j$), and the
cost of the imported input is P_i.

Introduce now a tariff system, where tariffs are imposed on
both the final good j and the input i. The tariff rate on j (referred
to as the *nominal* tariff) is t_j, and the amount of tariff per unit is
$T_j = P_jt_j$ ($=t_j$, since $P_j = 1$). The tariff rate on i (again referred
to as the 'nominal' tariff) is t_i, and the tariff per unit $= T_i = P_it_i$.
The domestic price of j rises to $P'_j = P_j + T_j$. The supply curve
of input i, which the domestic industry faces, rises by the
amount T_i from S_i to S'_i. The domestic supply curve of final
good j rises, accordingly, by the same amount, from S to S'. At
the new domestic price of j, P'_j, consumption is P'_jC', of which
P'_jB' is produced locally and $B'C'$ is imported.

We now come to our task: the measurement of the effect of
the tariff system on the domestic value added in the activity of
producing the good in question. The price of the value added
being the reward afforded to the primary factors involved in the
productive activity, it is this magnitude—and changes in
it—which affect the volume of factors attracted to the industry,
and thus the allocation of resources in the economy. The more a
tariff system increases this reward, the more it is likely to attract

resources into the industry under consideration. The basic
definition in the theory of effective protection is thus that of the
concept of the *effective protective rate*; this is the proportional
change, from a free trade to a tariff-ridden position, of the price
of the value added.[6]

In figure 20, $AB(=P_iP_j)$ is, we recall, the free trade value
added, designated by V_j. The introduction of the tariff
system—tariffs on both output j and input i—leads to a new
size of reward for the value added, V'_j, equal to $A'B'$ ($=P'_iP'_j$).
The effective protective rate of the activity of producing j,
designated by g_j, is thus

$$(2) \qquad g_j = \frac{V'_j - V_j}{V_j}$$

V'_j exceeds V_j by T_j, the amount of tariff on the final good j,
minus T_i, the amount of tariff paid for the imported input i;
hence,

$$(3) \qquad g_j = \frac{T_j - T_i}{V_j}$$

We recall that $T_j = t_j$, and that $T_i = P_i t_i$ and thus, from (1), $T_i =$
$a_{ij}t_i$. Also, $V_j = P_jP_i$, and from (1) $V_j = 1 - a_{ij}$. Equation (3) is
thus transformed into:

$$(4) \qquad g_j = \frac{t_j - a_{ij}t_i}{1 - a_{ij}}$$

Input i in figure 20 could be easily conceived—and presented,
had it not made the diagram too cumbersome—to consist not of
one but of many (n) inputs i, where $i = 1 \ldots n$. For each of
these, P_i would be a_{ij}, and hence T_i, the tariff paid on a unit of
input, equal to $a_{ij}t_i$. The input tariff rates t_i may, of course,
vary from each other. Instead of a single T_i we would now get
$\sum_{i=1}^{n} T_i$, and instead of a single a_{ij} we will have $\sum_{i=1}^{n} a_{ij}$.

Equation (4) would thus take the form

$$(4') \qquad g_j = \frac{t_j - \sum_i a_{ij}t_i}{1 - \sum_i a_{ij}}$$

Before proceeding with the main line of the analysis, it should be worthwhile to extend the coverage of the tax system by which effective protection is generated. First, it should be realized that a 'tariff' may either be positive or negative—a 'negative tariff' being a subsidy. Subsidies as well as tariffs are thus included in the formulation of the effective protective rate. A subsidy to imports of j, being a 'negative tariff', would show as a negative t_j and would tend to lead to negative protection. A subsidy to an imported input, being a negative tariff on the input, would appear as a negative t_i—raising the numerator in (4), and increasing effective protection.

Next, it should be pointed out that the analysis of effective protection applies to *exports* just as much as to import substitutes. In figure 20, no change would be called for if j is regarded not as an import but as an export good, facing infinitely elastic world demand at price P_j; and t_j would be an export subsidy rather than an import tariff. Likewise, no change would be introduced if i were not an imported input but an exportable one (namely, a good of which *some* exports exist), facing infinitely elastic world demand at price P_i, and receiving an export subsidy of T_i; and t_i would get a negative sign were it not a subsidy to the export of intermediate good i but, on the contrary, an export tax on it. Equation (4') is thus capable of yielding effective protection rates for export industries as well as taking into account exportable inputs. The theory of effective protection is designed to handle both importable (or import-substitutes) and exportable goods. It is thus the analysis of the effect of a tariff system on production of tradable (exportable and importable) goods.

Extending the coverage further, it should be realized that *production subsidies* granted to the final output are precisely equivalent to import tariffs, in their effect on the degree of protection. This may be easily visualized from figure 20, without burdening the diagram with new lines. Suppose that with the foreign price P_j no tariff is levied; instead, a subsidy of T_j per unit is granted to domestic production of j—but not to imports! The price of j in the home market will now be P_j, against P'_j with the tariff; and domestic consumption will remain at C, rather than fall to C'. But domestic production will increase to P_jE—equal to P'_jB, the tariff-induced production; and the reward for value added in units of production—which includes, of course, EB' $(=T_j)$ of subsidy—will be $A'B'$, just as with the tariff.

But the symmetry ends here, and does *not* apply to the input side. In the analysis of figure 20, the input i has been treated in a one-sided way, since its local production has been abstracted from. Let us introduce the possibility of such production. This would be entirely immaterial for the effect of the input's tariff on protection of the final good—as long as we assume, as we will, that at least *some* imports of the input exist; since a tariff would still increase the price of i to industry j by T_i, the local price being still equal to the foreign price plus the tariff. But allowing the possibility of domestic production of i adds one more point of view: it introduces the double role of tariffs on inputs. On the one hand, such tariffs serve—as the preceding analysis has shown—to reduce effective protection for the final good in the production of which the inputs are used. But on the other hand, these tariffs work to *increase* effective protection for the domestic activity of producing these inputs themselves.

Suppose, now, that instead of fixing tariff T_i per unit of input i, a subsidy of the same size is granted to local production of the input. The effect on protection of this input would be—just as we have seen earlier with regard to industry j—equivalent to that created by the tariff. But the effect on protection of j, the final good, would *not*: with a subsidy instead of the tariff on i, the price paid by industry j for i will be lower, by the extent of the (otherwise levied) tariff; and the reward for the value added in j will be to that extent higher. Thus, in a formula such as (4'), t_j should include, beside the tariff on j, also subsidies for domestic production of j; whereas the t_i's should include only tariffs (or *import* subsidies, which are negative tariffs)—and not subsidies to domestic production of the input.

Quite the opposite asymmetry exists where the impact of *excise taxes* is examined—taxes, that is, such as sales tax, which are imposed on consumption, so that they are levied on both domestic production and imports. Suppose, again, that in figure 20 no tariffs are imposed. Instead, excise taxes of the size T_j and T_i are levied on, respectively, final output j and input i. The price facing consumers rises, as before, to P'_j. The producer's price, however, remains P_j, since $P_jP'_j$ is paid as the excise tax by the domestic manufacturer (as well as the importer). The cost of production increases, on the other hand, by the amount of T_i—the excise tax on the input—per unit of production. The supply curve of output j (at prices excluding the output's tax) thus rises (supply falls) to S'—just as with a tariff on i. Domestic production of j now *falls*, from P_jB to P_jF; and the reward received per unit of value added in j falls by the amount of T_i—from AB to GB. Thus, the excise tax on the final output does not provide any protection to it; but the excise tax on the input yields *negative* protection to the production of the final output. The existence of excise taxes thus has, in general, an anti-protective effect. In a formulation, again, such as $(4')$ t_j would *not* include any excise tax on the final output; whereas the t_i's should include excise taxes on the inputs.

This discussion of the effect of local taxes may be summed up by stating that, in formula $(4')$:

(a) $t_j = t_{1j} + t_{2j}$

where t_{1j} is a tariff on j, and t_{2j} is a subsidy to domestic production of j; and

(b) $t_i = t_{1i} + t_{2i}$

where t_{1i} is a tariff on input i, and t_{2i} is an excise tax on the input.

In this formulation, the concept of protection takes into account the effect of *all* the economy's indirect tax structure.[7] The taxes designated by the subscript 1 form the *tariff system*, meaning all taxes and subsidies imposed on or granted to *trade*. Whereas the taxes designated by the subscript 2 may be referred to as *domestic taxes*, that is: taxes on (or subsidies to) domestic production, either not involving trade at all or treating trade equally with sales of domestic production in the local market.[8]

We may now proceed to draw some important inferences from the analysis of the effective protective rate. Once more, for brevity of exposition mostly imports and import taxes (namely tariffs) will be mentioned; but it should be remembered that, *mutatis mutandis*, the discussion and its results would generally be applied to exports as well, and to the tax structure as a whole rather than merely to tariffs. Equation $(4')$ above could be transformed into:

$$(4'') \qquad g_j = t_j + \left(t_j - \frac{\Sigma_i \, a_{ij} t_i}{\Sigma_i \, a_{ij}} \right) \left(\frac{\Sigma_i \, a_{ij}}{1 - \Sigma_i \, a_{ij}} \right)$$

From (4') and (4'') it is easy to observe some of the fundamental relationships within the tariff system.

(a) If $t_j > \Sigma a_{ij} t_i / \Sigma a_{ij}$, then $g_j > t_j$. The effective protective rate of the final good exceeds its nominal tariff rate when the latter is higher than the weighted average of the nominal rates of tariff on imports—each input rate being weighted by the input coefficient. When $\Sigma a_{ij} t_i = 0$, $g_j = t_j / (1 - \Sigma a_{ij})$. In the absence of tariffs on inputs (or when positive tariffs just cancel out negative tariffs) the effective protective rate exceeds the nominal output tariff rate by the inverse of the proportion of value added. Activities in which the value added is a small fraction of final output will, in this case, receive effective protection at a rate many times higher than the nominal tariff rate.

(b) If $t_j = \Sigma a_{ij} t_i / \Sigma a_{ij}$, then $g_j = t_j$. One obvious instance in which this equality is achieved is when all nominal tariffs are equal: a complete uniformity of the system of nominal tariff rates thus leads to a complete uniformity also of the system of effective protective rates—all the latter being equal to the (uniform) nominal tariff. But the equality under consideration could of course be achieved (for a single good) within a non-uniform system, when the weighted average input nominal rate happens to equal the nominal output rate of the tariff.

(c) If $t_j < \Sigma a_{ij} t_i / \Sigma a_{ij}$, $g_j < t_j$; moreover, when $t_j < \Sigma a_{ij} t_i$, $g_j < 0$. The existence of a positive nominal rate of tariff on the final output thus does not necessarily indicate a positive rate of protection: it could be outweighed by the anti-protection effect of the tariffs on inputs.

So far as importables are concerned studies of practically all countries[9]—regardless of the level of development—show a tariff structure of the nature indicated under heading (a). Nominal tariff systems are normally escalated with the stage of production—the closer the good to being a final product, the higher the nominal tariff levied on it, with little or no tariffs imposed on raw materials. Thus, whatever the stage of production of the good (except for the lowest), its effective protective rate would be higher than its nominal tariff rate.[10] This is not necessarily true, however, for exportables. Here, countries vary quite a lot from each other. In many, export subsidies are not granted (sometimes export taxes are even levied); in which case the existence of some tariffs on importable inputs leads to a situation described under (c) above, where effective protective rates are negative.[11] This impression about exportables would probably even be strengthened when, as will be explained in a later section, an exchange-rate adjustment is carried out.

3 Non-tradable inputs

One of the assumptions with which the analysis set out —expressed, in figure 20, by the horizontal shape of S_i—was that the produced input in the production of the final good is imported. As we have seen, it is of no consequence to the determination of the protective rate of the final good whether all or only part of the input is imported, although the existence of local production of the input introduces the role of the input tariff in protecting the input's production. Likewise, it would not change the analysis even to assume that all of the input is produced locally, provided that at least some of it is exported—signifying the existence, at the relevant price range, of a (foreign) infinitely elastic demand. In all these instances the input is tradable, and its price is determined (as it is in figure 20) by the foreign price plus the tariff or the export subsidy. We now examine, on the other hand, the situation in which the produced input is *non-tradable*—it is wholly produced and used at home, with no imports or exports, and would so remain at the relevant price range. This would be the case when transportation costs are relatively high; in some instances—such as electricity in many areas—these costs may even approach infinity.

When the input is non-tradable, its price is no longer given by the foreign price (which would be irrelevant) and the input's tariff (which most probably would not even exist). It may also be assumed that the price is no longer *given* to the using industry j:

a larger production of j, and higher demand by it for the input, would result in a higher price of the input. In other words, the elasticity of the input's supply (to the using industry j) is not infinite. Thus, any initial increase in the reward given to the value added in the activity of producing final good j is reduced, by the higher price which has to be paid for the input. By the same token, this affords some protection to the production of the input itself: the higher price received for it increases its own value added.

In principle, there are two alternative forms of incorporating this new element. One is to try and separate out the effective protection given to j between protection of value added in j and of value added in the production of input i. But this could (in principle—only with great difficulty in practice) be done also with regard to the separate components of the value added in the final stage of production, as will be seen in a later section. It could be regarded as a second step in the analysis, moving from the value added as a whole to its separate parts. We shall therefore not dwell here upon this method,[12] and examine only the other alternative, namely, to combine the two stages of production. Instead of asking how does the tariff structure related to good j affect the value added in producing this final output, we shall also ask how it affects the *value added in the production of the input* which the final-good industry uses. That is, we shall look at both values as being part of one activity.

Let us start, for simplicity, with the assumption that a single intermediate input—designated by h—is required for the output of j; and it is non-tradable. This input is, in turn, produced with the aid of a *tradable* input i and primary factors—the latter constituting the value added in the production of h. The effective protective rate we now look for is g_{j+h}—the protection afforded to the value added in both output j and input h. To determine it, we have to know not only the nominal tariff rate on j (t_j) but also the nominal tariff rate on imports of i into the production of h—the tariff on the input into the input (which was irrelevant when the latter was tradable). This is illustrated by figure 21, which is constructed in exactly the same way as figure 20, except that it shows now a rising supply curve of the (non-tradable) input S_h; the latter is derived from a horizontal supply curve of an imported input, S_{ih}, and a rising supply curve of the value added

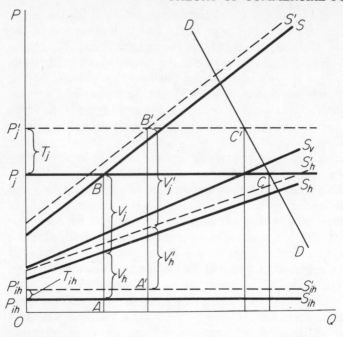

Figure 21

in the production of h, which is the difference between S_h and S_{ih}. Imposition of the tariff t_j on j works in precisely the same way as before. Tariff t_i on input i now raises, in turn, each of the supply curves S_{ih}, S_h and S, by the amount $t_i a_{ih} a_{hj}$ where a_{ih} is the free trade proportion of the cost of the imported input i in the production of input h, and a_{hj} is the proportion of input h in j. The effective protective rate, which is now defined as:

$$(5) \qquad g_{j+h} = \frac{(V'_j + V'_h) - (V_j + V_h)}{V_j + V_h}$$

thus turns to be:

$$(6) \qquad g_{j+h} = \frac{t_j - a_{ih} a_{hj} t_i}{1 - a_{ih} a_{hj}}$$

(6) is, of course, very similar to (4) except that the import component does not exist here directly, in the production of j, but indirectly through the production of input h used by industry j.

We may now combine the properties of figure 20 and figure 21; that is, we assume the existence of importable input i both as a direct component in the production of final output j (as in figure 20) and as an indirect component, through its participation in the production of non-tradable input h (as in figure 21). The effective protective rate thus becomes:

$$(7) \qquad g_{j+h} = \frac{t_j - (a_{ij} + a_{ih}a_{hj})\, t_i}{1 - (a_{ij} + a_{ih}a_{hj})}$$

The import coefficient is the combination of the direct and the indirect components. Expanding the analysis by admitting many importable inputs, we get:

$$(7') \qquad g_{j+h} = \frac{t_j - \sum_i (a_{ij} + a_{ih}a_{hj})t_i}{1 - \sum_i (a_{ij} + a_{ih}a_{hj})}$$

And, finally, admitting also not a single but many non-tradable inputs, the effective protective rate becomes:

$$(7'') \qquad g_{j+h} = \frac{t_j - \sum_i (a_{ij} + \sum_h a_{ih}a_{hj})t_i}{1 - \sum_i (a_{ih} + \sum_h a_{ih}a_{hj})}$$

The coefficient of importable inputs is thus the overall combination of all import components participating in the production of final good j, whether directly or through their contribution to non-tradable inputs which the industry producing the final good is using. Similarly, the value added (the protective rate of which is measured) is the aggregation of the value added (by primary factors) directly in the production of the final good, and indirectly in the production of all non-tradable inputs which the industry is using. The procedure could, of course, now be carried still another step backward—assuming non-tradable inputs in the production of non-tradable input h, tracing back the import components in these inputs, etc. In principle, this does not lead to any difficulty, but the formulation would, of course, soon become very cumbersome and awkward—and so may the actual computation required for the measurement of the protective rate.[13]

4 Protection of primary inputs

We have, until now, referred to protection of value added in an activity, and defined the degree of protection of this magnitude by the effective protective rate. It will be interesting to proceed and ask what this protection implies for the separate components of the value added—namely, the services of the various primary goods whose contribution constitutes the value added in the activity. We shall still stay within a partial-equilibrium framework. Specifically, we shall pose the question of how a given partial set of the tariff system, referring to one final good and the tradable inputs which participate in the process of its production, affects the prices of (the services of) the primary inputs which contribute to the activity—assuming all other segments of the tariff structure to be given, unchanged data.

Take the situation of positive protection. At the higher price for value added, equilibrium is reached only, of course, because the supply of value added (S_v in figure 20) is a rising schedule; otherwise, production is boundless.[14] A rising supply of value added is created, in turn, by rising supply schedules of the factors which contribute to the value added. The increased scale of the activity under consideration, due to protection, thus leads to increased prices of these factors; that is, it affords protection to the factors. The protection for the activity may thus be reinterpreted as an aggregate of protection given to the various productive factors.

The lower the elasticity of supply of a factor to the industry in question, the more will its price rise by a given effective protection to the activity; and the higher, therefore, will be the share of this factor in the total protection afforded. In an extreme case, if we assume (as we have *not*, in the analysis thus far, and will not in general) fixed proportions of the various primary factors, and fixed supply (zero elasticity) of one of the factors, the whole protection would go to this particular factor. We would then have a situation in which a fixed proportion of a factor specific to the industry prevents any expansion of production, and protection merely yields rent to the specific factor. This extreme situation is approached everywhere *in the short run*—the length of the 'short run' varying, of course, from one industry to another.

An opposite extreme would be the case of an infinite elasticity of supply of *some* of the factors. In this instance, all the protection accorded to the activity under consideration is enjoyed by the other factors, whose elasticity of supply is less than infinite. It may be assumed, for instance, that unskilled labour is in infinitely elastic supply to any single industry, so that it does not share in the protection given to the industry. Or, in a model distinguishing only two factors—labour and capital—that capital is perfectly mobile, hence supplied at a given price to any single industry; so that the protection is granted to labour only.[15] When some of the factors are supplied to the industry at a fixed price, and hence protection is enjoyed only by the remaining factors, the rate of this protection may be easily measured by treating the fixed-price factors (i.e. those with infinite elasticity of supply) as if they were *inputs* purchased with a zero rate of tariff. We would then also have to apply to this input the assumption of fixed proportionality with output. Let subscript 1 stand for services of factors with rising supply curves and 2 for services provided at infinitely elastic supply. The value added is allocated between the two:

$$V_j = V_{1j} + V_{2j}$$

Protection afforded to V_{2j} is, by definition, zero. Protection to V_{1j}, designated by g_{1j}, is

$$(8) \qquad g_{1j} = \frac{V'_{1j} - V_{1j}}{V_{1j}}$$

From (8), (2) above, and the knowledge that V_{2j} is fixed, we get

$$(9) \qquad g_{1j} = g_j \frac{V_j}{V_{1j}}$$

That is, the protective rate of the 'protectable' primary factors is higher than the effective protective rate of an activity by a multiple which is the inverse of the share of the protectable value added in total value added. In a more general way, it may be easily shown that (recalling that we assume here fixed proportions)

$$(10) \qquad g_j = g_{1j} \frac{V_{1j}}{V_j} + g_{2j} \frac{V_{2j}}{V_j}$$

from which, in the special case where $g_{2j} = 0$, we get (9) above.

With many factors, (10) may be written as

$$(10) \qquad g_j = \sum_s g_{sj} a_{sj}$$

where g_{sj} is the effective protection afforded to factor s, and a_{sj}—its share in the value added in j. The effective protective rate is thus a weighted average of the specific protective rates accorded to the various factors which participate in the productive activity. It may also be shown that the degree of protection of each factor is related negatively to its elasticity of supply, and positively to the elasticity of supply of other factors. The two cases discussed before—of zero elasticity and of infinite elasticity of one of the factors—are extreme illustrations of this principle.[16]

It should be emphasized that the degree of factor protection discussed here refers to the impact of protection on the factor's *price*. Conclusions about the impact on the *quantity employed* would, of course, be the reverse: the higher the elasticity of supply of the factor, the larger will be the expansion of its employment in the industry under consideration. In the extreme case of a factor whose supply is completely inelastic, no expansion at all would, by definition, take place. In analyzing the impact of protection on factors of production, it must indeed be specified whether the effect of protection examined is on the factor's price or on its employment in the industry concerned.

We may also investigate briefly the reverse question to the one we have pursued, and inquire what is the effect of taxes on and subsidies to *inputs of primary factors* on the effective protective rate of the value added in the final output. If fixed proportions of the primary factors are assumed, this problem becomes trivial: a subsidy, for instance, at a given rate to one productive input may be converted to a subsidy granted to the final output by multiplying the subsidy rate by the proportion (in value terms) of the primary input in question in the total cost (= price) of the final output. From then on, the analysis will proceed by treating this subsidy rate like any other component of t_j. If substitution among the productive factors is allowed, however (as it has been through most of the earlier discussion), the outcome is not that simple, but a few qualitative conclusions may be indicated. First, g_j, the effective protective rate of the activity, will rise *more* than in the proportion just indicated; substitution of the subsidized factor for other factors will take place, and the proportion of the subsidized factor in total output will be (at the margin) higher than before the subsidy. Second, the price and quantity employed of the subsidized factor will rise more than had the subsidy (calculated, as above, using the relevant factor's proportion) been given to the output, rather than to this input.[17] Third, the impact on the quantities of other factors employed consists of two opposite effects. As with fixed proportions, the subsidy to one factor will have a positive scale effect on the quantity demanded of other factors. On the other hand, assuming positive (scale-compensated) cross-elasticities of demand for the factors, the substitution effect will work in the opposite direction. We do know, however, that in the final outcome prices and quantities of other factors will *rise*, as if the subsidy were given to the output (although not, of course, to the same extent).[18]

This discussion, it should be re-emphasized, has been coined clearly in partial-equilibrium terms: it has raised the question of the impact of one partial set of the tariff structure, assuming all the other parts to be given. But in the analysis of the impact of protection on factor prices this is certainly a question of a rather limited scope. We shall re-examine the impact of the tariff structure on factors of production, as well as on goods, in the context of general equilibrium.

5 Scales of effective protection and effective exchange rates

The analysis thus far has discussed the effective protective rate of a given production activity. We now come to the second task of the theory, namely, to assess the impact of the tariff structure on the activity under consideration when account is taken of the effect of the tariff structure on other activities. This will involve both a comparison of protection of the various activities and, more important, the introduction of general-equilibrium considerations. The task will be carried out in stages: the required comparison, and some general-equilibrium considerations, will be introduced in the present section; whereas the general-equilibrium framework will be fully recognized only in the following section.

We have earlier stated that the existence of a positive protective rate—meaning an increase in the tariff-ridden situation, over the free trade position, of the reward for primary factors participating in the activity—leads to the attraction of factors into the activity under consideration. But this would obviously be true only in a very limited sense, namely, if only the impact of the particular segment of the tariff system which is related to the final output under consideration and its importable inputs is examined. In other words, if we assume that all other tariffs are given, and only the tariffs on the j good and the i inputs are imposed, and analyze the impact of this imposition, then the conclusions of the former analysis are valid. If, on the other hand, we wish to study the impact of the whole tariff structure on the good under consideration—as we most often will—the conclusions of the former analysis are premature, and possibly wrong.

Suppose, for instance, that the specific good j did receive positive effective protection; but that all other tradable goods receive even higher protection. The good in question is thus obviously discriminated against, by the tariff structure, rather than favoured, and factors of production will tend to move *away* from this activity, to other activities enjoying higher protection, rather than be attracted to the industry. Thus, in order to know whether a tradable activity is protected in relation to the tradable sector as a whole one would have to compare the activity's effective protective rate with the rates of other activities.

But this does not tell the whole story. It might be argued—for instance, in the example just given—that it is not at all clear that the industry in question, which has a positive but low protective rate, is indeed discriminated against. True, if it only had to compete for factors of production with other tradable (exportable and importable) industries, it would lose by the impact of the tariff structure. But its positive protective rate supposedly works in its favour in comparison with the *non-tradable* sector of the economy—which, since it does not compete with foreign goods, cannot be protected at all (positively or negatively) by the tariff structure. At this point, however, one should recall the important assumption of the maintenance of balance-of-payments equilibrium. This equilibrium is assumed to exist both at free trade and with the tariff structure. The latter, thus, is understood not to change the balance-of-payments position—and if it does, other measures will be taken, or developments will take place, to restore the balance of payments to its free trade (equilibrium) position.

The simplest way of conceiving this restoration is by using the device which Corden termed the 'exchange-rate adjustment'. To continue with our example, where all tradable goods enjoy positive protection: clearly, starting with an equilibrium balance-of-payments position (thus, by definition, with an equilibrium exchange rate) in free trade, the tariff-ridden position will be one of balance-of-payments surplus with the initial exchange rate; positive protection to all exports and all import substitutes (which, as may easily be seen, implies also by necessity that all nominal tariff rates are positive) leads to the expansion of exports and the reduction of imports, thus to a balance-of-payments surplus. To restore equilibrium, the exchange rate (i.e. the price of foreign exchange) is lowered (whether by act in a fixed-rate system, or in the market, in a flexible-rate system—this would be immaterial for the present purpose). This exchange rate adjustment favours the non-tradable sector, against tradable goods, thus leading to a new equilibrium position. Alternatively, it may be assumed that the exchange rate remains stable, but the general price level in the economy rises. Since prices of tradable goods are fixed (by the foreign price, the exchange rate, and the tariff, all remaining unchanged), prices may rise only in the non-tradable sector. This again leads to a relative rise of prices of non-tradables vs. tradables, which works to restore balance-of-payments equilibrium. For the present purpose, both methods of adjustment are equivalent, and we shall refer to both as 'exchange-rate adjustment' (in the sense that in both, the exchange rate—the price of foreign exchange—falls relatively to domestic prices).

Pursuing further our example, the specific industry subject to seemingly positive but particularly low effective protection would certainly be found, when the exchange-rate adjustment is taken into account, to have been negatively affected (by the combination of the tariff structure and the exchange-rate adjustment) in relation to the non-tradable sector, and not just in relation to other tradables. In general, to determine whether the tariff structure favours a specific tradable activity in comparison with the non-tradable sector, its effective protective rate would have to be compared with the size of the exchange-rate adjustment: only if the former is algebraically larger than the latter, would the activity's adjusted effective protection be indeed positive.[19] The effective protective rate from which the size of the exchange-rate adjustment is deducted has been termed by Corden the *net effective rate*.[20] Thus, an activity is protected in relation to other tradable activities if its effective protective rate is higher; and in relation to the non-tradable sector if its *net* effective rate is *positive*.

It should be noted that when the exchange-rate adjustment is performed so that, conceptually, balance-of-payments equilibrium is maintained, it is impossible for *all* tradable goods to have been found to be either positively or negatively protected: some activities will be found to enjoy positive net effective rates of protection, while others must be subject to negative net protection.

It is also important to realize that even if a non-tradable sector is assumed away (and recalling that full employment is always maintained), it is impossible for *all* (tradable) activities to have net positive (or negative) protection: if some activities are positively protected, others must be subject to negative protection, and vice versa. This was, of course, obvious in the two-good world in which our welfare analysis has been carried out.

At this point, it will be useful to introduce two concepts of the exchange rate: the *specific* exchange rate, and the *effective* exchange rate; and to re-coin the effective protective rate by use of these terms.

The *specific* rate of foreign exchange is the total price paid or received in trade per unit of foreign exchange. Thus, for instance, if the formal rate of exchange is kr 5 per dollar, and the nominal tariff rate on imports of textiles is 20 per cent, the specific rate of exchange in the import of textiles would be kr 6 per dollar (adding the 1 kr per dollar paid in tariff to the formal rate of exchange); or, if an export subsidy of kr 30 per bushel of wheat is granted, and the price received abroad is kr 60 per bushel, the specific exchange rate in export of wheat would be kr 7.5 per dollar.

The *effective* rate of exchange, on the other hand, is the price of a unit of foreign exchange of *value added* in a given activity.

The two measures are related to each other in precisely the same way that the effective protective rate is related to the nominal tariff rate:[21]

Designate:

R_{sj} = specific exchange rate (units of domestic currency per unit of foreign currency) in trade of final good j,

R_{si} = specific exchange rate for tradable input i in j,

R_{vj} = Effective exchange rate (exchange rate for value added) in activity j,

Then, with a single input:

$$(11) \qquad R_{vj} = \frac{R_{sj} - a_{ij} R_{si}}{1 - a_{ij}}$$

and with many inputs:

$$(11') \qquad R_{vj} = \frac{R_{sj} - \Sigma_i a_{ij} R_{si}}{1 - \Sigma_i a_{ij}}$$

To move from the effective exchange rate to effective protection, the equilibrium rate of exchange has to be introduced. An effective exchange rate higher than the equilibrium rate indicates positive *net* protection; and an effective rate below the equilibrium level—negative net protection. It should be noted, and emphasized, that the 'equilibrium level' is concerned with the *specific* rate of exchange, as it has been defined here (namely, a concept which goes beyond the formal rate, to include tariffs, subsidies, etc.). In a certain sense of the 'average', that will be discussed in the next chapter, the equilibrium rate is the average of the structure of existing specific rates. Designating this equilibrium rate by $\bar{R}$, we get for each activity j:

$$(12) \qquad g_j = \frac{R_{vj}}{\bar{R}} - 1$$

or, from $(11')$

$$(13) \qquad g_j = \frac{\left(\dfrac{R_{sj}}{R} - 1\right) - \Sigma_i a_{ij} \left(\dfrac{R_{si}}{R} - 1\right)}{1 - \Sigma_i a_{ij}}$$

where g_j is here the *net* effective protective rate. Formulation (13) is, of course, very similar to (4′): it merely replaces, in the appropriate places, nominal tariff rates by the ratios of specific exchange rates to the equilibrium rate. This formulation has a few advantages. First, it performs directly the exchange-rate adjustment—which, as we have seen, is a necessary step for inferences about protection of tradables vs. non-tradables: the equilibrium rate of exchange ($\bar{R}$) is arrived at, conceptually, after this adjustment has been carried out. It thus combines two steps that in the earlier formulation have been taken separately. It recognizes directly, moreover, that part of the tariff structure substitutes for the formal exchange rate. In other words, the assumption of free trade equilibrium *formal* rate of exchange is no longer needed. Instead, it is assumed that tariffs (and subsidies) replace to some extent (which may be zero) the formal exchange rate as a means of maintaining balance-of-payments equilibrium. To this extent, tariffs are added to the formal exchange rate (in the $\bar{R}$); and only a protection rate *higher* than this tariff level would then afford positive protection.

This leads, in a more general way, to the protective effect—positive or negative—of the foreign exchange rate, which is brought to the fore once the assumption of free trade equilibrium rate of exchange is abandoned. Suppose that a free trade situation exists, with no tariffs or other means of government interference in trade, except that the exchange rate is fixed (by the government), and that the currency is over-valued (that is, the exchange rate is below its equilibrium level). The earlier formulation of the effective protective rate either does not apply to this situation or, if used without regard to the balance-of-payments position, would show a zero protection all around. The formulation of protection through effective exchange rates, on the other hand—such as by (12) and (13)—would show *negative* protection of all tradables vs. the non-tradable sector. And this, indeed, is the correct inference: by its exchange-rate policy, the government leads in this case to the drawing away of resources from tradable to non-tradable activities—in comparison, that is, with a *completely free trade* situation, in which not even government interference through the fixing of the price of foreign exchange takes place.

Finally, it may be noted that the exchange-rate formulation

handles directly and very conveniently the protective structure created by the existence of a (formal) multiple-exchange rate system. This, to be sure, could be carried out with the earlier formulation of the effective protective rate;[22] but through a less direct or obvious and more complicated procedure.

A formulation such as (12), in sum, yields the effective protective rate of (in principle) all measures of government interference in foreign trade. Suppose a set of effective protective rates is thus derived for all tradable productive activities in the economy. Could it then be inferred, from this set, which industries will be drawing resources from the non-tradable sector (having positive protection) and which would be losing (having negative protection)? Or that an activity with a higher protective rate would be more likely to attract resources than an activity with a lower rate? Despite the exchange-rate adjustment, the answer cannot be an unqualified yes. This will be analyzed now, by introducing fully general-equilibrium considerations.

6 Protection in a general equilibrium framework

We have tentatively asserted that primary productive factors will be pulled to activities which enjoy higher protection than others, and prices of these factors will rise. By the same token, however, factors will move out of activities which are negatively protected (whether other tradables or non-tradables); and prices of these factors will fall. Some of the factors may be specific to each activity, and with these alone we might have been able to end the analysis here. But other factors will participate in many activities, including both those with positive and those with negative protection, and we would then reach the conclusion that prices of these factors both rise and fall—an untenable conclusion in a situation (which we assume all along) of perfect competition, and with homogeneous factors. The answer which seemed to be straightforward in a partial-equilibrium context thus does not apply in a general equilibrium, when the impact of the tariff structure as a whole is examined.[23]

In a two-good, two-factor world, it would be simple to show rigorously what the correct answer is now. In this model, one good is positively protected, and the other negatively (by definition—barring the case of no protection at all—since protection of an activity is relative to other activities).[24] The former will expand, and the latter contract. Assuming varying factor proportions between the two goods, the price of the factor in which the former (expanding) activity is intensive will rise, and the price of the other factor will fall. This, of course, is nothing but the well-known Stolper–Samuelson theorem, reached by the simple device of the Edgeworth box diagram.

With many goods and many factors, no such clear-cut demonstration is possible. But the essence of the conclusion would still hold. The tariff structure will tend to encourage some activities, and contract others. Different activities will vary from each other in their factor intensities. Thus, thought of in terms of weighted averages (that is, weighted by both size and the degree of factor intensity), factors in which expanding industries are intensive will face increased demand and rising prices, whereas the prices of factors in which contracting activities are intensive will fall.

Let us move back now to the impact of the tariff structure on various activities. In view of the impact of the tariff structure on factor markets, it will now be realized that once the analysis is coined in general-equilibrium terms, the ranking of activities by the size of their effective protective rates does *not* carry necessary implications about the directions in which resources will tend to move among the activities; that is, it does not necessarily tell us which will be the expanding and which the contracting activities. Take a world of four tradable activities, A, B, C, D, arranged in a descending order of their (net) effective protective rates (with A's the highest and D's the lowest).[25] Is it possible to assert that if C expands, B definitely will? The answer is negative. Suppose that A and B have roughly the same factor intensities, varying greatly from those of C and D; and that A is a large industry, which gets a rate of protection considerably higher than B's. The expansion of A will raise substantially the prices of factors in which it is intensive, thus raising in particular costs in activity B, which is intensive in the same factors and this may more than offset the protection with which activity B is granted. The reverse may be true, on the other hand, in the relationship of C and D to each other: the fall in the prices of factors in which C is intensive will more than offset its negative protection. Hence, C will expand and B contract. This may be put in terms of cross-elasticities of supply. These elasticities are high (in absolute terms—they are negative) among industries which, in a loose manner of talking, use the same factors of production, that is, which have similar factor intensities. Factors will be attracted to the expanding activity from activities with which it has high cross-elasticities of supply; in our example, they will be drawn to A from B.

Moreover, it is not even possible to assert with certainty that the activity with the *highest* effective protective rate will expand or that the one with the lowest protection will contract. Suppose, in our example, that A still has the highest protective rate, but it is only slightly higher than B's; that B is a relatively large activity; that B uses (to make it extreme—in a fixed proportion) a factor whose total elasticity of supply is very low; and that A is very intensive in this factor. The expansion of B will raise the price of the factor in question, and thus the costs of producing A, which is intensive in this factor; and this rise in costs may more than offset A's protection, even though it is the highest in the ranking. Hence, activity A will contract, despite its protection: B's expansion has drawn from it a factor of primary importance, thus leading to the contraction of the activity. And a symmetric example may be constructed to show an expansion of D, the activity with the highest negative rate of protection.

It thus appears that, within a general-equilibrium framework encompassing the whole tariff structure, the conclusion arrived at is that anything could happen: the position of a good in the ranking of effective protective rates does not necessarily indicate the expansionary or contractionary impact of the tariff structure on this activity.[26] Does that deny any validity from the effective-protection analysis and measurement?

If rigorous, firm conclusions are to be drawn from the analysis, the answer would have to be: unfortunately, yes. But if lesser demands are made on the analysis, it could still be of very valuable service. Specifically, the inferences of the analysis would have to be interpreted as statements of *probability*, rather than of certainty. If tariffs are fixed at random, and no bias is involved, there is no reason why (on average) an activity with a high protective rate should have high cross-elasticities of supply (that is, similar factor intensities) with other industries enjoying high protection, rather than with industries subject to low or negative protection. If no such bias is suspected or demonstrated, it may thus be stated that it is *probable* that an activity with positive protection would tend to expand and to attract resources, and that this tendency would be stronger the higher the rate of protection. The reverse statements would hold for activities with negative protection.

In practice, judgement (as well as much empirical knowledge) will have to be used. In general, it may be said that the more important is the sub-set of tariffs concerning a given activity within the general structure of tariffs, the closer we are to the partial-equilibrium circumstances, and the less likely the deviations from the partial-equilibrium conclusions introduced by general-equilibrium considerations. To cite an extreme example: if all industries but one have no protection, and the remaining one has a positive protection (so that all the rest have, in relation to it, equal negative protective rates), the industry with positive protection should expand. Also, as a general rule, the validity of the 'probabilistic' conclusion about any specific industry would have to be tested primarily by comparing its protective rate not just within the ranking of all other industries, but specifically with activities of similar factor intensities to the one examined.

It should finally be noted that within a general-equilibrium context, it is easy to introduce the effect of the tariff structure on the non-tradable sector of the economy. The exchange-rate adjustment compensates for the effect of the tariff system on this sector as a whole, in comparison with the tradable sector. But this does not imply, of course, the absence of effects on allocation of resources among activities *within* the non-tradable sector. Some activities are influenced directly, we have seen, by producing inputs into tradable activities. But more generally, some non-tradable activities are better substitutes (in production) to tradable activities which enjoy positive protection; whereas others are close substitutes to tradable activities with low or negative protection. The former will be *negatively* protected, and the latter positively. In other words: non-tradable activities intensive in factors whose prices rise, due to the tariff structure, will be negatively protected; and conversely with activities intensive in factors whose prices fall. To this will have to be added the effects of substitution in demand. But it will be remembered that demand effects of the tariff structure are via *nominal* tariff rates, and not the rates of effective protection.

In the rest of the discussion of this chapter, we revert again mostly to the partial-equilibrium context. But the qualifications introduced by general-equilibrium analysis should be borne in mind.

7 Substitution between primary factors and produced inputs

Throughout the analysis, except in a few specified instances, substitution among the various components of the value added has been assumed. But we have, on the other hand, retained all the time the assumption that intermediate inputs are required in fixed (physical) proportions to the final output. Thus, no substitution was allowed between intermediate inputs and the value added as a whole or any of its components. We shall now examine the impact of such substitution, assuming first substitution between inputs and the value added as a whole, but not its separate components; that is, we assume that the value added is either produced by a single factor or contributed by several factors in fixed proportions to each other. For simplicity, we shall assume a single produced input.

Two separate, though closely interrelated issues, have to be distinguished. One is how the introduction of substitution affects the degree of protection of an activity, and the second is how substitution is reflected in the measure of the effective protective rate. Starting with the former problem, it is easy to see intuitively that the possibility of substitution *increases* the degree of protection of an industry (that is, reinforces a positive protection, or diminishes the degree of negative protection).[27] The simplest way of grasping this is by looking at the process in two stages. First, suppose the tariff structure operates (as we had earlier assumed) without substitution, and an equilibrium is reached. At this point, substitution is allowed. With no change in relative prices of all inputs, this would be immaterial. But with such a change, the minimum-cost combination would be lower (than the cost without substitution) by substituting the input which became relatively cheaper for the one which became expensive. With the lower cost, the existing situation is no longer an equilibrium one: an impetus is added here for a further expansion.[28] The direction of substitution will be determined by the relationship of the tariff on the final output (t_j) to the tariff on the produced input (t_i). We recall that if $t_j > t_i$, then $g_j > t_j > t_i$. Since g_j is the proportional change in the price of the value added (i.e. of the primary input), and t_i the proportional change in the price of the produced input, the former thus becomes relatively more expensive and the latter cheaper. Hence, there will be substitution from the former to the latter—the coefficient of the produced input should increase, and vice versa if $t_j < t_i$.[29]

The other, related problem is how substitution affects the *measure* of the effective protective rate. What should be truly measured is the proportional change in the price of the value added from the free trade to the tariff-ridden situation. With a change in the proportions of produced inputs and of value added brought on by the tariff system, however, actual estimates would vary from this 'true' measure. The *observable* input coefficients (the a_{ij} components) are conceptually two: these are based either on the production process observed, under free trade, before substitution; or on the process found under protection, when substitution has taken place. It can be seen that regardless of whether t_j is larger or smaller than t_i, hence whether g_j, the effective protective rate, is larger or smaller than t_j (and whether it is positive or negative), the use of the post-tariff, cum-substitution imported-input coefficient always yields a higher effective protective rate than the use of the free-trade, pre-substitution coefficient.[30] The only case where the two methods yield the same result is, of course, when $t_j = t_i\ (=g_j)$: in this case the ratio P_i/P_j remains unchanged by the tariff, so that no substitution takes place. Neither of the two methods will, however, measure correctly the 'true' effective protective rate; the former understates and the latter overstates it. The former disregards the added impact of substitution, which works to increase the effective protective rate; whereas the latter treats the production process as if it incorporated the substitution already in the free-trade situation—involving, thus, production cost in the free-trade position being assumed higher than it actually was, and so yielding an apparent higher increase in profitability with the move to the post-tariff position. We have a familiar index-number problem, where use of the weights (the coefficients of inputs, in this case) of the original position underestimates the gain; whereas the use of weights of the final position overestimates it. The 'true' change would thus be somewhere in between the magnitudes shown by the two indexes; and this, in turn, would be yielded by the use of weights—the imported-input (vs. value added) coefficient, in our case—somewhere in between the two positions.[31] But as will normally be the case in such an index-number problem, there is no method of actually determining the true coefficients to be used. Whether the problem is of major importance, leading to substantial biases, is of course a matter for empirical investigation and judgement.[32]

The analysis thus far has assumed, for simplicity, a single intermediate, imported input. No new element would be introduced by allowing many such inputs and substitution among them. Like substitution between imported inputs and the value added, substitution among the various inputs *raises* the effective protective rate: if input tariffs, the t_i's, vary from each other, inputs with lower tariffs will replace inputs with higher tariffs, thus lowering the cost of imports (and total costs) and raising the reward to value added. Likewise, the index-number problem will exist in this case in exactly the same way as before: using the individual input coefficients of the free-trade situation would underestimate the true effective protective rate, whereas the use of tariff-ridden, cum-substitution coefficients would exaggerate the measure of protection.

The allowance, on the other hand, of varying degrees of substitution between the imported input (whether it is one or many) and separate components of the value added does introduce, within a general-equilibrium context, additional problems and complications. As has been shown earlier, in a general-equilibrium framework it does not *necessarily* follow that an industry with a higher effective protective rate is more likely to attract resources than an industry with a lower rate. When the possibility of substitution between imported inputs and the individual factors *at varying elasticities* is admitted, this may provide another source of a 'perverse' result in which an industry does not expand but rather contracts with a positive protection. The difference of this argument from the earlier one is that, although it too is demonstrated within a general-equilibrium context, it does not concern itself with the whole tariff structure but only with the sub-structure pertaining to one industry; that is, it is argued that, all other parts of the tariff system remaining unchanged (or not existing altogether), the granting of positive effective protection to one industry may lead to its contraction, rather than to its expansion.

In an intuitive way, this possibility may be illustrated by the following example.[33] Suppose we have two industries, producing final goods j and X. Imported good i is an input to j, but not to X. Both industries employ labour and capital to produce the value added, and j is the capital-intensive activity. Substitution in j is possible, and it is much easier (that is, the elasticity of substitution is much higher) between the imported input and capital than between the input and labour. Suppose now protection is granted to j (and none to X), by imposing tariffs on both output and input, so that $t_j < t_i$ but g_j is still positive (that is, $t_j > a_{ij}t_i$). Since the ratio P_i/P_j rises, the import coefficient will fall by substitution: the imported input will be replaced by domestic factors. This, however, by the assumption of varying elasticities of substitution, will not be done in a 'neutral' but in a 'biased' fashion; namely, it will be mainly capital which will be substituted for the imported input. The capital/labour ratio in j will thus tend to rise—and the price ratio of capital to labour will tend to fall. In equilibrium, the capital/labour ratio will tend to rise in industry X as well. But with given amounts of capital and labour in the economy, the capital/labour ratio cannot rise everywhere except by the expansion of the labour-intensive activity and the contraction of the capital-intensive activity. In our example, this means a contraction of j—the industry receiving protection—and the expansion of the other industry X. This is what Corden termed the 'bias effect'—a bias working, in this example, against the protected industry. The 'normal effect' of protection, which has been considered all along, is still in operation. But it may be more than outweighed by the bias effect, so that the net result in the example on hand would be perverse—the protected industry will contract, and the unprotected (meaning, in this two-activity model, the activity with negative protection) will expand.

Thus, it is conceivable that a positive protection (or an increase in it), in the sense of a measured positive protective rate, would not attract domestic resources to the protected activity but, on the contrary, would drive resources away from it. Judgement as to whether this is a likely phenomenon would require an empirical basis, which not only is not currently available but may be conceptually difficult to provide.[34]

8 Negative value added

It is logically possible, and not infrequently found in empirical investigations, that the value added in a protected activity is negative: the value of the imported input used in the production process will exceed the value of the final output—both measured *at foreign (world) prices*. This phenomenon merits some explanation; and it raises a problem in the measurement and interpretation of effective exchange rates, which should be dwelt upon.

Negative value added could be explained by a number of factors. First, production functions and processes may differ among countries; where differences are extreme, negative value added may result. This is, in other words, a case of extreme inefficiency and waste: the raw material is transformed into a final product so much less efficiently at home than abroad, that the value of the final product resulting from the production process at home is less—when sold at world prices—than the value of the raw material.

Another possible reason is differences between world prices faced by the country concerned and prices with which foreign economies are faced. This, in turn, may be due mainly to two sources. One is transportation costs. When the raw material is bulky and expensive to transport, whereas the final good is not, the imported input coefficient (in value terms, and valued at c.i.f. prices)—the ratio P_i/P_j—would be considerably higher in the home country than abroad. Combined with the existence of other significant imported inputs, which would lower the value added, this may turn an otherwise small positive value added into a negative value added. An obvious example of this sort—although much less important today than a century ago—is coal: a bulky raw material which physically disappears altogether in processing the final output. By a proper definition, this case could be said to be a variation of the former: if transportation of the raw material is regarded as part of the productive process, this would be termed not a case of different prices but one of different production functions and processes, where the process in the home country involves an obvious waste. The other major source of different prices is monopolistic pricing practices abroad—from which the analysis has thus far abstracted by assuming that there is a single world price. In many instances, no perfect world market exists, mainly because the goods involved are differentiated rather than homogeneous. This would be particularly true for a relatively small home economy, where each industry consists of a small number of firms—possibly even a single firm, which may be associated in one way or another (being a subsidiary, or using patent or marketing rights, etc.) with a single foreign firm. The latter may then set prices of the imported inputs at a higher level than it sets in other markets.[35]

When value added is found to be negative, it is self-evident that in free trade the industry concerned would not have been producing as it does under protection. With fixed input coefficients—that is, with fixed, unalterable production processes—the industry would not have existed at all in free trade. When substitution is recognized, however, it is possible that the industry would have been operating in the free trade position as well, but it would have used different input coefficients, with which value added would have been positive. Thus, in that sense, negative value added may be said to be the result, in such cases, of substitution arising from protection.

This may be illustrated more rigorously by means of figure 22, where j_1 is an isoquant which shows the alternative combinations of i (the imported input) and v (the value added) which produce one unit of j. We shall assume constant returns to scale, so that this isoquant represents completely the production function. The slope of the line $P_f^{ji} P_f^{jv}$ represents the world price ratio of P_i to P_v (which is directly derived from the price ratio P_i/P_j, and the world input coefficients). In free trade equilibrium, price will equal cost, and the minimum-cost combination would be A: the unit of j will be produced with an amount OP_f^{ji} of i and OP_f^{vv} of V. The former is the cost of input i, in terms of this input, of

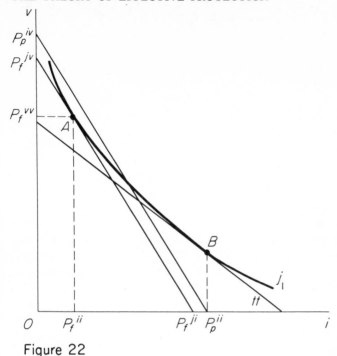

Figure 22

producing the unit of j; similarly, the latter is the cost of the value added, in terms of units of value added, in producing a unit of j. With the given foreign prices, the price (= cost) of a unit of j could be represented either by P_f^{ji} in terms of units of i or by P_f^{jv} in terms of units of V. Now a tariff system is imposed (consisting, for instance, of a tariff on j without a tariff on i) which lowers the (home) price ratio P_i/P_j, therefore also lowering the price ratio P_i/P_v; the new latter price ratio is represented by the slope of tt. Substitution towards the use of i takes place, and production of a unit of j is now made at the point B, which is the new minimum-cost combination. The number of units of i now used in a unit of j becomes OP_p^{ii}, and it is higher, as shown in this case, than the world value of j, which is only OP_f^{ji} of i. Similarly, if measured in terms of v, the world value of input i used in producing a unit of j exceeds the value of j by $P_f^{jv} P_p^{iv}$. Hence, a negative value added is found. And this is due, in this example, *only* to substitution: the production function represented by the j isoquant might well be similar to the one existing abroad, and foreign prices (of j and i) facing the country are assumed to be the same as those facing the foreign countries themselves. This is, thus, a case of extreme waste resulting not from any differences in production functions (or transportation costs), but from making the imported input relatively very cheap, leading to such a large use of this input per unit of output as to make the value added negative.[36]

The problem of measurement and interpretation of effective protection when negative value-added exists arises from the fact that with it, the *denominator* in the definition of effective protective rate, $g_j = (V'_j - V_j)/V_j$, would be negative, making the effective protective rate appear as a negative number. But in this instance, the negative protective rate does not, of course, mean negative protection: on the contrary, an industry manifesting negative value added must have positive (probably heavy) protection, since in free trade it would not have operated at all, or at least not on the protection scale. Likewise, a smaller algebraic (larger absolute) number would not mean lower protection but, on the contrary, higher protection. The standard definition and measurement of effective protection is thus not applicable to the case of negative value added. It is clear, first, that these cases have to be separated from all the rest—a separation which normally should not face much difficulty in practice, being distinguished from cases of truly negative protection by having the negative sign found in the denominator rather than the numerator.[37] But the problem of interpreting the findings in this group will still remain. If the problem analyzed is that posed when the subject matter of the theory of effective protection was defined—namely, to learn from the size of effective protection the *direction* of movement of resources induced by the tariff system—then the very existence of negative value added provides an answer: it indicates a pull of resources into the activity under consideration—regardless of the actual size of the 'negative' protective rate found in such an instance. Thus, within this context, it is enough to separate out the whole group of negative value-added activities, lumping them all together at the top of the effective protection scale.[38] Although being a correct procedure and answer within this context, it leaves the impression that once the denominator in the effective protective

rate definition is negative, its size and the size of the numerator
are of no consequence. If our interest extends beyond the question posed, to the problem of the *cost* of protection, these
magnitudes would indeed be relevant.[39]

9 Effective protective rates and domestic resource costs

The 'domestic resource costs' (DRC) is a method, developed in
Israel in the early 1950's, of evaluating contemplated investment
projects and estimating the social costs of existing industries.[40]
In the latter role, it seems to belong to the same family as the
effective protective rate (EPR)—an affinity which has led recently to a controversy about the similarities and differences of the
two measures, and the superiority of one over the other.[41] A
comparative analysis of the two measures may provide a useful
framework for pointing out the potential use and the limitations
of the concept of EPR, and some of the adjustments called for in
the practical application of the concept. We shall start by stating
briefly the nature of the 'rival' method of DRC.

The DRC concept is addressed to a tradable industry, and
applied in a regime of government interference in international
transactions either by way of tariffs, subsidies, etc., or by the
maintenance of a disequilibrium exchange rate (or multiple
rates). The industry is producing, normally, some net earnings of
foreign exchange:[42] it yields gross receipts (if the tradable is an
export good) or saving (if it is an import substitute) of foreign
exchange of the (world) value of the final product, and carries an
expenditure of foreign exchange of the value of the imported (or
exportable) input used in the process of production, the difference
being net foreign-exchange earnings. To produce the net earnings,
the domestic value added was employed. The 'domestic resource
cost' is the cost, in terms of value added, of producing a unit of net
earnings of foreign exchange. It is, hence, the value added divided
by the net foreign-exchange earnings.[43] In symbolic terms, we
have:

(14) $$C_j = \frac{DVA}{V}$$

where C_j is the domestic resource cost, DVA—the domestic value added in local currency, and V—the value added ('earned' or 'saved') in foreign exchange (C_j is thus denominated in units of local currency per unit of foreign exchange). Normalizing the foreign price of the final good at unity, we thus have

$$(15) \qquad C_j = \frac{DVA}{1 - \sum_i a_{ij}}$$

where, as usual, the i's are imported (tradable) inputs in the production of j.[44] Now, *if* the domestic value added is *defined by using actual market prices*, we fall back to our formula (11′) above, where the concepts of specific and effective exchange rates were used: since DVA would then be $R_{sj} - \sum_i a_{ij} R_{si}$, C_j would be precisely R_{vj}, and (15) turns to be (11′). And, as we have seen, the transformation from R_{vj} (or C_j) to g_j, the effective protective rate, is then straightforward. Any ranking by g_j would then be exactly equal to the ranking by C_j, and vice versa. The two concepts will become one and the same thing.[45] Even then, however, it should be recalled that the R_{sj}'s and R_{si}'s, the specific exchange rates, are *not* determined solely by the existing tariffs. On the one hand, they include the price effects of practices such as import quotas. On the other hand, they do not necessarily include all existing tariffs. When prohibitive tariffs exist—a case from which the analysis has abstracted all along—it will be only an accident if the specified (nominal) tariff rate is exactly the one which turns out to be prohibitive. Normally, the prohibitive level will be *below* the nominal rate; that is, part of the nominal rate will be meaningless—the situation known as 'water in the tariff'. And it is only the *utilized* part of the tariff which is relevant, and which forms a component of the specific exchange rates. This utilized part would be found, like the implicit tariff of an import quota, by defining the tariff as the ratio of the local price to the foreign price (at the formal exchange rate); whereas the rationale of a definition of EPR's by something like (4) above, is the opposite transformation—from tariff levels to local prices. This demonstrates again the usefulness of the specific and effective exchange-rate concepts. But in essence, these are still within the EPR approach.

The crux of the difference between the concepts of EPR and DRC lies in the italicized proviso above—'if . . . defined by using actual market prices'; and, similarly, in the difference between *measured* EPR's and those implied by the assumptions on which the analysis of this concept has hitherto been based. The DRC concept is meant to measure the *social cost* in the economy under consideration of the various productive activities. Under conditions of perfect competitive equilibrium—which have been assumed throughout most of the present discussion of effective protection—market prices *will* measure social cost, and the EPR and DRC concepts will become equivalent. When these conditions are not met, on the other hand, market prices will no longer accurately reflect social cost. In *actual* EPR estimates, market prices will nevertheless be normally used for the calculations. In the DRC concept they will be replaced—in principle, at least—by 'correct' shadow prices of the productive services. This would mean, in general, correction of factor prices for elements of rent, tax, or subsidy.

Recall, for instance, the discussion of a positive protection granted when one productive factor (required in a fixed proportion) has a completely inelastic supply (to the protected industry). All of the protection will then result in rent to this specific factor, without any change in the total size of the activity, or in the production process (hence, also, in quantities and prices of other factors). No change has thus resulted in the *social* cost of the protected activity, although the price does, of course, rise: it is now higher than the social cost by the rent element. The DRC concept would value, in this case, the specific factor at a shadow price excluding its rent, and will be lower than the EPR by the rent element. Or, to take another example, certainly of much practical relevance: when the industry concerned is not fully competitive but is dominated by a monopolistic firm, monopolistic profits will result. The price of the product, being higher than marginal revenue, will be higher than marginal cost—which, in turn, being the opportunity cost, measures the (marginal) social cost of production. Hence, the DRC concept will assign lower (than the market price) costs to this activity, by abstracting from monopolistic profits, which are the rent element in the price of enterprise in this instance. Other important examples will be found in imperfections in factor markets. Thus, due to institutional restrictions, a factor price facing each industry may be higher than its opportunity cost; an obvious instance would be unskilled labour having a positive market price in economies where this factor is in long-run unemployment. An opposite case would be a factor market price lower than its opportunity cost due to a (direct or implicit) government subsidy. As we have seen in our earlier discussion, a subsidy to a factor *in one activity* may be transformed into a rate of subsidy to the activity (although not without difficulties, when substitution exists); but a general subsidy to a factor will not appear in any activity's EPR. The DRC would then be higher than the EPR, due to a use of a higher shadow price of the factor—the difference being more significant the more intensive is the activity in the subsidized factor. Here, a very frequent concrete example would be capital, when it is subsidized by the government.[46]

Thus, when the correct shadow prices differ from market prices of factors, DRC's will differ from EPR's. The former ones, being designed for the purpose, will provide the correct ranking of activities by their social cost.[47] It will thus yield ranking of activities by their comparative advantage in the economy. But since these estimates do not necessarily reflect market prices, they will *not* provide a measure of the way in which government interference—by way of the tariff structure in its broadest sense—affects the location of resources in the country's various activities. For this purpose—and strictly speaking, only for this—the EPR concept is designed; and this is the function it, rather than the DRC, will fulfil. It is only in the case of a perfectly competitive market all parts of which are in long-run equilibrium, and in which the government interferes in the goods rather than the factor markets, that the two measures will coincide. Both will give the same ranking, signifying both the degree of encouragement given by the tariff structure to the various activities and (in reverse order) the degree of the economy's comparative advantage in these activities.

10 Effective protection: concluding remarks

The concept and the theory of effective protection are designed to assess the effect of a tariff structure on the allocation of the economy's resources among the various activities. How well do they succeed in this role?

We have seen that, strictly speaking, effective protective rates by themselves cannot fulfil this function. In a general-equilibrium context, a scale of effective-protective rates does not, without additional information, necessarily tell us where and out of where will resources have moved due to the imposition of a tariff structure. This conclusion is strengthened if the possibility of varying elasticities of substitution among various inputs in the production of each good is taken into account. This does not mean, however, that the concept of effective protection loses its value; it rather calls for a redefinition of the role assigned to it. Instead of looking for a certain, rigorous answer, *probable* effects should be looked for. In that sense, the concept retains its usefulness. But this, of course, introduces an element of judgement into the analysis. If the directions of movement of resources indicated are only probable, then only large differences among protective rates should be considered, and small variations be overlooked—the determination of 'large' and 'small' being a matter of judgement. The redefinition also implies that as far as possible, studies of effective protection have to be supplemented by additional information about interrelationships among activities and factors.

The effective protection theory is primarily a *positive* theory of commercial policy. Following a long period of concentration on normative aspects of commercial policies, this new emphasis has definitely helped in improving the balance in the analysis of commercial policies. But the emphasis has probably been carried too far. In actual problems for which theories should be useful, the question will rarely be: what would be the effect of removing (or imposing) a *whole* tariff structure? And even if this is asked, the question will probably not stop at the effect on reallocation of resources, and certainly not merely on *directions* of this reallocation. The typical question is likely to be: what would be the effect of removing a tariff (or part of it), or of imposing a tariff, in one industry or one group of industries? It will likely be, hence, a question of *marginal* changes, rather than an all-or-none question posed for the whole tariff structure. Moreover, and this is probably of even larger importance, the question of *costs and benefits* to the economy is likely to be posed as an inseparable part of the problem, which is bound to be not just how a tariff (or its removal) will reallocate resources, but whether this benefits or injures the economy—and by how much. The problem of the *cost of protection* is thus likely to be essential.

The theory and measurement of effective protection would be useful for this function. To some extent, actually, the theory may provide better answers to the normative issue of the cost of protection than to the positive issue originally assigned to it. If we ask what the cost of removing one tariff is, general-equilibrium considerations may by and large be disregarded. And, if the question is related to part of a tariff—to a marginal reduction (or imposition)—substitution effects may not be large enough to be of much significance. The effective rate of protection will thus provide a reliable estimate of costs borne or saved by the contemplated change in the tariff system.

This would be disturbed, as we have just seen, by distortions in factor markets, with private costs being different from social costs. The concept of domestic resource costs (DRC) is designed to handle this difficulty. Indeed, if a set of DRC's is available, the demand upon the analysis of effective protection to indulge in normative aspects would become much less justified. But more often than not, this would not be the case. In comparison with DRC's, EPR's are easy to construct, and are much more likely to be available. In these instances, the second-best analytic policy would be to adapt the effective protective rate, introducing to it some of the necessary and obvious adjustments in each case, so that it would be able to fulfil the added normative function.

Appendix: Some problems in constructing estimates of effective protective rates

Transforming the analysis and definitions of protective rates into operational guidelines for the construction of estimates would require an elaborate manual. This is *not* the purpose of this brief appendix, which is rather meant to give a sample illustration of problems that have to be faced in this transformation, and to comment on certain biases that may be involved in the procedures followed in overcoming the problems.

In principle, EPR's could be constructed by examining in detail the production of a given good (j), determining the physical quantities of each intermediate input required for the production of a unit of the final good, and observing the foreign prices of each input and of the final output. This would provide enough information for estimating the size of the a_{ij} coefficients. This procedure is, however, as may be gathered, quite laborious and expensive, and is rarely followed.[48] Instead, use is made of available input-output tables for the economy. This raises a number of issues.

One of the problems, the adjustment of input coefficients for deviations from international prices, is quite easy to overcome. We recall that with physical units of final output j defined to make the foreign price unity, and physical units of input i defined so that one unit of i is used in the production of one unit of j, the input coefficient appearing in the definition of g_j, the EPR, is P_i—the foreign price of a unit of i. The input-output table, on the other hand, would most often show input coefficients calculated by dividing the value of the input by the value of the output—both valued at *local* prices. This coefficient must, hence, be adjusted.[49] A unit of input is valued, in the input-output table, not at P_i but at the local price $P_i (1 + t_i)$; likewise, a unit of output is valued at $P_j (1 + t_j)$. The input-output coefficient, designated by a'_{ij}, would hence be:

$$a'_{ij} = \frac{P_i (1 + t_i)}{1 + t_j}$$

instead of the correct valuation by which $a_{ij} = P_i$. We get:

$$a_{ij} = \frac{a'_{ij} (1 + t_j)}{1 + t_i}$$

and thus, the available input-output coefficients are used for the estimate of EPR by calculating:

$$g_j = \frac{t_j - \Sigma_i \, a'_{ij} \left(\dfrac{1 + t_j}{1 + t_i} \right) t_i}{1 - \Sigma_i \, a'_{ij} \left(\dfrac{1 + t_j}{1 + t_i} \right)}$$

This procedure raises no severe difficulty. But it may require, as we shall see shortly, the use of somewhat different measures of tariffs (t_j and t_i) in the various components of the formula.[50]

A much more serious problem is raised by the fact that input-output tables are aggregated, often highly so.[51] Any tariff would then be some average—normally a weighted average, where import values are used for weights. But with escalated tariff structures, this would introduce a bias, in practice of probably quite significant size, into the estimates. Suppose, for instance, that aggregate good i consists of two items, i_1 and i_2. The former is an intermediate input, and the latter a final good. Assume the former is free of tariff, whereas the latter is subject to tariff. We have some average positive tariff for i, which we shall apply to the coefficient a_{ij} as received (after the aforementioned adjustment for local prices) from the input-output table. But in effect, a_{ij} should be a_{i1j}—since, by assumption, i_2 is a final good, thus $a_{i2j} = 0$. Hence, we should have applied to a_{ij} the tariff rate $t_{i1} = 0$, rather than a positive tariff. By applying (for lack of better data) the wrong input tariff t_i, we would *underestimate* g_j, the protective rate for final good j. In turn, by applying t_i to both i_1 and i_2, we *underestimate* g_{i1}, the protective rate for final good i_1; and *overestimate* g_{i2}, the protective rate for intermediate good i_2. If i_1 and i_2 are produced in the same proportion as they are imported, this would not bias the estimate of the average protective rate for the activity of producing good i. If, on the other hand, as might normally be expected, i_1 (the final good) will have a higher share of home production than its share in imports of i, this procedure would involve an *underestimate* of protection of industry i as well. The use of (aggregate) input-output coefficients thus leads to an underestimate of effective protective rates.[52]

Besides this problem of weighting in aggregation—that is, assuming that we have as detailed information about input coefficients as we would wish—other issues are involved in estimating nominal tariff rates. One method of obtaining the rate is by dividing tariff revenues from the imported item by the value of imports (at the formal rate of exchange) of the item. In practice, this raises a severe problem of timing: data on tariff revenues for a given period (say, a calendar year) and the size of imports are likely not to be related exactly to each other. But even abstracting from this difficulty (assuming, that is, that revenue data actually refer to duties imposed on imports of the same period), the tariff rate yielded by this procedure is likely *not* to be identical with the rate posted in the tariff schedule.

This would be due to the fact that some imports of the item—ranging from relatively unimportant personal imports by returning tourists to substantial magnitudes such as imports used in exports—may be exempted from the tariff, or subject to special tariff provisions. What, then, is the 'correct' tariff rate to use—the one posted in the schedule, or the (lower) one yielded by the ratio of revenue to imports? For the purpose on hand, it is the former—the posted tariff rate. Since we are interested in the EPR's as indicators of the effect of a tariff structure on allocation of resources, it is prices *at the margin* which would be of interest. Assuming that the posted tariff rate is the highest (from which, that is, there could be only exemptions, partial or complete), this would be the relevant tariff for decisions (at the margin), leading to expansion or contraction of the activity.[53]

Notes

1 Corden's analysis is developed fully in his book (1971a); but the tool has been presented, and the fundamental elements of the theory exposed, in an earlier paper (1966a).

2 B. Balassa (1965, 1967, 1971); and H. G. Johnson (1965d, 1969); a forerunner in the English language literature is a paper by C. L. Barber (1955). A concise history of the development of the concept, and a comprehensive bibliography, appear in Corden's book (1971a, Appendices I and III). It may be added that an early analysis by B. Ohlin (1943, Appendix IV) of the Swedish tariff policy before 1914 has applied in essence the effective-protection idea.

3 W. M. Corden (1971a). With this general statement, specific references to Corden's work will mostly be dispensed with.

4 Based on W. M. Corden (1971a, figure 3, p. 30).

5 Note, however, that no such assumption is made about the separate components of the value added—the contributions of the various production factors. These could be substituted for each other.

6 Under present assumptions this will also be the rate of change in the reward received by domestic factors of production for their contribution to the production of a unit of the final good. But this will not necessarily be true when substitution between the intermediate input and the value added is allowed.

7 Income taxes may also be designed to afford protection to certain domestic activities (for instance, by a complete or partial exemption of

exporters' profits from the tax). Both the definition and, much more so, the measurement of the protective effect of such income tax regulations are rather complicated and will not be dealt with here. In practice, it may be assumed that overlooking income taxes altogether, in the examination of protection, would not have grave consequences in most countries. Still other taxes (or subsidies), beside those examined in the text and the income tax, may also have protective effects. One such impact will be analyzed later, in section 4.

8 In addition, the measure of effective protection is designed also to take into account the effect of non-tariff devices of interference in trade, of which the existence of import quotas may be the most important example. Quota profits on imports of a final good should be added as if they were a tariff on the good—at a rate implied by the ratio of these profits to the formal price of the good; and quota profits on the import of an input should be similarly treated as a tariff on the input. This procedure assumes, it should be noted, that imports of inputs and production of the final good are carried out independently. Very often, however, import licences for inputs would be granted only to producers of the final good, in proportion to the size of their production. In such instances, quota profits on inputs should *not* be considered, since they do not work to subtract from the reward for the productive activity; and only the quota profits on imports of the final good should enter the calculation.

Under a quantitative-restrictions regime imports of the final good may often be prohibited altogether. In these cases, quota profits on the final good would have to be *implied*; but this carries the argument somewhat beyond the framework used until now.

9 See, for instance, B. Balassa (1965, 1967, 1971).

10 But not necessarily higher than the *effective* rate at the earlier stage: for this to happen, an escalation of the rate of escalation would be required.

11 Provided that export industries do pay the tariffs on inputs. Very often they do not, under a 'drawback' scheme.

12 But see, on this, W. M. Corden (1971a, pp. 152–163).

13 The analysis presented here follows W. M. Corden's (*ibid.*, and 1966a) and this approach to non-tradable inputs became known as the 'Corden method'. An alternative, the 'Balassa method', has been suggested by B. Balassa (see especially 1971, pp. 16–18 and 321–324), and partly followed in his own studies. Balassa treats non-tradable inputs as if they were tradable inputs subject to a zero rate of (nominal) tariff. The justification of this approach is on the pragmatic level: it facilitates considerably the calculations (and data gathering) involved

in estimating protective rates, and may on occasions be the only feasible way. But Balassa's defence of this method on the conceptual level, based on making the assumption that the inputs in question are provided at constant cost, does not seem well taken. First, there is no empirical support for such an assumption. Second, if this assumption is made, it should logically be applied also with regard to the final outputs—in which case the theory of protection breaks down completely.

A rigorous proof that the Corden method does indeed yield the index required (for the task of evaluating the impact of tariffs on the shift of resources), under specified conditions, has been provided recently in A. Ray (1973).

14 Or, in the present context: otherwise, local production would immediately displace all imports, making the present analysis of protection invalid.

15 G. Basevi (1966) has attempted a measurement of the effect of the US tariff structure on US labour, based on such an assumption.

16 Assuming that the value added consists of the contribution of two factors, (1) and (2), in fixed physical proportions, we will get:

$$g_{1j} = g_j \left/ \left(\frac{e_1}{e_2} \frac{V_{2j}}{V_j} + \frac{V_{1j}}{V_j} \right) \right.$$

which may also be transformed into

$$g_{1j} = g_j \left/ \left[\frac{V_{1j}}{V_j} \left(1 - \frac{e_1}{e_2} \right) + \frac{e_1}{e_2} \right] \right.$$

where e_1 and e_2 are the respective elasticities of supply of the two factors. g_{1j} is higher the lower is e_1/e_2; that is, the lower is e_1, its own elasticity of supply, and the higher is e_2, the elasticity of supply of the other factor. There is no unequivocal conclusion, on the other hand, about the impact of the share of the factor in the value added. It may be seen that a higher share of the factor, V_{1j}/V_j will yield a higher rate of protection for it if $e_1/e_2 > 1$, that is, if $e_1 > e_2$—the factor's elasticity of supply is the relatively higher; if $e_1 < e_2$, on the other hand, the higher factor's share will lead to a *lower* degree of protection for it.

17 This conclusion seems only too obvious; but note that it does *not* hold for the case of fixed proportions of productive inputs.

18 Assume again two factors, (1) and (2). We know that in equilibrium, $P_1/MP_{1j} = P_2/MP_{2j} = P_j$, where the MP's are marginal physical productivities of the factors.

The subsidy to (1) lowers P_1 for the producer, hence (by substitution) MP_{1j} is lowered; by the same token, MP_{2j} is raised (more units of (1) and fewer of (2) are engaged in the production of a unit of j). But since P_j is fixed, in this case (it is the unchanged foreign price), we get necessarily $P_2' > P_2$, which also implies necessarily $Q_2' > Q_2$.

19 The 'exchange rate' is used here, in conformity with the convention mostly (but not universally) accepted, in the sense of the price in units of local currency of a unit of foreign exchange. To make the statement in the text correct, the degree of exchange-rate adjustment would thus have to be defined as the proportional change of the *inverse* of the exchange-rate (that is, of the price in units of foreign currency of one unit of local currency).

20 W. M. Corden (1971a, pp. 106–114 and 122–125).

21 The term 'effective rate of exchange' has been used—by the present author, *inter alia*, on other occasions—in the meaning defined here as the 'specific rate of exchange'. The definition used in the present context is adopted in order to emphasize the relationship of this magnitude to the effective protective rate, and facilitate the transition from one concept to another. To emphasize the equivalence of the terms even more, the 'specific' rate of exchange should have been termed the 'nominal' rate—being of the same character as the nominal tariff rate. It is probable, however, that such a concept would tend to mislead, being intuitively interpreted as what is called here the *formal* rate of exchange.

22 See W. M. Corden (1971a, pp. 87–92).

23 A general-equilibrium analysis does not imply necessarily that the tariff structure as a whole is studied. We could ask, for instance, what would the impact of one tariff (or one sub-set of the structure) be on the economy as a whole (rather than the direct effect on the activity concerned, as we have done in the partial-equilibrium context), tracing out all the reverberations of the tariff; and this would be, strictly speaking, a general-equilibrium analysis. But such a study would add only little to the partial-equilibrium analysis at the present stage.

24 It should be noted that protection is meant here in its 'net' sense.

25 This means, of course, that some of the protective rates—at least D's—are negative.

26 It should perhaps be emphasized that this inconclusiveness is *not* due to the shift from 'nominal' to 'effective' protection which results from the introduction of intermediate inputs, but to the shift from a world of two goods to a multi-good world. In the absence of intermediate goods, nominal tariff rates would also be rates of effective protection, and the same inconclusiveness in the interpretation of the

results of a tariff structure would then apply to the ranking of industries by their nominal rates of tariff.

27 The formal proof, however, is more elaborate. See W. M. Corden (1971a, pp. 131–142).

28 With substitution, the change in price of the value added (which is the effective protective rate) and the change in the value added per unit of the final product are no longer identical: the latter is affected by both the former and the change of the physical proportion of value added in the final product (which will be rising with $t_j < t_i$ and falling with $t_j > t_i$). If we denote, following Leith, the change in the value added per unit of final output by h_j, and σ is the elasticity of substitution between the produced input and the value added, we get the following relationships:

	$t_j > t_i$	$t_j < t_i$
$0 < \sigma < 1$	$g_j > h_j > t_j$	$g_j < h_j < t_j$
$\sigma = 1$	$g_j > h_j = t_j$	$g_j < h_j = t_j$
$1 < \sigma < \infty$	$g_j > h_j < t_j$	$g_j < h_j > t_j$

See J. C. Leith (1968, pp. 593–595).

29 In equilibrium, $P_i = P_j \, MP_i$ (where MP_i is the marginal physical productivity of input i). If $t_j > t_i$ then, by definition, the proportional change in P_j is higher than in P_i. To restore equilibrium MP_i must then fall. And this means, in turn (assuming constant returns to scale) a higher ratio of input i to the value added (the input of the primary factor), and vice versa for $t_j < t_i$.

30 Recall that we may write g_j in the form

$$g_j = t_j + \frac{a_{ij}}{1 - a_{ij}}(t_j - t_i).$$

If $t_j > t_i$, g_j will be higher the higher is $a_{ij}/(1 - a_{ij})$; and the latter will, in turn, be higher the higher is a_{ij}. Substitution is in this case *towards* i; hence a_{ij} will be higher in the post-substitution than in the pre-substitution (free trade) measure. When $t_j < t_i$, g_j will be higher the *lower* is $a_{ij}/(1 - a_{ij})$. But in this case, substitution is *away from i*, thus showing a_{ij} [and $a_{ij}/(1 - a_{ij})$] to be lower in the tariff-ridden, post-substitution situation than in free trade.

31 J. M. Finger (1969) was the first to demonstrate the relationship between the three magnitudes (the 'true' effective protective rate, the rate's measure by free trade coefficients, and the measure by post-tariff coefficients) as an index-number problem and relationship. W. M. Corden (1971a, pp. 131–142), along with his proof that substitution raises the rate of protection, also shows diagrammatically the

relationship of the three measures and the position of the 'true' measure.

32 In actual measurements, normally only the post-tariff, post-substitution coefficient would be found: the production process subject to observation is, of course, one that reflects the existing tariff structure. Even if there were, on occasions, observations of a former situation, where the tariff system had not existed, these would be too far removed in the past to suggest that they would reflect the present production structure had tariffs not existed. For this reason, most researchers use the available, post-tariff coefficients, noting the bias involved. An important exception are the studies of B. Balassa (1965, 1967, 1971), in which production coefficients of Belgium and Netherlands are used for estimates of protective rates in other countries. Balassa argues that since these economies are close to being in a free trade situation, and since their overall structure and attributes are similar to those of other countries, the Belgium–Netherlands coefficients would be reasonable approximations of free-trade coefficients in other countries. This argument suffers, however, from two flaws. First, there is no *a priori* reason to believe that the free-trade coefficients are closer to the 'true' coefficients required (namely, those that would provide the 'true' measure of the protective rate) than are the tariff-ridden coefficients. Second, even assuming (which we are always able to, by approximate definitions) that production functions are identical in Benelux and in the country under consideration, Balassa's conclusion that free-trade coefficients in the two would be equal requires that either (a) no substitution exists, or (b) free-trade factor prices are similar in the two. The first case may be ruled out: without substitution, no problem exists and the country's post-tariff coefficients should be used without qualifications. The second possibility—of similar factor prices—seems rather unlikely (especially if we recall that for the production functions to be similar in two countries, factors have to be defined in a narrow, specific rather than broad manner). It should be noted, however, that in his later studies Balassa constructed *both* sets of estimates; that is, those derived from Benelux input–output coefficients as well as from domestic (tariff-ridden) coefficients.

33 This follows the discussion in W. M. Corden (1971a, pp. 146–151).

34 The possibility of a 'perverse' result was first demonstrated, through the construction of a specific counter-example, by V. K. Ramaswami and T. N. Srinivasan (1971). The discussion was then taken by R. W. Jones (1971). More recently, the issue has been analyzed, within a wider context, in a symposium consisting of the contributions of J. N. Bhagwati and T. N. Srinivasan (1973), M.

Bruno (1973), and C. Khang (1973). The conclusion which emerges from this symposium is that the 'perverse' outcome *cannot* occur if the production function is of a separable type. The function in which input coefficients are fixed (i.e. no substitution can take place at all) is one example of such a type. The Cobb–Douglas function, as well as the CES—the two most-widely used for empirical research—are other examples of separable production functions.

It has been noted above (note 26) that the inconclusiveness in predicting the resource-pull effects of a tariff structure, within a general-equilibrium framework, is not specific to a world with intermediate goods, and would apply just as well to a system of nominal rates in a world of many final goods. The 'perverse' result discussed in the present section is, on the other hand, peculiar to a world which *does* contain intermediate goods: it is a possibility which arises, we recall, only due to the substitution among such inputs and the services of primary factors.

35 To cite one illustration: during the late 1950's and early 1960's car manufacturing in Israel—very heavily protected, of course—consisted mainly of an assembly plant for a French car of a specific model. The price of the imported components amounted to about 80–85 per cent of the foreign price of the finished car—all prices recorded according to the lists of the foreign manufacturer. This would supposedly leave (disregarding other imported inputs) a domestic value added of 15–20 per cent of the final product. The specific model under consideration was sold, however, not in free markets but in other protected markets, and its price was thus higher than the price of equivalent cars which were sold freely in the international market. Were the latter price taken as the basis for calculation—as it should—the apparent positive value added would turn into a negative value added even without taking into account other direct or indirect imported inputs.

A rather similar instance, concerning the assembly of a Fiat car in India, is mentioned in J. N. Bhagwati and P. Desai (1970, p. 366). See this source (Appendix to Chapter 17, pp. 363–367) also for a more exhaustive list of the possible reasons for the appearance of negative value added.

36 For alternative methods of demonstrating the relationship between substitution and negative value added see W. M. Corden (1971a, pp. 142–144) or S. E. Guisinger (1969).

37 There has been an attempt (R. Soligo and J. Stern, 1965), to avoid this separate treatment of negative value-added cases by using an alternative definition of the effective protective rate. Instead of $(V' - V)/V$, Soligo and Stern define and measure effective protection by $(V'$

$- V)/V'$; that is, the denominator of the ratio is defined as the value added in local prices, after protection, rather than the value added at the free trade (foreign) prices. Since value added in local prices must be positive—or else the industry would not exist—the denominator here would always be positive. Negative rates would then, by necessity, indicate the existence of truly negative protection. This solution is not, however, entirely satisfactory: in cases of negative value added (at world prices)—that is, when V is negative—an added protection will show a *lower* rate of protection by this definition. An increase of t_j, for instance, will raise V', thus raise by equal amounts the numerator and the (smaller) denominator, hence lowering the ratio. See S. E. Guisinger (1969).

38 To this group could be added those industries with extremely high protective rates though with positive value added. An unusually high (say, over 10) effective protective rate most probably—although this is not a logical necessity—indicates a very low fraction of value added; and the difference between this and a small fraction of negative value added may often be a matter of inaccuracies in measurement. Also, an increase of an extremely high protective rate to a still higher rate is probably of very little consequence so far as the pull of added productive resources is concerned.

39 This is analyzed in M. Michaely (1975).

40 The clearest exposition of the method is found in M. Bruno (1963). For the history of the development of the concept and its application in Israel, see N. Halevi (1969). An identical approach has been applied independently by A. O. Krueger (1966).

41 See B. Balassa and D. M. Schydlowsky (1968), M. Bruno (1972), A. O. Krueger (1972), and again Balassa and Schydlowsky (1972).

42 That is, unless it has a negative value added, a problem in measurement facing the DRC concept just as the EPR.

43 This calculation could be done—for normative issues such as the selection of investment projects it ought to be—in marginal rather than average terms. The meaning of 'marginal' would change, of course, from case to case: a whole plant may be considered marginal, or an addition to the output of an existing plant, and so on.

44 A. O. Krueger (1972, p. 53, formula (3)) subtracts in the denominator also the payments received by foreign factors (labour, capital) employed in the domestic production. This is in principle a correct procedure to follow *both* in the definition of DRC and of EPR. In the latter, payments to imported services of productive factors should be treated, if by 'value added' we refer to the contribution of

domestic factors, just as the cost of imported produced inputs. For simplicity, we have disregarded this element throughout the presentation of the EPR—and will continue to do so in the following discussion. But since in actual estimates of EPR's too this element has tended to be disregarded, Krueger is apparently right in claiming that this is one of the sources of differences between EPR's and DRC's.

45 A difference which has been pointed out among the two is that in the DRC concept the net value added (V in (14), or $1 - \Sigma_i a_{ij}$ in (15)) is derived by subtracting both direct and indirect import components; whereas in the EPR concept only the direct component is taken into account. It will be recalled, however, that by the Corden method of analysis of non-tradable inputs, indirect import components are treated just like the direct component—as is seen clearly from (7″) above. This alleged difference thus exists only if the Balassa method of referring to non-tradable inputs is followed in constructing the EPR concept. The allegation was probably helped by an ambivalent approach in B. Balassa and D. M. Schydlowsky (1968): they seem to recommend the use of the Corden method ('. . . . one may then apply the method suggested by Corden'—p. 354) but at the same time to defend the use of the direct import component alone (pp. 351–353).

46 Although *in principle* all factor prices are corrected in the DRC concept, in actual use of these measurements the two most familiar corrections would be concerned with the last two examples; namely, assigning lower (than market) prices for labour, at least of certain categories, and a higher price for capital. Such corrections would be appropriate probably in most less-developed economies, where labour (of certain varieties) is partly unemployed and where capital is subsidized (through lending at low interest rates, or by provision as equity capital) by the government. Other important prices which may often be corrected are those of land, water, or electricity.

47 B. Balassa and D. M. Schydlowsky (1968, 1972) introduce a concept of the 'social effective rate' of protection which, in distinction from the 'private effective rate' uses shadow factor prices where factor markets are imperfect. Such procedure, as will be argued shortly, may indeed be desirable. But if followed, the 'social effective rate' would simply become the DRC. Hence, it should be noticed, it would *not* necessarily fulfil the assigned role of the EPR, namely, the indication of directions of resource pull and push by the tariff structure. If such basic assumptions as the existence of perfect competitive equilibrium, or the absence of externalities, are not fulfilled, no single index would be able to serve both as an indicator of social costs and of the impact on the direction of resource allocation.

48 It is more indispensable for DRC estimates—which is at least one of the explanations why these are much less common than estimates of EPR.

49 This should not be confused with the problem of substitution and the difference between free-trade and post-tariff input coefficients: it is accepted here that the latter would be used (since only they are available)—but they have to be calculated by evaluation at international rather than home prices.

50 See note 53.

51 An input–output table of, say 100×100 would be regarded as a rather detailed one.

52 It should be noted that the latter bias—involving the use of a wrong tariff for the final good—could be avoided if each t_j (in the formula of g_j) is calculated by using for weights not imports but local production (this will be discussed further in the next chapter); but this corrected weighting would still leave intact the former bias, involved in applying too high input tariff rates. And, it should be noticed, the correction would imply using *different* t_i's when the effective protective rates for j and for i are studied.

It may also be mentioned that when aggregation is considerable (as it normally is), one high a_{ij} coefficient is likely to be a_{jj}, that is, purchases of inputs from the j industry itself. For instance, if both yarn and clothing belong to a j industry called 'textiles', the highest input coefficient in textiles would be purchases from the textiles industry. For this particular a_{jj}, we have of course $t_j = t_i$, and if that were the only input, we would have $g_j = t_j (= t_i)$. But in fact we may have a much higher protective rate than nominal rate for clothing if the tariff on clothing is high and the tariff on yarn low (or absent altogether).

53 Note, however, that valuations of commodity flows in the input–output table are likely to have been carried out at the actually-paid local prices—which take into account all exemptions. If this is the case the transformation of the a'_{ij} to a_{ij}, which has been discussed above, would have to be carried out by using t_j's and t_i's yielded by the second method—that is, derived by dividing tariff revenue by the size of imports.

5

The Measurement of Protection

This chapter will analyze the possibility of quantifying some of the normative considerations pointed out in the earlier parts of the book, incorporating into it the concept of effective protection which was discussed in the last chapter. We shall begin with a model of two goods, move later to the measurement of cost of protection in a world with many goods, and then discuss the representation of the tariff system by various indexes.

1 The cost of protection: from theory to measurement

In the following analysis we shall assume throughout a situation in which free trade is unequivocally the best policy, and trade restriction a policy which reduces welfare. This is, thus, a situation in which all other Pareto-optimum conditions are fulfilled—no domestic distortions are found—and where the country is small, having no effect on its terms of trade with the outside world. Our task will be to give the welfare loss from trade restriction (or the welfare gain from their removal) a quantitative expression.

By the very definition of the task and the problem, we shall have to start by making a major departure from the basic concept adopted in the discussion of welfare implications of free trade and trade restrictions. There, 'welfare' was not cardinally measured or measurable; hence, it could also not be aggregated for a community of many individuals. Now, on the other hand, we set out to measure the loss or gain from a policy and we must, therefore, use some cardinal measure. This will be either one good or an aggregate of goods reduced, through market-price valuations, to a common denominator. The problem, and the method, are not unique to this specific measurement. It is similar to the adoption of the measurement of the economic well-being of an individual by his income, or the well-being of a community by the national income, which is the availability of a certain bundle of goods (expressed by a common denominator). We thus do not measure the immeasurable—the impact of a policy on the welfare level. We switch, instead to measure the impact of policies simply in terms of the amount of goods they make available to the economy.

The method we shall use is the following. We shall ask what is the value of the goods (in terms of one of them) which could be taken away from the community when it pursues a free trade policy and still leave it as well off as it is under tariff protection. This value will represent the loss from the tariff (or conversely, the gain from moving from protection to free trade).[1]

Figure 23, which in part reproduces the relevant parts of figure 3, illustrates the shift from the welfare comparison to the loss estimate. PQ is, in a two-good world, the transformation curve. With free trade conducted at the world prices represented by exchange line ww, production will be at point B, and consumption somewhere to its left on the budget-restraint line ww. This is precisely equivalent to a situation in which a quantity OR of X is produced by the economy (or in any other way made available to it), and the economy is free to move along exchange line ww—that is, every individual is free to trade at the given world price. For this full equivalence to be maintained, however, it is required that the (hypothetical) production of OR of X will involve the same income distribution as at production point B. For simplicity, we shall assume for the moment that the community consists of a single consumer, so that this problem is circumvented—at least at the present stage.

With a tariff on import good M, tt represents the domestic exchange line, and A will be the production locus. The consumption locus is C, to the left of A on the cum-restriction budget-restraint line $w'w'$.[2] The economy (the single consumer) *could* be

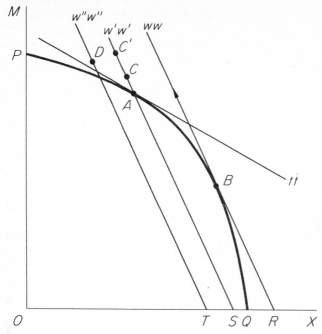

Figure 23

at this consumption locus had it produced (or had it otherwise received) the quantity OS of X, and traded part of it freely, at the existing world prices. The difference of SR is thus a measure of loss of the economy: while employing all its resources, as under free trade, it acquires a bundle of goods worth SR units of X less than the bundle of goods acquired under free trade. This is defined as the *production cost* (or loss) of trade restriction.

But suppose the economy had indeed produced OS of X, and traded it *freely* at world prices represented by exchange line $w'w'$. The price of the import good would then be lower, and of the export good higher, than at the cum-tariff price ratio tt. Hence, consumers (our individual consumer, under the present assumption) would *not* consume the bundle C, but some combination to the left of it—such as C'—representing more of M and less of X. Since C would still be an open consumption possibility, this would mean that C' is superior to C; that is, a welfare gain will be realized from the removal of distortion faced by consumers.[3] To find a position which is not superior to C but equivalent to it, we look for a point like T. Had the economy produced OT of X, and traded it freely at the world price, the consumption locus would be at D—which is thus the best possible location on $w''w''$; and this, we assume (so was point T selected) provides the consumer with just the welfare level afforded by consumption locus C.[4] Thus, TS is an *added* loss from trade restriction—defined as the *consumption cost* (or loss). The welfare of the community is equal, under trade restriction, to what it would have been with the production (the availability) of OT of X, and free trading at world prices. The total loss from trade restriction is thus TR of X, divided between a production loss of SR and a consumption loss of TS.

Assuming that we have information about the transformation curve (which is derived, in turn, from knowledge about production functions and the economy's factor endowment) and the consumer's preferences, as well as data about international prices and the rate of tariff, we are now able to measure the cost of protection—in the sense of 'cost' just illustrated. It will greatly facilitate the measurement, however, if this information is presented by way of conventional supply and demand schedules, which may be derived from the transformation curve and the consumer's preference function. This is done in figure 24, where M, the import good, is represented on the quantity axis, and the price of M in units of X on the price axis. The quantity of X, which we have adopted as the measuring yardstick for losses or gains, is thus given by the relevant *area* in each case (the area being M times X/M, thus yielding units of X).

The curve DD, derived from the consumer's preference function, represents a 'compensated' demand curve for M, the import good; that is, with each price change the consumer's income (which is originally OS units of X, in figure 23) is adjusted so that his welfare will be unaffected, and the resulting change in the quantity demanded reflects purely the substitution effect. We know that with a demand curve so constructed, the area bound by the curve above any designated price represents (in terms of units of X) the amount of 'consumer's surplus' at this price.[5] The price of OP of M is the world price of M (derived from exchange line ww in figure 23). At this price, the consumer would have bought OE ($=P\mathcal{J}$) of M. The tariff raises the home

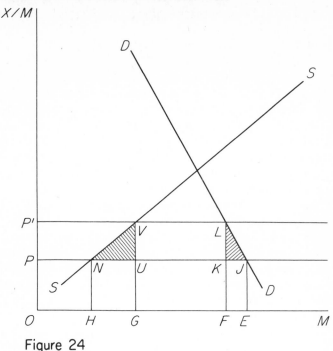

Figure 24

price to OP' (derived from exchange line tt in figure 23). At this higher price, consumption of M will fall to OF ($=P'L$). It may now be shown that the number of units of X yielded by the shaded area JKL is identical with the amount TS in figure 23; that is, this area represents the consumption loss involved in the imposition of the tariff.[6]

SS, in figure 24, is the home supply curve of M, derived from the transformation curve of figure 23: the quantity produced is read off the transformation curve, as the price of M in terms of X varies. At the free trade price, OP, home production of M will be OH ($=PN$) (and imports of M will be HE—the difference between consumption and home production). The tariff, which increases the home price to OP', raises home production to OG ($=P'V$) (and lowers imports to GF). It may again be shown, in a similar way, that the shaded area NUV is equal to SR units of X (in figure 23); that is, this area measures the production loss. Thus, the total loss from protection—TR units of X in figure

23—is yielded by the combination of the shaded areas JKL and NUV.[7]

Let us now define units so that OP, the world price, is unity. Assume, for simplicity, that DD and SS, the demand and supply curves, are straight lines at the relevant range (which they will approximately be if the range is relatively short); the two areas under consideration are thus two triangles, the size of which is to be estimated (indeed, this is known as the 'triangles method' of estimating losses). We turn, first, to the triangle JKL: this area is equal to *half* of the area yielded by the multiplication of the change in price, due to the tariff—the tariff itself, PP'—by the change in the quantity demanded. The latter is, in turn, yielded from the information known: it is equal to the relative change in price ($\Delta P/P = \Delta P$, since $P = 1$) and the elasticity of the demand curve (the average, or arc elasticity over the range JL). Designating the free trade demand (OE) by C_0, the change in quantity demanded (JK) by ΔC, the change in price by t, the tariff rate (since originally $P = 1$), and the elasticity of demand (defined to be positive) by η, we have:

(1) $\Delta C = t\eta C_0$

and since we know that the area of triangle JKL is half of $t\Delta C$, we get:

(2)   area $JKL = \frac{1}{2} t^2 \eta C_o$

In a similar way, we get the area NUV: designating the free-trade production of $M(OH)$ by Q_0, and the elasticity of supply at the relevant range by ε, this area will be:

(3)   area $NUV = \frac{1}{2} t^2 \varepsilon Q_0$

The total loss from the imposition of the tariff—the combination of the two areas—becomes therefore:

(4) $JKL + NUV = \frac{1}{2} t^2 (\eta C_0 + \varepsilon Q_0)$

We thus get an estimate of the loss. It will be higher, we see, the higher are the tariff rate, the elasticities of demand and supply of the good, and the free-trade quantities of consumption and production.[8] We may prefer to put this loss in *relative* terms—relative, that is, to either production or consumption. If, for instance, we chose the former, the relative loss will become $\frac{1}{2}t^2/(\eta C_0/Q_0 + \varepsilon)$. It is a function of the tariff rate, of the two elasticities, and of the ratio of free trade consumption to home production of the import good.

We have assumed, for simplicity, that the community consists of a single consumer. But the argument, and the conclusions, will not be affected by the admission of many consumers—so long as for each of them the same demand experiment is carried out —namely, that each individual's demand curve is 'compensated', leaving *him* on the same welfare level regardless of price changes, thus yielding the change in quantity demanded by him due to the substitution effect. Such individual demand curves could be aggregated, to an income-compensated demand curve for the community; and the latter will form—as it did in the case of a single consumer—the basis for the calculation of the consumption loss from protection. But it should be emphasized that such an income-compensated aggregate (community) demand curve assumes a very specific form of income compensation: it assumes that each and every individual is compensated (positively or negatively) so that his own welfare level remains unchanged when the relative price changes.

We have made no assumption about the number of producers—which could be many. Indeed, the background assumption of absence of distortions implies the existence of many producers.[9] No correction of the measurement of production loss is thus required on this score. Once we admit, however, a world of many goods—rather than the two assumed until now—additional amplifications and qualifications are called for, of the nature indicated in the preceding discussion of the theory of effective protection.

2 Protection of many goods with many tariffs

When many imports and exports exist, with many rates of tariffs, subsidies or export taxes, the first qualification of the former analysis is called for by the realization that imports and exports are not exclusively of final goods—as is inevitably assumed in the two-good world: part of the trade is in intermediate inputs. This necessarily complicates the calculation of the cost of the system.[10]

When a final good is imported, the elements which determine the *consumption* loss remain those which were pointed out in the two-good analysis: the rate of the *nominal* tariff on the good, the elasticity of (compensated) demand for the final good, and the free trade quantity of its consumption. No change is called for, since consumption is of the *final* good, regardless of where and how it is produced, and because the nominal tariff rate is the factor which (together with the foreign price) determines the local price of the good facing the home consumer. *In production*, on the other hand, the relevant magnitudes are now the *value added* in each activity, rather than the total value of the output, since it is the value added which the home industry contributes; and the *effective protective rate*, rather than the nominal tariff rate—since it is the former which affects the quantity (of value added) supplied by the home industry. In a definition of production cost such as in (3) above, t, the tariff rate, will have to be replaced by the effective protective rate; ε will stand for the elasticity of supply of value added; and Q_0 will be the free-trade production of value added.

An import duty imposed on an intermediate input, on the other hand, has no consumption cost at all: given that the country is 'small' it does not affect, either directly or indirectly any price (of tradable goods) facing the home consumer. The duty on an intermediate input will thus form a loss element only through its impact on production, which consists, we recall, of two parts. Such duty first lowers the effective protective rate of the value added in the activity in which the good serves as an input, and on the other hand raises the effective protective rate of the activity of producing this input itself, thus leading to a production loss in this activity.

It has also to be recalled that, once many goods and a whole tariff structure are introduced, the correct magnitudes to be used are *general-equilibrium* values—as was assumed all along in the analysis of the two-good world. As one aspect of this statement, it should be emphasized that all prices are *relative*, though some numeraire (money) is used. Thus, if any positive protection exists in the system, there must be somewhere a negative protection—since positive protection is in relation to some other good or goods. In the measurement, this fact will be taken into account by the introduction of the exchange rate adjustment.[11] In the most general way, this will be carried out by deducing all nominal tariffs from the ratio of each specific rate of exchange to the equilibrium rate and, likewise, each effective protective rate from the ratio of the effective exchange rate in the activity to the equilibrium rate.[12]

It is important to note, in this connection, that when relative prices are not expressed directly but through a numeraire—as they must when many goods exist, if any price of a good is to be presented by only one index—the measurement of the cost of protection involves the estimate of costs of goods and activities with *negative* tariff rates (nominal or effective protective rates, as the case may be). In the two-good world, this would have amounted to double counting: the positive protection of imports was a negative protection of exports; but all the loss of this protection was accounted for in looking at the import good—as it might, instead, have been by viewing the export good. This was so because the price of the import good was in terms of the export good, demand for imports was a supply of exports, and so on. In the multi-good world in which prices are expressed by a numeraire, this is no longer true: the changes in relative prices, and their impact—introduced by the tariff system—will be accounted fully only by including both the positively and the negatively protected goods and industries.[13]

The loss from negative protection is measured in a parallel way to that used for measuring the loss from positive protection. This is shown in figure 25 in relation to an export industry X, in a two-good model. OP is the international price of X; at this price, PV of X is produced, of which PL is sold at the home market and LV is exported. An export tax is imposed, at the rate PP', which lowers the producer's (and home-consumer's) price to OP'. Production of X falls to $P'N$, of which $P'J$ is consumed at home and JN is exported. Producer's surplus (measured in units of M) falls, following the tax, by $PP'NV$. Consumer's surplus, on the other hand, rises by the area $P'PLJ$; and the government now collects a tax of the amount $JKUN$. When these two gains are offset against the producer's loss, the resulting net loss is represented by the two shaded areas JKL and NUV. Assuming for simplicity, as before, straight-line supply and demand curves in the

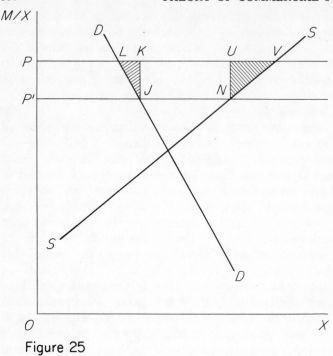

Figure 25

relevant range, these two areas are estimated in exactly the same way as in formula, (2)–(4) above. In the world with many goods, the nominal tariff rates will be replaced here by (nominal) tax rates on exports, and negative protective rates will replace the positive rates. In general, thus, the cost-of-protection formulae include both nominal import and export taxes, for the estimate of consumption losses, and negative as well as positive rates of effective protection for estimates of production losses.[14]

The general-equilibrium nature of the impact of the tariff system also implies, following the discussion in the previous chapter (and as is obviously assumed in the two-good analysis), that factor prices change, readjusting to the structure emerging from the imposition of the tariff system. As has been pointed out, this in turn disconnects the rigorous association of effective protective rates, as they are in fact measured, with the strength (or even direction) of movement of resources into an activity or out of it. What remains is merely a statement of probability: that the higher is an effective protective rate, the more likely it is that the activity concerned will expand rather than contract, and the larger is the expansion likely to be.

We should also recall, on the other hand, the remark made at the end of the previous chapter: when *marginal* or *partial* changes are concerned, the general-equilibrium considerations are of only limited importance. When the cost of imposing one particular tariff, or the gain from removing one, or the gain from a small overall reduction of many tariffs, are considered, general-equilibrium effects may be disregarded without introducing a substantial error. Existing prices may thus be used for such estimates without much damage.

This, however, leads to the recollection of another important distinction. It is assumed, all along, that existing prices are at their *competitive equilibrium* levels. As was noted in the discussion of the last chapter, this assumption may very often not hold, even after allowing a long time for adjustment: subsidies to factors or taxes on them, factor price rigidities, monopolies, and so on, will establish gaps between existing prices and those that would be found in a free, competitive equilibrium. As we have seen, the concept of DRC (domestic resource cost) is designed—in principle, at least—to handle this problem, by using correct 'shadow' prices instead of existing prices in the market. For the estimate of production losses, thus, not the effective protective rates but the DRC estimates[15] would have to be used.[16]

Finally, it should be mentioned that the general formula for estimating production losses, by the use of EPR's or DRC's, is not applicable for an industry where a negative value added is found. An appropriate formula for this situation is developed in Michaely (1975).

3 The aggregate cost of a tariff system

Following the discussion of the preceding two sections, we may now sum up the cost of individual tariffs in a many-good world, by aggregating the losses involved in these tariffs. Instead of formulae (2) and (3) above, we will have, first, the consumption loss:

(5) $$CL = \frac{\Sigma_j \, r_j^2 \, \eta_j \, C_j}{2}$$

CL is the aggregate consumption loss; r_j is the nominal tariff rate of an individual good, as measured by the ratio $R_{sj}/\bar{R} - 1$, where R_{sj} is the specific exchange rate of good j, and $\bar{R}$ is the equilibrium rate of exchange;[17] η_j is the elasticity of demand for j; and C_j is consumption of j.

Similarly, we will have the production loss:

(6) $$PL = \frac{\Sigma_j \, g_j^2 \, \varepsilon_j \, Q_j}{2}$$

PL is aggregate production loss; g_j is the effective protective rate, yielded by $R_{vj}/\bar{R} - 1$, where R_{vj} is the effective rate of exchange (or, alternatively, the domestic resource cost) of j; ε_j is the elasticity of supply of value added in j; and Q_j is the value added in production of j.

The total loss is the combined value of the two. To indicate its significance, it may be expressed as a ratio to the national product (or to national expenditure—the two will be equal under the assumption of equality of exports and imports). Thus,

(7) $$L = \frac{\Sigma_j \, r_j^2 \eta_j C_j + \Sigma_j \, g_j^2 \, \varepsilon_j Q_j}{2 \Sigma_j Q_j}$$

where L is the relative measure of total loss, and $\Sigma_j Q_j$, the aggregate of value added in the various industries, is the national product.[18] It should be recalled that consumption loss is involved only in *final* goods whereas the production loss appears in industries producing intermediate goods as well.

What could be the expected application of this method of measurement of the loss from a tariff system? If precise or even approximate estimates of the overall loss are required, formulae such as those presented here may, in all probability, be of only little help in any concrete situation. It should be recalled that some crucial assumptions have been made along the way. Thus, for instance, the demand schedules whose elasticities appear in the estimate of consumption loss are derived from 'compensated' demand functions. The likelihood of finding even a large number of estimates of elasticities of conventional demand schedules is small, and a compensated demand curve—where compensation is required for each individual consumer separately—is certainly a concept which, though useful in welfare analysis, cannot be subject to actual estimation.[19] Similarly, all prices have to be assumed to be corrected for general equilibrium effects—again a step which cannot be reasonably expected to be carried out in practice. Thus, while partial-equilibrium estimates of selected, individual goods may hopefully yield reasonably close approximations, it would be illusory to expect a similar performance from an aggregate, general-equilibrium estimate of the impact of a whole tariff structure.

Instead, formulae such as (5), (6) or (7) above may be used to point out the important elements which participate in determining the size of the loss from a tariff structure and the sensitivity of the estimate to changes in these elements, and to attempt, in an illustrative manner, to find out reasonable boundaries to the size of loss yielded by this method of estimate.

From expressions (5)–(7), we may see that the loss from protection is a rising function, first, of the size of individual tariffs—nominal and effective (and negative as well as positive). Second, it is a function of the size of protected industries: when high tariffs are found in large industries—in terms of, respectively, local production or local consumption—the loss from the tariff system will tend to be high. Likewise, the loss is a function of the elasticities of supply and demand; when these elasticities are in general high, or when high tariffs happen to concentrate in industries in which elasticities (of supply or demand) are particularly high, the loss will tend to be high. Later on in this chapter, we shall discuss concepts of an 'average' tariff. Even without this more precise analysis, however, it may be seen that the loss is thus a rising function of the average level of the tariff—provided this average considers in its weighting system not only the size of industries but also the various elasticities involved.

But beyond this average level, another factor appears to be involved. It will be noticed that in the cost formulae, the tariff levels (the r's, or the g's) appear in the *second power*—thus giving added weight to particularly high tariffs. The cost of protection is thus seen to be not only a function of the *average* (in some sense) level of tariffs, but also of the degree of *dispersion* of the tariff system: with any given average, the less uniform is the tariff structure (recalling that by this we mean also export taxes or subsidies, or any other form of interference in trade) the higher will be the loss from the system. Indeed, since both positive and negative tariffs are taken into account, the *level* of the tariff is reduced to the degree of dispersion. Against every positive tariff there is a negative one; a complete uniformity means necessarily a zero tariff all around; and higher tariffs on some goods, implying high negative tariffs on others, mean inevitably higher dispersion.

The role played by the degree of dispersion of the tariff structure is probably of particular significance when the production loss and effective protective rates are involved. Since tariff systems tend to be escalated, effective protective rates tend, as we have seen, to be higher than nominal rates at 'advanced' stages of production. This by itself, as was just argued, means a larger dispersion (when negative protection is taken into account). But beyond that, since effective rates are not specified directly and explicitly, they are probably—at least in part—at levels which are not determined by design but by accident. And this, in turn, is likely to imply a higher degree of dispersion in the system. If this is true, this factor would tend to make production losses a more important element than consumption losses. This conclusion would be reinforced if, as is most often assumed, supply elasticities (at least in the long run) tend to be high relative to demand elasticities (particularly since the latter, we recall, refer in the present context only to the substitution effect of price changes). This conclusion would be reinforced even further if it is assumed—as would seem reasonable—that supply elasticities tend to be higher at the more advanced stages of production.

Following is a hypothetical table designed to illustrate, through a numerical example, the principles involved. The economy is assumed to produce four goods, B, C, D and E; the former two are export industries, and the latter two are import competing industries. Good A is an input (the sole intermediate input) in the production of all four industries, and it is not produced at home at the relevant price range: it is wholly imported. Tariff structure I is yielded by assuming a schedule in which only two tariffs are posted: on imports of D, at the rate of 50 per cent, and of E, at the rate of 55 per cent. An exchange-rate adjustment of 30 per cent shows, however, that this posted system implies—as shown in column (6)—lower tariffs for D and E; and *negative* tariffs on imports of input A and on exports of B and of C, at the rate of 30 per cent. From this schedule, and the coefficients of the imported input assumed in the table, follows the schedule of effective tariffs in column (7).

Assume, now, that all demand elasticities are uniform and equal to 0.7, and, similarly, that all supply elasticities are uniform and equal to unity. Application of formulae (5)–(7) will show, under these assumptions, a consumption loss of about 2 per cent of national income (the latter being the sum of value added in the four industries; which is also equal, as the table is constructed, to the size of consumption, since exports equal imports). The production loss is 8 per cent; and the total loss is, thus, about 10 per cent of national income. The much higher loss in production than in consumption is due, primarily, to the higher dispersion of the schedule of effective protective rates than the schedule of nominal rates, and, to a small extent, to the fact that supply elasticities have been assumed to be somewhat higher than demand elasticities.

Tariff structure II, in columns (8) and (9), is a slight variation. One of the exported goods, B, is assumed to face now an export tax of 10 per cent; whereas the other, C, is granted a (posted) export subsidy of 10 per cent. In imports, one tariff—on D—is lower than before; and the other—on E—is higher. The exchange-rate adjustment is assumed to remain 30 per cent; and the two separate (weighted) averages, of negative tariffs for exports and of positive tariffs for imports, also remain approximately as before. The degree of dispersion in the system rises, however: the coefficient of variance for nominal tariffs rises from 0.258 to 0.300, and for effective tariffs from 0.403 to 0.456. The consumption loss rises, with the same assumed elasticities, from about 2 to about 3 per cent; the production loss rises from 8 to 10 per cent; and the total loss rises from 10 to 13 per cent of national income.

This example illustrates the effects of the elements involved in the estimate of loss from a protection structure. The size of the

Table 1 *Hypothetical illustration*

Industry	Value added (1)	Imports of input A (2)	Imports of final good (3)	Exports (4)	Home con-sumption (5)	Tariff structure I		Tariff structure II	
						Nominal tariff (r_j) (6)	Effective tariff (g_j) (7)	Nominal tariff (r_j) (8)	Effective tariff (g_j) (9)
A	—	—	—	—	—	−0.30	—	−0.30	—
B	20	3	—	12	11	−0.30	−0.30	−0.40	−0.41
C	20	5	—	13	12	−0.30	−0.30	−0.20	−0.18
D	10	5	2	—	17	+0.20	+0.45	+0.05	+0.22
E	10	7	3	—	20	+0.25	+0.63	+0.40	+0.89
Total	60	20	5	25	60				
Weighted average						+0.03	−0.02	+0.03	−0.01

loss in this illustration—some 10 or 15 per cent of national income—is, of course, the outcome of purely hypothetical tariff schedules and arbitrary assumptions about elasticities or about the composition and structure of the economy. But this illustrative example is probably not a gross deviation from some concrete cases of economies in which protection is widespread.[20]

4 The level of a tariff system

We have met on a number of occasions during the discussion the concept of an 'average' level of the tariff. The study of the measurement of a tariff structure will now conclude with a somewhat more systematic analysis of this concept. We must start by emphasizing that 'the' average tariff level, as a *single* concept, which purports to represent the whole structure by some index number, does *not* exist: the proper index will depend on the purpose for which it is designed, and different concepts, or indexes, will be indicated by different uses.[21]

It is convenient to start with the simplest yet quite important concept of the average level of tariffs which measures the extent of import restriction. This concept concentrates on that part of the tariff system which falls within the conventional definition of the term 'tariff'—that is, taxes on imports—and is concerned with what has been termed earlier 'posted' tariffs; that is, with tariff rates which are not corrected by an exchange rate adjustment. The concept is defined as the *uniform* (posted) tariff rate which, if replacing all the individual tariff rates on the various commodities, will maintain imports on the same aggregate level as they are under the heterogeneous tariff system;[22] or, in other words, it is the uniform tariff which will have the same restrictive effect on the size of imports—in comparison with free trade at the current exchange rate—as the existing tariff system. While this restrictive effect is not a measure of loss from trade restriction for the country itself, it is important from the point of view of the country's trade partners, and is thus a very popular concept in trade negotiations.[23] Likewise, it is important when the balance-of-payments effect of the tariff system is considered.

Take commodity 1. M_1^f will represent the *free trade* size of imports[24] (measured in terms of one currency or another—this would be immaterial with a given exchange rate). The elasticity of demand for imports of this good, in the region of the free-trade price and quantity, is η (defined to be positive).[25] A tariff at the rate t_1 is imposed on the good. With this tariff, imports will fall, from their free-trade level, by $t_1 M_1^f \eta_1$. Suppose, instead, that a uniform tariff t^* is imposed, replacing tariff t_1. The fall of imports, from their free-trade level, will then be $t^* M_1^f \eta_1$. The replacement of tariff t_1 by tariff t^* will thus lower imports (if $t^* > t_1$) or raise them (if $t^* < t_1$) by

$$(8) \qquad (t^* - t_1) \, M_1^f \eta_1$$

The same is true for good 2, where the replacement of its tariff t_2 by the uniform tariff rate t^* will lower imports by $(t^* - t_2) M_2^f \eta_2$. And so on for any other good (in a system of n goods). We look, by definition, to that uniform rate t^* which, if replacing all existing individual tariffs, will make the aggregate *net* change of imports zero (that is, will maintain the same aggregate size of imports). Thus,

$$(9) \qquad (t^* - t_1) \, M_1^f \eta_1 + (t^* - t_2) \, M_2^f \eta_2 + \ldots$$
$$+ \, (t^* - t_n) \, M_n^f \eta_n = 0$$

Some of these changes will, of course, be positive—where the uniform tariff rate will be lower than the existing tariff rate for the good—whereas others will be negative. Solving (9), we get:

$$t^* = \frac{t_1 M_1^f \eta_1 + t_2 M_2^f \eta_2 + \ldots + t_n M_n^f \eta_n}{M_1^f \eta_1 + M_2^f \eta_2 + \ldots + M_n^f \eta_n}$$

or

$$(10) \qquad t^* = \frac{\sum_j t_j \, M_j^f \, \eta_j}{\sum_j M_j^f \, \eta_j}$$

Expression (10) thus gives us the proper, or 'ideal', method of estimating the average tariff level as the concept is presently defined. On the abstract level, there is little to add to this presentation. But its concrete application faces serious problems and these, when not solved satisfactorily, would lead to certain biases in practical measurements. These problems and biases will now be briefly discussed.

Of the three elements in (10)—t, M^f, and η—data about the t's (tariff rates) are generally easiest to obtain—although collection and construction of such data are not free of major problems.[26] The η's, on the other hand—elasticities of demand for imports of individual goods—will be found only infrequently. Moreover, available estimates will refer to partial-equilibrium sets of observations, whereas the 'ideal' measurement—such as in (10)—is of a *general-equilibrium* nature: *all* tariff rates are changed simultaneously, and imports of individual goods adjust themselves to the resulting changes in the economy. This factor, as we have remarked on a number of occasions, would be of minor importance if the system concerned contains primarily low tariffs, but it may be crucial when tariffs are high and widespread. The inaccessibility of estimates of demand elasticities for imports, and the possible deficiency of available estimates, are important not only because these data are required by themselves but also because they are essential for the estimate of the third element—the M^f's: these are, it should be emphasized, the *free trade* levels of imports of individual goods. Available observations, on the other hand, refer to *cum-tariff* imports: only in rare cases (where the tariff on a given good is relatively new) could it be hoped at all to have a direct estimate of the free-trade size of imports. With reliable, or even approximately reliable estimates of elasticities over the relevant range, the free-trade imports could have been derived from the data of existing imports, existing tariff rates, and the demand elasticities; but in the absence of the latter, this procedure is not generally feasible.

Expression (10) is thus not likely to lead to concrete, good (or approximately reliable) measurements of the average tariff level looked for. It may serve, on the other hand, a number of related purposes. One is to point out, as we have done, the elements which participate in the determination of the tariff level. Another is to make possible very rough estimates—in the nature of informed guesses—of the tariff level, by replacing actual estimates of the elasticities of demand by arbitrarily selected magnitudes which seem 'reasonable' in given circumstances. Still another purpose is to compare this 'ideal' measurement with those which are used in practice, thus seeing whether the latter may have any value, for the measurement of the average tariff level as it is defined here, and what biases they do contain. Three such measurements may be mentioned.

One, which is probably the most widely practised, is the measurement of the tariff level through a weighted average, in which observed sizes of imports of the individual goods serve as weights; this is equivalent[27] to the division of total tariff revenues by the aggregate value of imports (at international prices)—and may indeed often be derived in this way. Designating observed (post-tariff) imports by M^p, this measurement is thus

$$\sum_j t_j M^p_j \Big/ \sum_j M^p_j$$

Two differences are seen between this and the ideal measure of expression (10). First, here *observed* post-tariff rather than free trade imports are used for weighting (M^p rather than M^f). This necessarily leads to a *downward* bias in the actual estimate, in relation to the ideal: the higher the tariff of a good is, the more its imports are likely to fall, and the lower therefore will be the weight accorded to it in the actual measurement in comparison with the ideal.[28] The other difference is the absence of demand elasticities (the η's) from the actual measurement. This is, of course, an element which tends to lead to a deviation of the actual from the true measure, but it is not clear whether a bias is involved—and if so, in what direction. If tariffs are imposed at random (in the sense relevant here), no bias exists. But tariffs may have some relationship to demand elasticities. It may be assumed, for instance, that higher tariffs are imposed when they are expected (through their impact on effective rates) to lead to a relatively substantial expansion of local production—that is, where the elasticity of domestic supply of the industry is high. But a high elasticity of domestic supply contributes to a high elasticity of demand for imports; such policy would mean, therefore, that high tariffs tend to be imposed when demand elasticities for imports are high. If true, this will be another source of downward bias in the actual estimate in relation to the ideal measurement. The tariff may, on the other hand, be directed—an aspect of tariff policy which has been consistently overlooked in the present analysis—towards the achievement of maximum *revenues* for the government. In such a case, high tariffs will tend to be imposed on imports whose demand elasticity is low, and the bias will be reversed. Be that as it may, the possible bias here is an empirical question, varying probably from case to case, whereas the aforementioned bias—involved in the use of post-tariff observations—is a logical necessity.

One other measure which is sometimes used is the simple arithmetic, unweighted average of individual tariffs (that is $\sum_j t_j/n$). This estimate will be free (that is, in the sense of logical necessity) from the bias involved in weighting by observed import values. And, if the possible biases generated by the exclusion of elasticities from the weighting system are not realized, the estimate would not contain any bias, in relation to the correct measurement. But the relationship between the two will be a matter of accident. The 'accidental' element will be weaker—and the usefulness of this measure thus higher—when 'goods' are classified in very minute detail, and no single good (or the aggregate of a small number of goods) constitutes a substantial fraction of total imports.

Sometimes, a measure is suggested in which the weights of individual tariffs are assigned by the share of the imports of each good in *world* imports (that is, the measure will be $\sum_j t_j M_j^w/\sum_j M_j^w$, where M_j^w are the world imports of goods j). Once more, the relationship of this to the true measure will at best be accidental. Here, moreover, an implied assumption is involved; namely, that in free trade, import composition of the various countries will be similar—an assumption which cannot be empirically supported and (if 'goods' are defined to be homogeneous) must be rejected on *a priori* grounds. Furthermore, if countries tend to impose high tariffs on similar goods—a possibility which does not seem unlikely—the weighting system of this measure will also contain a downward bias: world imports of high-duty goods (which are then, by assumption, similar all around) will be a lower fraction of the world's (and each individual country's) imports after duties have been imposed than in the free-trade position.

In a way entirely similar to the construction of the index of the 'level of the tariff', in the sense defined, we may construct an index of the 'level of effective protection'. As before, this will refer only to a *partial* effect of the existing tariff structure: no exchange-rate adjustment is performed, and effective rates of protection are based on deviations from the existing exchange rate.[29] In other words, in the absence of the set of tariffs measured, home free-trade prices are assumed to be international prices at the existing exchange rate. We now look, thus, to a uniform effective rate of protection which, if replacing all the existing rates, will maintain the same aggregate output (i.e. value added) of the protected activities. Without repeating the step-by-step procedure carried out before, it may be easily seen that this uniform effective protective rate will be equivalent to (10). That is,

$$(11) \qquad g^* = \frac{\sum_j g_j Q_j^f \varepsilon_j}{\sum_j Q_j^f \varepsilon_j}$$

where g^* is the uniform effective rate; g_j is the (unadjusted) effective rate in industry i, Q_j^f is the *free-trade* size of value added in the industry, and ε_j is the elasticity of supply of value added (in relation to changes in its price) in the industry. The practical problems of measurement of this average are similar to those mentioned earlier—coupled, this time, with the fact that data of effective protective rates (the g's) are more scarce, and less precise or reliable, than data of nominal tariff rates. Once more, it is interesting to point out the bias involved in the use of a measure which is constructed as a weighted average based on existing production; that is, a measure in which the average level is defined as $\sum_j g_j Q_j^p / \sum_j Q_j^p$. Here, the logically inevitable bias will be the opposite of what it was in the formerly analyzed measure: post-protection production (value added) will exceed the free-trade value the higher is the rate of protection of the activity. Hence, the use of post-protection weights, instead of free-trade values, will lead to an *overestimate* of the 'true' average rate of protection. The symmetry between this and the average tariff is not found, however, in relation to the other (possible) source of bias. If, as has been stated before to be a likely possibility, high protective rates are granted to industries in which supply is relatively elastic, the exclusion of elasticities would create a *downward* bias in the use of this concrete estimate rather than the ideal. If this is true, then the two elements of difference between the average rate under consideration and the true, or ideal, average—the use, in the former, of post-protection rather than free-trade sizes of production for weighting, and the exclusion of supply elasticities from the weighting system—would lead to biases in offsetting directions; whereas, with similar assumptions, the two biases were found to operate in the same direction (downward) in the analysis of the average rate of nominal duties.

Using the same method, we may now investigate the more comprehensive index of the *average change in the rate of exchange*—the 'devaluation equivalent' of the tariff system.[30] We pose the question: suppose all tariffs, in their broadest sense (including, *inter alia*, export subsidies or taxes) were abolished, what would be the change (positive or negative) of the rate of foreign exchange which would maintain the same trade *balance* that exists with the tariff system?

Let us look at imports of a given final good. A change in the rate of exchange, like a tariff, will lower imports of the good by the combined value of the fall in home consumption and the rise in *value added* in home production of the good: it is the value added rather than gross value of production because the increase in production of the final good will require the use of an intermediate imported input, which has to be offset against the fall in imports of the final good. Following the same pattern as before, we know first that the fall in home consumption of the good, when its tariff is replaced by a change in the rate of exchange, will be:

$$(12) \qquad \Delta C_1 = (r^* - t_1)\, C_1^f\, \eta_1^c$$

where ΔC_1 is the fall in consumption; r^* is the change in the rate of exchange—the uniform devaluation (i.e. the rate of increase in the price of foreign exchange); t_1 is the (unadjusted) nominal tariff rate of the good; C_1^f is free-trade home consumption of the good; and η_1^c is the home elasticity of demand for the *good* (*not* for *imports* of the good, as the demand elasticity involved earlier). Similarly, the increase in value added in home production will be:

$$(13) \qquad \Delta Q_1 = (r^* - g_1)\, Q_1^f\, \varepsilon_1$$

where Q_1 is the increase in value added; g_1 the effective protective rate; Q_1^f the free-trade size of value added; and ε_1 the elasticity of supply of value added.

The fall in imports—the combination of these two

changes—will hence be:

$$(14) \qquad \Delta M_1 = (r^* - t_1)\, C_1^f \eta_1^c + (r^* - g_1)\, Q_1^f \varepsilon_1$$

The increase in exports, due to a change in the rate of exchange, will likewise be the combination of a fall in home consumption of the (export) good and the rise of value added in production. No new formulae have to be developed: expression (12) above could represent an export, as well as an import industry, where t_1 will now stand for the rate of export *subsidy* (export subsidy, we recall—like an import duty—raises the home price of the good); whereas expression (13) could represent an export good without any amendments. Thus, (14) sums up the effect on the export industry—with the only proviso that here t_1 will represent the export subsidy.

The combination of all changes in imports and exports of individual goods will yield the change in the trade balance; and we require r^* to be such that this change in the balance will be zero. That is,

$$(15) \qquad \begin{aligned} &(r^* - t_1)\, C_1^f \eta_1^c + (r^* - g_1)\, Q_1^f \varepsilon_1 + (r^* - t_2)\, C_2^f \eta_2^c + \\ &+ (r^* - g_2)\, Q_2^f \varepsilon_2 + \ldots + (r^* - t_n)\, C_n^f \eta_n^c + (r^* - g_n) \\ &Q_n^f \varepsilon_n = 0 \end{aligned}$$

This yields the change looked for:

$$r^* = \frac{t_1\, C_1^f \eta_1^c + g_1\, Q_1^f \varepsilon_1 + t_2\, C_2^f \eta_2^c + g_2\, Q_2^f \varepsilon_2 + \ldots}{C_1^f \eta_1^c + Q_1^f \varepsilon_1 + C_2^f \eta_2^c + Q_2^f \varepsilon_2 + \ldots}$$

or

$$\frac{+ t_n\, C_n^f \eta_n^c + g_n\, Q_n^f \varepsilon_n}{+ C_n^f \eta_n^c + Q_n^f \varepsilon_n}$$

$$(16) \qquad r^* = \frac{\sum_j (t_j\, C_j^f \eta_j^c + g_j\, Q_j^f \varepsilon_j)}{\sum_j (C_j^f \eta_j^c + Q_j^f \varepsilon_j)}$$

The 'devaluation equivalent' is thus a weighted average of all (unadjusted) nominal tariff duties or export subsidies and effective protective rates, where both the (free-trade) sizes of consumption and of value added and the elasticities of demand for consumption and supply of value added appear in the weighting system. Since effective protective rates are a function of nominal tariff rates, (16) could also be put in terms of nominal tariff rates alone ('tariffs' interpreted in the broadest sense), but this would complicate the expression without offering any substantial advantage.

The difficulties involved in the calculation of the devaluation equivalent, and the biases inherent in any method which uses available information, may be inferred from the earlier discussion of the separate elements, and need not be repeated here. On the other hand, the relationship of this concept to the earlier analyses of effective protection and the measurement of protection should be pointed out: this average change of the exchange rate, or the devaluation equivalent, is precisely the size of the 'exchange-rate adjustment' which appeared earlier. If, with the existence of the tariff system, the foreign-exchange market is in equilibrium,[31] then the change of the existing rate of foreign exchange by the rate defined as the devaluation equivalent, would yield the equilibrium rate of exchange without the tariff system.[32]

Finally, we may discuss what could perhaps be termed, somewhat awkwardly, an 'equal-cost uniform-tariff equivalent'; that is, a uniform tariff which will lead to the same welfare loss as the existing tariff system. Such a concept must apply only to a partial set of the tariff system: as we have seen earlier, if *all* tariffs, in the broadest sense of the term (including, *inter alia*, export subsidies or taxes) are uniform, and the exchange-rate adjustment is (conceptually) performed, no loss at all will be found. But we may confine our view to, say, just the import sector, and ask: suppose all import tariffs are replaced by a uniform tariff—which will also necessarily make all effective protective rates uniform—what would be the size of such a tariff which will leave total welfare loss unchanged?

We recall expression (7) above, which estimates the welfare loss from a tariff system:

$$L = \sum_j t_j^2 \eta_j C_j^f + \sum_j g_j^2 \varepsilon_j Q_j^f$$

With a single, uniform tariff t^*, this will be

$$L = t^{*2} \left(\sum_j \eta_j C_j^f + \sum_j \varepsilon_j Q_j^f \right)$$

Hence the two losses will be equal when:

$$(17) \qquad t^* = \sqrt{\frac{\Sigma_j \, t_j^2 \, \eta_j \, C_j^f + \Sigma_j \, g_j^2 \, \varepsilon_j \, Q_j^f}{\Sigma_j \, (\eta_j \, C_j^f + \varepsilon_j \, Q_j^f)}}$$

It will be noticed that the elements which appear in (17) to determine the level of the equal-cost uniform tariff equivalent, are mostly similar to those found in the determination of the earlier indexes considered (say, of the equal-imports uniform tariff equivalent, or the devaluation equivalent): the levels of individual tariffs (nominal and effective protective rates); the free-trade levels of consumption and production of individual goods; and the elasticities of supply and demand. But the fact that in (17) tariff rates appear in the second power, adds here the element of *dispersion* of the tariff system. Compare, for instance, two alternative situations, in both of which we have two goods of equal free-trade size of consumption and equal demand elasticities; but in one situation, the two goods are subject to the same rate of duty, whereas in the other one good is subject to a duty twice as high while the other good is free of duty. For, say, the determination of the devaluation equivalent, these two situations will be entirely equivalent; not so, on the other hand, for the measure of the equal-cost uniform tariff rate. This illuminates, once more, the important role of the degree of dispersion in determining the welfare cost of a tariff system.

Notes

1 See J. Bhagwati and H. G. Johnson (1960) for a discussion of this as well as other methods of estimating the loss from the tariff. Of the three alternative concepts analyzed there—the 'Marshallian surplus', and the Hicksian 'compensating variation' and 'equivalent variation'—it is the second which is adopted here.

2 It may, if so desired, be assumed that the tariff under consideration is prohibitive. A will then be the autarky position, and the cost of protection measured will be the cost of complete elimination of trade. A and C, the consumption locus, will then coincide.

3 This repeats the argument (in Chapter 2), where production subsidy was proved to be superior to tariff.

4 Since we assume at present a single consumer, the device of the in-difference curve could legitimately be used at this juncture (although it is not essential—and is dispensed with in the text). Consumption locus C would be described as the point on $w'w'$ at which an exchange line of the slope of tt is tangent to an indifference curve. Budget-restraint line $w''w''$ would then be that exchange line, of the same slope as ww or $w'w'$ (representing the given world price ratio), which is tangent (at point D) to the same indifference curve. C and D will then be two alternative equilibrium positions representing the same welfare level.

5 See, on this, D. Patinkin (1963).

6 See E. E. Leamer and R. M. Stern (1970).

7 This follows the presentation in E. E. Leamer and R. M. Stern (*ibid.*). An alternative way of arriving at this conclusion—used in the original development of the measurement by Corden (1957a) and Johnson (1960), is as follows. The imposition of the tariff, which raises the home price from OP to OP', reduces consumer's surplus by the area $PP'LJ$. At the same time, however, producer's surplus rises, with this increase in price, by the area $PP'VN$. In addition, a 'surplus' is ac-crued to the government, which now collects revenues from the import duty: this revenue (again, in terms of units of X) is equal to the size of imports ($UK = GF$) times the tariff per unit (PP'), that is, to the rectangle $UKLV$. When these additions—to producers and to the government—are offset against the consumer's loss, the net loss to the community is found to be the combination of the two shaded areas, JKL and NUV. It should be recalled that we assume here a communi-ty of one consumer, so that the producer's gain and the government's revenue are indeed the property of that consumer.

8 It may easily be seen that

$$\eta_m = \frac{\eta C_0 + \varepsilon Q_0}{M_0}$$

where η_m is the elasticity of demand for imports and M_0 is the free-trade size of imports. Hence, (4) may be rewritten in the form

(4') $JKL + NUV = \frac{1}{2} t^2 \eta_m M_0$

The size of the loss appears here as the function of the tariff rate, the elasticity of demand for imports, and the size of imports.

9 The provisional assumption of a single consumer thus involved an inconsistency but, as we have just seen, it was required only for simplification.

10 For the treatment of this new element, see H. G. Johnson (1965a, 1969), R. Dardis (1967), and R. H. Snape (1969).

11 See the discussion in section 5 of the previous chapter. Such an exchange-rate adjustment is always implied in the analysis of the two-good world, by the assumption that balance-of-payments equilibrium (equality of values of imports and exports) always exists.

12 As could be inferred from the discussion of this procedure (*ibid.*), this will also lead to the measurement of loss in a system in which no tariffs, export taxes, or other direct means of interference in trade are practised, but the exchange rate is not in equilibrium. A related issue, discussed in the literature, is the cost of exchange-rate stabilization; that is, of a system in which the exchange rate may follow a long-run trend of equilibrium, but it shifts between positions in which it is either below or above equilibrium level, because it is changed only in long intervals whereas local prices change continuously and gradually. See J. C. Hause (1966), and H. G. Johnson (1966b).

13 Suppose, for instance, that we have two goods, and money is used for price quotation. A duty of 100 per cent is imposed on the import good, doubling its price in terms of exports (this is the ratio that would appear, in the two-good world, when relative prices are used directly, without recourse to money). Assume now that equilibrium in the balance of payments, disrupted by the duty (which lowers imports), is restored by the fall of the exchange rate (the price of foreign exchange). With an exchange-rate adjustment, the import price will appear to have risen by less than 100 per cent; whereas the export price will appear to have fallen (by the extent of the exchange-rate adjustment). A calculation of the cost based on imports alone will thus not reveal the doubling of the price of imports in terms of units of exports, whereas the addition of the cost involved in the negative protection of exports will correct for it.

14 We have referred here to a negatively protected export industry. But the same method of analysis may be used in the case of negative protection of an import-substituting industry; and the same outcome will follow. Figure 24, slightly modified, may be used for this purpose. Suppose that P' is the *international* price; and that a *subsidy* is granted to the import of M at the rate $P'P$. The post-subsidy home price will be OP. Consumer's surplus will now increase by $P'P\mathcal{J}L$. Against this, producer's surplus will fall by $P'PNV$ and, in addition, a subsidy amounting to $N\mathcal{J}$ times PP' will be paid by the government. When these two losses are offset against the consumer's gain, a net loss will be found, equal—on the assumption of straight-line supply and demand curves—to the areas of the two triangles $\mathcal{J}KL$ and NUV.

15 Or what B. Balassa and D. M. Schydlowsky (1972) termed the 'social' EPR.

16 In this application, in a formula such as (3) above, t will stand for the ratio: $(DRC - \bar{R})/\bar{R} - 1$, where $\bar{R}$ is the equilibrium rate of exchange.

A fundamental inconsistency should, however, be pointed out here. The 'loss' measurement still implicitly assumes free trade to be an optimum policy—an assumption which is not necessarily valid where distortions exist (and no other policy measure, such as tax or subsidy, is added). The use of correct 'shadow' prices does *not* resolve this inconsistency.

17 See, again, section 5 of the last chapter.

18 It may be noted that (7) is not similar to (4) above: in the two-good world, the same tariff rate applied for the estimates of consumption and production losses whereas now one rate is nominal and the other is effective.

19 It is sometimes argued, as a simplifying step, that income effects of price changes may be assumed to be zero (for each individual consumer, and in each individual good)—in which case the observed demand curve and the compensated curve will be identical. But this appears to be carrying simplifications too far.

20 See, for instance, the tariff structure in underdeveloped countries in the study of B. Balassa (1971). To cite another example (from M. Michaely, 1971): the coefficient of variance of (unadjusted) nominal tariff rates in Israel between 1949 and 1962 ranged from 0.142 to 0.468 (and was mostly in the upper part of this range). For effective protective rates, the range was most probably far higher.

It will be noted that two categories of goods (not mutually exclusive) are overlooked, in the text as well as in the numerical illustration: capital goods and non-traded goods. Capital goods present the less difficult problem; they provide capital services, which are intrinsically similar to other intermediate inputs. The incorporation of capital goods into the theory of measurement of losses from protection thus faces no fundamental obstacle, although it adds several specific viewpoints as well as some technical complications. This analysis is carried out in E. Kleiman and M. Michaely (1973).

The non-tradable sector, on the other hand, will require a major modification: the framework in which the method of estimating losses from protection is developed is a model in which a good is either exported or (partly) imported, with no room for a non-tradable good. In exercises similar to the illustration presented in the text, it has been a tradition—starting with the paper of H. G. Johnson (1960)—to treat the non-tradable sector in a particular manner which has contributed to a downward bias. The estimated losses from protection of tradable goods have, in these illustrations, been divided by the *total* of national income (or national product). This implicitly assumes that the tariff structure leads to no loss whatsoever so far as the non-tradable sector is concerned. But we know, from our general-equilibrium analysis, that this could not be true: through substitution and complementarity in production and consumption, non-tradable activities must be affected by the impact of the tariff structure on the tradable sector. Although we do not know how to handle these effects, and how to incorporate them into the measure of loss from protection, the assumption of no loss is clearly unwarranted. It is as arbitrary as—and probably even less justified than—an assumption that the proportional loss in non-tradable activities is equal to that found in the tradable sector.

21 A recent contribution to this analysis, on which the present discussion will partly draw, is W. M. Corden's (1966b). But the 40-years-old discussion in G. Haberler's classic book (1936), under the title 'The Concept of "the Height of a Tariff" and the Methods of Measuring it' (pp. 355–359), is well worth reading. Although it does not develop any formula for measuring, it does point out most of the important conceptual problems, and the essential ingredients in the solutions. This discussion also contains references to some of the earlier literature in this field.

22 Corden (*op. cit.*) has termed this the 'uniform-tariff equivalent'.

23 This would presuppose that the country concerned is not 'small'; if it were, other countries should not care about its policies or the size of its imports. Yet, for convenience, we shall still maintain the small-country assumption in the following discussion.

24 That is, quantity and price—hence value—are those maintained under free trade. For simplicity, prices of all import goods may be thought of as normalized to unity, so that quantities and values are identical.

25 This elasticity is itself a function of the elasticity of demand for the *good*, as such, and the elasticity of supply of local production of the good (see note 8), but we shall not make this separation in the present discussion.

26 For a sample of these, see again the brief discussion in the Appendix of the last chapter. One important problem that has not been mentioned there is the conversion of specific or 'mixed' tariffs—which are quite common—into *ad-valorem* rates of duty.

27 With certain qualifications—see again the Appendix of the last chapter.

28 It should be noticed that some aggregation is likely to be involved in the construction of *individual* tariffs: if many thousands of separate items in the customs code are presented by way of, say, a few hundred tariff rates, each of the latter would refer to an aggregate of many items. Since the aggregation, or averaging, will normally use current imports as they are observed, such averages will be estimates which suffer from a *downward* bias, for the same reason pointed out in the discussion of the average of the country's imports as a whole.

29 Otherwise—this is the essence of the exchange-rate adjustment— 'average' (or aggregate) protection is by definition zero: full employment and equality of exports and imports exist by assumption.

30 See W. M. Corden (*op. cit.*) for the term—although the method there is slightly different from the one used here.

31 This is not the appropriate occasion for a precise definition of this 'equilibrium'. For simplicity, it may be assumed that no autonomous capital movements exist, so that equilibrium is maintained when the values of exports and imports are equal.

32 See, again, section 5 of the last chapter.

6
Geographic Discrimination: Trade Preferences and Customs Unions

1 Framework of the analysis

Thus far, the analysis has dealt with interferences in international trade which discriminate among *goods*. In a two-good world, one good was assumed to be favoured (say, by tariff) at the expense, necessarily, of the other; or in a world with many goods, each good was encouraged or discouraged at a different rate. Geographic discrimination, on the other hand, has been entirely absent: all foreign countries have been assumed to be treated equally. Indeed, the analysis has been conducted by regarding all foreign countries as a single unit—'the' foreign country, or the outside 'world'. In this final chapter, the differentiation, or discrimination, among various components of the outside world will be introduced.

Obviously, some interference in trade must be taking place to make any geographic discrimination possible: if free trade is pursued, there could, by definition, be no discrimination either favourable or unfavourable. But the existence of *discrimination* among goods is not a *logical* necessity for geographic discrimination. Thus, take a two-good world in which the home country imposes a tariff duty on the import good and grants an export subsidy at the same rate to the other good. When the outside world is a single unit (or many units treated equally), this policy would lead to the free-trade outcome and would imply no discrimination between the two goods.[1] Suppose now, however, that the outside world is separated into units in which there is policy discrimination, that is the import duty is levied on imports from some countries but not from others; and the export subsidies are similarly treated. In this situation, the outcome will be different from the free-trade result, due to the geographic discrimination alone. But although this is not a logical inevitability, it will be assumed all along that geographic discrimination is preceded (or accompanied) by commodity discrimination.

Geographic discrimination may take a variety of forms. For convenience, three categories are usually distinguished. The weakest form of discrimination is an agreement between two or more countries for partial exemption from duties of their imports from each other; that is, an exemption of some imports from some part of the duties imposed on them.[2] The strongest form is that known as a 'customs union', the definition of which is presented, following long-accepted conventions, succinctly by Viner:[3]

> A perfect customs union must meet the following conditions:
> 1 the complete elimination of tariffs as between the member territories;
> 2 the establishment of a uniform tariff on imports from outside the union;
> 3 apportionment of customs revenue between the members in accordance with an agreed formula.

In between is the category defined as 'free-trade area', in which only the first of the three conditions for the existence of a customs union is met. Technically, the fulfilment of 1 without 2 is made possible by a proviso which confines the elimination of tariffs on the intra-union trade to goods 'originating' with the union members; that is, in which some minimum proportion of the value of the traded good is value added in the union member which exports it.

Most of the post-war literature on the theory of geographic discrimination usually comes under the heading of 'the theory of customs unions', and we shall mostly use the same term in the present discussion. But in effect, this theory usually analyzes not a customs union but a free-trade area: the act analyzed most often is the fulfilment of condition 1; less frequent is the analysis of 2; whereas the effect of 3—the distribution of customs revenues—rarely forms part of the topic of discussion. The present chapter will largely follow this focus of attention. It will assume, by the term 'customs union', a complete elimination of the tariff among members. This greatly simplifies the exposition without affecting the important aspects of the analysis, which would apply just as well to the case of a partial reduction of the tariff. Only scant attention will be paid to the effect of unifying the tariff scales of the union members in their trade with the non-union world, and the question of distribution of the customs revenue will be completely disregarded.

In the main part, the discussion will employ the assumptions with which the analysis of Chapter 2 started. Primarily, it will assume a two-good world, in which conditions are such that free trade is the optimum policy. In part of the analysis, the small-country assumption will be relaxed, so that an optimum policy would entail some positive tariff rather than a free trade. One inevitable change in assumptions will be an increase in the number of countries from two to three: the home country and *two* foreign countries (rather than one). This, of course, is the minimum number required for the introduction of geographic discrimination.

The addition of geographic to commodity discrimination complicates the analysis. The scope of combinations of situations is greatly widened, and the analytic techniques become more intricate. The present chapter should be viewed not as aiming at anything approaching a comprehensive discussion of geographic discrimination, but rather as an introduction portraying the skeleton of the theory. On a few occasions the directions which the existing theory takes will be pointed out, although not followed at any length.

2 Trade creation and trade diversion

Of the set of conditions enumerated in Chapter 2 (section 5), which must be met for the attainment of 'Pareto optimality' (thus maximum welfare, in the sense discussed there), the four 'closed-economy' conditions listed there are assumed to be fulfilled. The fifth, we recall, the 'open-economy' condition, reads as follows: 'marginal rates of transformation should be equal in domestic production and in trade'. With the division, now, of the outside world into sub-units, and the existence of separate trade flows between the home country and each of these sub-units, a further, sixth condition for optimality has to be added, namely:

(f) marginal rates of transformation should be equal in the home country's trade with each foreign country.

When a uniform tariff is imposed by a 'small' country on the import good, whatever its foreign source of supply, condition (e) is not satisfied. But the new condition (f) *is* fulfilled (this has been implicitly taken for granted in the analysis thus far): with a uniform tariff duty and a uniform domestic price, the price (transformation) ratio of the import good in trade with each foreign country must also be uniform.[4]

The elimination of the tariff on imports from one part of the outside world, while the tariff is retained for imports from the other part, reverses this order: the first condition (e), will now be fulfilled in trade with the country from which imports are now duty free.[5] But with a non-uniform tariff (i.e. a zero tariff in one trade flow and a positive tariff in the other), and a uniform domestic price, transformation ratios in the alternative trade flows will no longer be equal.

Could any welfare implication be suggested now, for the effect of the discriminating removal of the tariff? From our previous discussion (in Chapter 2), we know that no such general inference could be drawn; since, we recall, 'situations of varying forms of distortions cannot be ranked'.[6] The specific issue on hand has also served as a prime example in the development of what became known as the 'theory of second best',[7] illustrating the similar proposition that 'there is no *a priori* way to judge as between various situations in which some of the Paretian optimum conditions are fulfilled while others are not.'[8] The contradicting forces created by the shift from the uniform tariff to the customs union have been termed by Viner, who was the first to note and emphasize that a customs union does not necessarily lead to a welfare improvement, as 'trade creation' and 'trade diversion': the former leading to an improvement, the latter to a deterioration.[9] Much of the analysis of customs unions is indeed conducted by reference to these two forces. It will be convenient to start with the presentation of these factors in the simple context in which they were suggested by Viner.

Viner's implicit model runs strictly along Ricardian lines, except that it introduces the division of the outside world into sub-units. Accordingly, while the model manages to present the essence of the 'trade creating' and 'trade diverting' effects just as the Ricardian model puts across the nature of 'comparative advantage', it is similarly deficient for a fuller exploration of the effect of tariff changes.[10] The analysis overlooks entirely the possible effect of the tariff change on consumption, and is restricted to the impact on production. In terms of our former analysis, it asks for the welfare implications which may be drawn from the positions of the budget-restraint *lines* (rather than positions on the lines) before and after the tariff change. The model implicitly incorporates a cardinal assumption, in the Ricardian tradition, of straight-line transformation curves, namely that of constant marginal (and average) costs of production in each country.[11]

Viner's model is presented in figure 26. The world consists of three countries: home country A; foreign country B, with which a customs union is concluded; and the 'third' country C. The transformation curve of the home country is PQ, and the transformation ratio between the two goods X and M is given by the slope of aa. In autarky, the production and consumption location in the home country is at point H. The price of M is assumed to be lower in B than in the home country, and still lower in C; the two prices are represented, respectively, by bb and cc.

Before the union, with a uniform tariff imposed on the imports of M, two situations only are possible (given that PQ is a straight line): either the tariff is prohibitive, in which case production and consumption is at autarky point H; or it is not, in which case the home country specializes completely in the production of X and buys M from the cheapest foreign source, namely country C, so that production is at point Q and consumption somewhere along cc.

We shall now introduce an *effective* customs union, namely an elimination of the tariff on imports from the union partner which makes the home price of these imports lower either than the home production cost of the good or of the (cum-tariff) price of

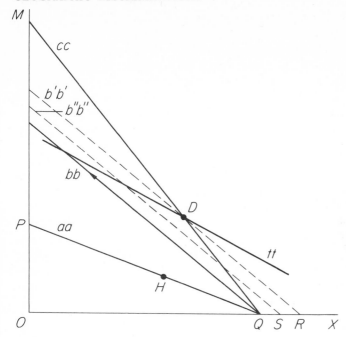

Figure 26

imports from the third country C. Production will now be at Q, with X being sold to B for M at the price indicated by bb, and consumption somewhere on bb. If the pre-union position was point H, the union results in the specialization of the home country in the production of X, the elimination of home production of M and the purchase of M from B. This is the case defined as *trade creation.* If, on the other hand, before the union production was at Q and consumption along cc, home production will remain unchanged by the union; trade with C will, however, be replaced by trade with B—the imports from the latter now becoming cheaper—and consumption will be along bb. This is the case defined as *trade diversion.*[12]

Trade creation leads to a welfare gain: consumption possibilities superior to H become open when the country trades along bb, the slope of which represents also the price faced by home consumers. Trade diversion lowers welfare in the special sense used by Viner: abstracting from the actual consumption baskets, Viner comes to the conclusion of a welfare loss by the fact that budget-restraint line bb is contained within the budget-line cc. These results are intuitively obvious. Trade creation takes place, in this model, when the pre-union position is that of autarky, and the opening of the country to trade (although not with the cheapest source of imports) must raise welfare. Trade diversion on the other hand takes place when, *disregarding consumption effects*, the country trades along free-trade lines; this is, by assumption, an optimum position, and any move from it must involve a welfare deterioration.[13]

But the disregard of possible effects on consumption invalidates inferences drawn about welfare changes. The introduction of these effects leaves Viner's conclusion intact for the case of trade creation; but his other assertion, of a welfare loss in the case of trade diversion, is no longer necessarily true.[14] The demonstration of the welfare impact of the effect on consumption, though similar to analyses carried out earlier in this book when essentially similar problems were treated—such as the demonstration of superiority of subsidy over tariff, or of the loss from non-prohibitive tariff in a Ricardian model[15]—will be restated here.

Turning back to figure 26, assume the pre-union consumption locus to be at point D on cc. Prices faced by home consumers are not, however, those represented by the slope of cc but rather those of tt—the cum-tariff domestic price. We thus know that, with a given income distribution combination D is preferable to (or, in the limit, as good as) any other combination on the line tt; and, *a fortiori*, to any combination below this line. After the union, with the source of imports diverted from country C to country B, consumption will be somewhere on line bb, the slope of this line now representing both the international price and the home price. Had the consumption locus been below the intersection of bb with tt, it would indeed be inferior to consumption basket D, and Viner's conclusion of welfare deterioration would follow. Consumption could, however, be above this intersection, in which case it *may* represent a position of increased welfare. In the general case, thus, it is not possible to rank the pre-union and post- (trade-diverting) union consumption positions—either could represent a higher welfare than the other.

This could be stated in a somewhat different way, giving

quantitative expressions to the two opposing factors at work.[16] With the diversion of imports to country B, the price in trade with which is represented by bb, the home country would have to produce OR of X (rather than OQ) in order to be able to provide the pre-union consumption basket D. The difference QR is thus the *production loss* from trade diversion—and it is only this loss which Viner takes into account. But had the country actually traded from R along $b'b'$ (parallel to bb)—this being also the price faced by home consumers—consumption will not be at D but, with the change in relative prices, somewhere above D on $b'b'$, at a point yielding a (potential) higher welfare for any and all consumers. Construct now line $b''b''$ (parallel to bb and $b'b'$), so that the best possible consumption locus on it represents a welfare level just equal to that of D; that is, with $b''b''$ being the country's budget-restraint line, the welfare level would be unchanged from the pre-union position. The line $b''b''$ originates from point S, on the X-axis. RS may thus be regarded as the *consumption gain* due to the elimination of discrepancy between the country's relative prices in trade and in the home market. In the general case, S could be either to the right of Q, as it is shown in figure 26, or to its left (and $b''b''$ to the right or left of bb); that is, the production loss due to the trade diversion could exceed the consumption gain or fall short of it (or the two may, in a limiting case, just happen to be equal). The pre-union and post-union consumption positions thus cannot be generally ranked.

It will be very easy to see that a consumption gain appears also in the situation of trade creation. A customs union which leads in this direction would then increase welfare on two scores—by both production and consumption gains.

Once varying production costs are admitted—that is, a concave rather than a straight-line transformation curve—Viner's conclusions must be further qualified, and the terms of 'trade creation' and 'trade diversion' further clarified.[17] With a concave transformation curve (or increasing marginal costs), the pre-union position could still be that of a 'corner solution'; that is, the country could still completely specialize in the production of one good. In this case, the analysis would be basically similar to that presented for the situation of a straight-line transformation curve: only trade diversion is possible, yielding the welfare im-

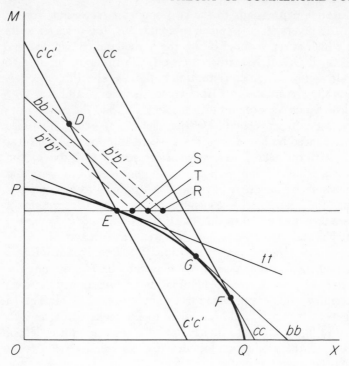

Figure 27

plications which have just been presented. Or the tariff may be prohibitive, with production and consumption being at the autarky point; in which case, again, the analysis would resemble that applied for the straight-line transformation curve. Only trade creation would be possible, in this instance, with a welfare improvement resulting from both production and consumption gains. But the introduction of increasing costs enables the analysis of the more interesting and more general situation of the incomplete specialization with a non-prohibitive tariff: the country produces both goods, but imports part of its consumption of one of the goods.[18] In the Ricardian world of constant costs *either* trade creation *or* trade diversion could result, whereas now *both* trade creation and trade diversion will follow from the establishment of a customs union. This analysis is presented with the aid of figure 27.

PQ is, as usual, the home country's transformation curve. The small-country assumption—fixed foreign prices—is maintained. Imports of M from country C are cheaper either than imports from country B or from the production price of M in the home country under autarky.[19] With free trade, home production would be at F; trade would be with C, at the price prevailing in the latter, and consumption somewhere on budget-restraint line cc. With a (non-prohibitive) tariff on M, home price of the good is represented by the slope of tt. Production will take place at E. Trade will still be maintained with C, at the price prevailing in it, and the consumption locus will be somewhere to the left of E on $c'c'$ (parallel to cc). The introduction of an effective customs union with B will now make, by assumption, the home price of imports of M from B lower than the (cum-tariff) price of M in its purchase from C. Trade with C will stop, and trade with B will take place instead. The new production point will be G, where marginal costs in home production of M are equal to its price in trade with B, represented by the slope of bb; and the consumption combination will be somewhere to the left of G on bb.

Two forms of replacement are seen to have taken place here. One is the replacement of trade with C by trade with B—Viner's 'trade diversion'. The other is the movement in the home country from the production of M to the production of X; that is, the replacement of domestic production of the import good by imports from the partner country. This is Viner's 'trade creation'.

It is immediately apparent, as in the case of constant marginal costs, that no general conclusion emerges about the direction of change of welfare. If the pre-union consumption locus lies within the country's post-union budget restraint, bb, the union has resulted in a welfare gain. Otherwise—hence, also, as a general conclusion—the welfare levels of the pre- and post-union positions cannot be ranked.

As before, it should be worthwhile to designate the quantitative impact, in terms of units of good X, of the various (contradicting) effects. Suppose the pre-union consumption locus is D. After the establishment of the union, with the shift of trade to a more expensive source of imports, the country would have to possess the basket of goods R, rather than E, in order to reach consumption basket D by means of trade (with country B, along the line $b'b'$). ER may thus be designated the *trade-diversion effect* on production—a negative impact. On the other hand, the post-union shift of production from E to G makes the goods available to the economy equivalent (by way of trade with B) to combination T, rather than E. The distance ET is the *trade-creation effect* of the union on production, and it is of course positive—it is a welfare gain. The net outcome of these two changes—the distance TR—may be termed the *net production effect* of the union on welfare, and it could be either positive or negative. In the case demonstrated in figure 27, the net production effect is negative. But had D been contained within bb—rather than being above it, as it is shown in the diagram—the net production effect would have been positive: it would show an amount of X which could be taken away from the economy and still enable it to acquire the same basket of goods as before the union. In this case the net production effect alone—overlooking, that is, the impact of the union on consumption—would imply an increase of welfare.

To this now has to be added the consumption effect, which acts to raise welfare just as before. Similar to the analysis in the constant-costs model, a line $b''b''$, originating in S, is constructed so that the best consumption basket available on it would leave consumers just as well off as with consumption basket D. The distance RS is thus a measure of the *consumption effect* of the union on welfare, and it must always be positive. If the net production effect is negative—T is to the left of R—the combined effect of production and consumption may still be positive. Graphically, this combined effect is represented by the distance ST. If S is to the left of T, the total effect of the union is an increase of welfare, and the opposite if S is to the right of T. The distance ST measures, in terms of units of X, what could be taken away from the economy when welfare is increased by the union, or what would have to be added to it when welfare is diminished, to leave the economy's welfare unchanged by the formation of the union.

3 Likelihood of gains from a union

The conclusion reached has thus been that 'anything can happen': a customs union may raise welfare, lower it or, in the limiting case, leave it unchanged. The separation of the factors at work and the identification of the offsetting tendencies facilitates, however, the determination of the *likelihood* of one outcome or the other. In this section, we shall enumerate the circumstances which contribute to a higher likelihood of a 'success' of the union, that is, to its resulting in raising rather than lowering welfare. Most of the inferences may be derived using the analysis the skeleton of which was presented in figure 27. Others may be due to more elaborate models, which will not be presented, or based on a more intuitive reasoning. The discussion will be confined throughout to the small-country case—retaining, that is, the assumption of fixed prices in all foreign markets; and, as hitherto, will be presented from the point of view of the single (home) country.[20]

(i) First—and probably most important—the customs union is more likely to increase welfare the higher the level of the pre-union (uniform) rate of tariff. In figure 27, this may be easily seen in the following way. The higher the tariff rate, the further to the left will be the pre-union production point E; that is, the more the country will produce of its import good M and the less of its export good X. The post-union production point G, on the other hand, is not affected by the pre-union tariff rate (which following the union is imposed on imports from C alone). The distance ET will thus be larger; that is, the trade creation effect on production, leading in the direction of welfare gain, will be stronger. At the same time, the pre-union trade with C (the vector ED) will be smaller with a higher tariff; E is expected to be higher (more production of M) and D lower, less of the import good M being consumed at the higher domestic price associated with the higher tariff. The distance ER will thus also be accordingly shorter; that is, with a smaller amount of (pre-union) imports, the trade diversion effect, which contributes to a welfare loss, will be weaker. The net production effect of the customs union is thus more likely, due to tendencies in both its components, to be positive (i.e. to lead to a welfare gain) the higher the pre-union tariff.[21]

It cannot be shown as an inevitable outcome of the model, but would seem likely to be generally true, that the higher the discrepancy between the home price and the international price before the union—the higher, that is, the tariff rate—the stronger will be the effect of removal of this discrepancy on welfare; in other words, the stronger is the (always favourable) consumption effect of the union. This would combine with the net production effect to make the outcome of a welfare gain more likely the higher the pre-union tariff.

(ii) The likelihood of a welfare gain is higher the smaller the size of imports (from the non-partner world) before the union is established.[22] Small imports could be due, as we have seen, to a high tariff rate—in which case this is simply part of the effect of the former factor—but they could also result from other circumstances, such as the structure of demand. With all other variables given, the trade creation effect on production will be given; whereas the (negative) trade diversion effect will be smaller, and the net production effect of the union more likely to be positive. In the extreme case, when no (pre-union) trade exists, only the two positive effects will be found—no trade diversion at all is then possible.

This proposition has been discussed in the context of a two-good world in which it is assumed beforehand that the price of import good M is higher in trade with country B, the union partner, than in trade with country C—the non-union outside world; whereas the possibility of the opposite order has been overlooked. If country B is indeed the cheaper source of imports of M, and the pre-union tariff is not high enough to be prohibitive, pre-union trade will have taken place with B rather than with C. If the tariff is prohibitive no trade will have taken place at all, by definition. In both instances the establishment of the (effective) union will have only positive effects—the trade-creation effect on production and the consumption effect—trade diversion being impossible. Thus, given the amount of pre-union imports, the likelihood that the union will lead to a welfare gain is higher if the good is imported before the union from the future partner rather than from the rest of the world: the gain is certain in the former case, whereas the outcome is unknown in the latter. With many goods, some will be imported (before the union) from the union member, some from the rest of the world (while for still others the tariff may be prohibitive). The proposition derived before should therefore be amended to read as follows: the likelihood of the union resulting in a welfare gain is higher the smaller the size of pre-union trade, but the higher is the proportion of the total of trade with the (future) union members.[23]

(iii) The third set of circumstances is rather obvious: the union is more likely to result in welfare gain the closer the relative prices in trade with the partner country (B) are to those prevailing in trade with the outside world (country C). In figure 27, this would mean a slope of bb closer to the slope of cc. The closer these two, the further to the right will be the post-union production point G; and the larger the trade creation effect (distance ET). At the same time, the closer this resemblance, the smaller will be the (negative) trade diversion effect (distance ER)—the given amount of imports will be bought at only slightly higher prices. The net production effect of the union is thus more likely to be positive. Likewise, the (necessarily favourable) consumption effect is likely to be stronger, since the change in relative prices facing the consumer (the difference between tt and bb) is larger. In the limiting case, the relative price of M in trade with B will be equal to the price in trade with C—the case in which the union turns to be equivalent to a move to a completely free trade.

(iv) Stepping out, for the moment, of the three-country two-good model, it intuitively follows from the former argument that the larger the number of partner countries to the union, the more likely is a welfare gain. In the two-good context, this may be thought of as follows: each of the countries joining the union will have a relative price, such as bb, between the two goods. With the union, trade of the home country will take place with that partner country whose price of import good B is lowest—that is, whose bb price line is closest to that represented by cc. The more partner countries there are, the closer we may expect the 'best' price line bb to be to cc (indeed, the more likely it is that the union will include country C and price line cc itself). In a multi-commodity context, this may be thought of in a slightly different way: for each pair of two goods, a price ratio such as that represented by bb (or cc) will exist. The larger the 'economic size' of the country's partners to the union (whether due to the number of partner countries or to the size of each), the larger we may expect the number of goods to be in which the bb ratios would be closer to the cc ratios, so that the net production effect of the union will be more likely to be positive. A corollary of this argument is that the *more diversified* the structure of the country's partners to the union, whether due to the number of countries joining the union or to the degree of diversification of economic structure in each, the more likely it is that the union will result in a welfare gain.

(v) A welfare gain is more likely the less the marginal costs rise with an increase in production. In figure 27, the more constant the marginal costs, the flatter is the transformation curve PQ. Given the pre-union production point E, the flatter PQ is, the further to the right will be the post-union production point G, the larger the trade creation effect (distance ET), and the more likely it is that net production effect of the union will be positive. Intuitively, this is rather clear. The increase in costs of production following trade and specialization acts to restrict the degree of specialization and to reduce the gain from it; the less the costs rise with the expansion of production (of the good in which the country specializes), the higher therefore the gain from trade.

(vi) Similarly, the likelihood of a welfare gain will be higher the more the consumption patterns in the home country are affected by changes in relative prices.[24] This, again, though seeming to be intuitively correct, cannot be proven to follow inevitably from the assumptions of the model. A larger change in the consumer's optimal basket due to a given change in relative prices would (probably) imply that a larger portion of the consumer's initial basket could be taken away from him and still leave his welfare unchanged. In terms of figure 27 this would mean, with the given change from tt to bb in the relative prices faced by home consumers, that the distance RS would be larger. The consumption effect of the union—necessarily positive—is thus larger, and the likelihood of a welfare gain from the creation of the union higher. In terms of the consumer's surplus discussed in the last chapter this is again intuitively clear: the increase in this surplus following a reduction in the price (of the import good) faced by consumers will be higher the higher the elasticity of the (compensated) demand curve. A larger response of quantities to changes in relative prices indicates a larger measure of substitutability among the goods under consideration; this rule implies that the success of a customs union is more likely the more substitutable in consumption the import goods are with goods of domestic production.

(vii) The analysis thus far was concerned with a 'union' entailing a full elimination of the tariff within it. As has been stated earlier, and could readily be verified, no change in the direction of conclusions would emerge had only partial rather than complete elimination of the tariff been involved. But the partial elimination will be introduced now, in the context of the discussion of likelihood of success of the union, to examine the following question: is a 'union' (in the loose sense, of course, of any tariff preference) more likely to lead to a welfare gain when the removal of the tariff is partial or complete? In the literature of customs unions, the assertion that a welfare gain is *more likely* with a *partial* preferential reduction of the tariff seems to enjoy general endorsement.[25] As will be demonstrated presently, in the two-good world the opposite of this proposition is true. In a multi-good world, on the other hand, it seems that no general proposition could be offered.

The analysis in the two-good framework is undertaken by means of figure 28, which incorporates parts of figure 27 (abstaining from a fuller reconstruction to avoid cluttering).

Consider the removal of tariff on imports from country B, the union's partner, to take place in two stages. First the tariff is lowered from the original (uniform) level to a still positive level t_1; then, in the second stage, the tariff is removed altogether. At the first stage, the home price ratio will change from that represented by the slope of tt to that of t_1t_1, indicating a lower price of import good M. Production will shift from E to G_1. Trade—now with country B rather than with country C from whom M was bought before the union—will take place from G_1 in the northwest direction along line b_1b_1, whose slope (like that of bb) represents the price ratio in trade with B. Just as in our earlier analysis, the move may be shown to include three components: a negative trade-diversion effect on production; a

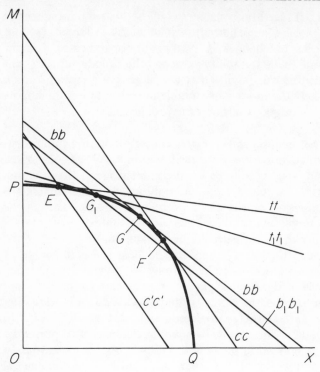

Figure 28

positive trade creation effect on production; and a positive consumption effect, the latter being due to the change of prices
faced by home consumers from tt to t_1t_1. The combined, total
effect on welfare is, of course, unknown—it could be, in the
general case, either positive or negative.

Now proceed to the second stage of removing the tariff t_1 on
imports from B. The slope of bb will now represent the price
ratio both at home and in trade (with B). The production point
will move from G_1 to G, and trade will take place along bb, the
consumption locus being somewhere on it to the left of G. This
leads to the usual impact of a tariff removal on welfare.
Specifically, *no* negative trade diversion effect exists in this move
at all. Only a positive trade creation effect is found, and inevitably a positive net production effect, and a positive consumption effect. This move must, therefore, lead to a welfare

gain—regardless, it should be stressed, of whether the earlier move (the partial lowering of the tariff) led to a welfare gain or a welfare loss. Thus, to recapitulate: the first stage, of partial removal of the tariff, may lead either way; the second stage, of a complete removal of the (remaining) tariff, inevitably leads to a welfare gain. Hence, a union involving the combination of the two stages, namely the complete elimination of the tariff, is obviously more likely to lead to a welfare gain than a union in which only a partial reduction of the tariff is granted. In exactly the same way, it would be easy to establish the more general rule, namely: the higher the proportion of the tariff removed in the union trade, the more likely it is that the union will lead to a welfare gain, a complete elimination of the tariff being the limiting case.

In a multi-good world other considerations have to be added, and the result seems to be indeterminate—at least so far as the intuitive reasoning which will be developed here is concerned. In the two-good world, we have always assumed an *effective* union—one which shifts the source of imports from C to B—to make the union relevant. In the multi-good world, we may divide all import goods into three classes. One will include all the goods which even before the union (that is, with a uniform tariff) are imported from B. Another group, the opposite, includes those goods which even with no tariff at all on imports from B will still be imported from C (while the pre-union tariff on imports from C is maintained throughout). The third group, on the other hand, includes those goods which are potentially affected by a customs union: before the union, they are imported from C, and some preferential lowering of the tariff on B will make the latter replace C as the source of imports. For the sake of brevity, we shall refer to the first group as 'B goods'; to the second, as 'C goods', and to the third as 'potential B goods'. It is primarily the latter group with which we shall be concerned.

The group of 'potential B goods' consists of a continuum of goods, which may be ranked according to the proximity of their price in B to that of the price in C. The price in B of the good at the top of the rank is just a shade higher than its price in C, whereas the price of the good at the bottom is just a shade lower than the *cum-tariff* price of the good in C, when imported by A. We shall now suppose, again, the lowering of tariffs on A's imports from B to take place in stages, each successive stage being of a size just sufficient to make the customs union effective for one additional good in the 'potential B' group. The first stage will make B replace C as the source of A's imports for the good at the top of the rank, the second stage will add to it the good next to the top, and so on until the final stage, of a complete removal of the tariff on imports from B, which will make the union effective also for the good at the very bottom of the list.

The first stage of tariff reduction will have the following consequences. For the good at the top of the rank in the 'potential B' group, only trade diversion will exist—the reduction of the tariff having been, by assumption, just sufficient to lead to this diversion (hence with no change in the home price in A). The loss from this trade diversion will be small, since the B and C prices are close to each other for this good. In addition, there will be gain from both production (trade creation) and consumption in the markets for all the goods in the 'B group', the tariff on all these imports having been lowered. In the next stage, there will be loss from trade diversion in the market of the good next to the top in the 'potential B' group; and this loss will be larger, for each value unit of trade diversion, than it was for the former good, since the gap between B's and C's price is now larger. On the other hand, additional gains are realized in production and consumption in the market for all the goods in which B has been the source of imports, and these markets include now not only the 'B group', but also the good at the top of the rank of the 'potential B' group, which has become an import from B at the former stage. These additional production and consumption gains will, however, tend to be lower (per unit of tariff reduction) in each of the separate markets than in the former stage.[26] In each successive stage we shall thus have the following tendencies, in comparison with the effect of the preceding stage: a larger loss from trade diversion (per unit of such diversion); positive trade creation and consumption effects on welfare in a larger number of markets; but, finally, a smaller (additional) impact of these positive effects, per unit of tariff reduction. The first and last of these three comparisons indicate a larger loss and lower gains; whereas the second comparison indicates larger gains than in the preceding stage.

To this now has to be added the impact on goods which we

have termed the 'C group'. Our favourable consumption effect was derived from the substitution, in consumption, of imported goods for the domestically produced good (the X-good in the two-good analysis). But the lowering of price of a good in the 'potential B' group also leads to a substitution of consumption of this good for that of goods from the 'C group'; and this involves a *loss* which becomes bigger (at each successive stage of tariff reduction) as the goods in the 'C group' are replaced by goods the tariff on which is gradually lower. On the other hand a loss is also involved, at each successive stage, in the substitution of consumption of goods imported from B for that of goods in the 'potential B' group for which the union has *not* yet become effective; and the list of these goods keeps getting shorter at each successive stage of tariff reduction. These are thus, again, factors working in opposite directions in the comparison of the effect of successive stages of tariff reduction.

The upshot of this rather involved—and certainly imprecise—analysis is that the comparison of the likelihood of a net gain or a net loss resulting from successive stages of removal of the tariff on imports from B, the partner union, reveals tendencies in opposite directions, and no clear-cut outcome seems to emerge. Hence, no proposition is offered on whether the likelihood of gain from a preferential tariff reduction is higher or lower the larger is the extent of this reduction.[27]

(viii) The likelihood of success of the union is often debated in relation to the degree of 'complementarity' vs. the 'competitiveness' or 'rivalry' among the union members. The substance of the conclusions which may be derived in this context is in fact implied by the propositions listed thus far. But due to the importance of this formulation, and the debate around it, in the literature of customs-union theory, a further discussion under a separate heading may be worthwhile.[28]

To start with, 'potential complementarity' (or 'dissimilarity') and 'rivalry' ('similarity') have to be clearly defined, to avoid ambiguity (which may be at least a partial source of disagreement on this issue). The simplest definition, and the one which is most probably usually implied, is to be phrased in terms of *relative prices* (or their equivalent under perfect competition, relative costs) *in the autarky situation* in each country. The closer these prices in two countries are, the more 'similar', or 'competitive', are these economies; and the further apart these prices are, the more 'dissimilar', or 'complementary' the two countries.

Differences in relative prices, we recall from the Heckscher–Ohlin model, may arise from two sources. One is a (non-proportional) difference in the transformation curves of the two countries, reflecting differences in the proportions of factors of production available to each economy. In the discussion under consideration (as well as in the original Ohlin presumptions), this is assumed to be the primary source of similarity or the lack of it. The other potential source is differences in demand patterns (which do not happen to counteract the former source). The more similar are individual tastes, income levels and patterns of income distribution which determine the community's demand patterns, the more similar, 'competitive' and the less 'complementary' will the two economies be.

With the aid of figure 27 above, it is easy to see—and in fact it has already been shown—that the less similar, more 'complementary' the two economies joining the union, the more likely it is that the union will result in a welfare gain. The more B's prices (which, by assumption that A is 'small', are not affected by trade with A) differ from A's prices, the stronger will be both the (positive) trade creation effect and the (positive) consumption effect of the union. At the same time, given A's (autarky) prices and C's prices, the larger the discrepancy between A's and B's prices, the smaller the discrepancy is between the latter and C's prices (or the more likely it is that B's price of the import good M is *lower* than C's price); hence, the weaker the (negative) trade-diversion effect is, or the more likely it is to be absent altogether. The conclusion is thus clear-cut and unambiguous. It is, of course, not surprising, recalling that dissimilarities between countries are both the motivation for trade and the source of gain from it.

In what sense is it relevant that the two countries are 'actually very competitive'? If this refers to the situation in which both countries compete in the home country's market, the necessary implication would be that before the union import good M is bought from (future) union partner B rather than from C: country B is the cheaper source of imports. In this case, of course, no trade diversion will appear, and the union must result in a welfare gain. But this is simply stating that a union is likely to (in fact, it must) lead to a welfare gain to the country if concluded with the foreign country which is the cheapest source of its imports, and has nothing to do with 'complementarity' and 'competitiveness'. If, on the other hand, the position implied by being 'very competitive' is that before the union relative prices in both union partners (A and B) are close to each other, then of course the opposite of the alleged rule would be justified. The closer these prices (tt and bb) are, the weaker will be the positive trade-creation and consumption effects, the stronger the (negative) trade-diversion effect, and the more likely a welfare loss from the establishment of the union. Probably the kindest (although a bit stretched) interpretation of being 'potentially complementary but actually competitive' is simply that the home country in question changes relative prices substantially from what they would be *in free trade* by imposing a high tariff—in which case, as we have seen, the union is indeed more likely to lead to a gain.[29]

It may be recalled on this occasion that the customs union is more likely to lead to a gain in the home country the more 'similar to', or 'competitive with', the union partner (country B) and the *rest of the world* (country C) are: the larger this similarity—the closer, that is, line bb to line cc in figure 27—the stronger the positive trade-creation effect and consumption effect and the weaker the negative trade-diversion effect. By this rule, the home country should seek for partnership in the union foreign countries which do not possess unique features, but are rather similar to the part of the world excluded from the union. As noted, the chance of the partner having this attribute is greater the larger the economic size of the partners and the more diversified their economic structure.

4 Customs unions under variable international prices

All the circumstances under which the home economy has been assumed hitherto to operate would make free trade an optimum position. These included, *inter alia*, the assumption that the country is 'small'—the amount of its trade having no effect on the prices in which it trades. We shall now examine briefly the

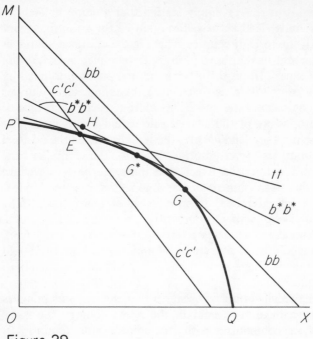

Figure 29

result of the relaxation of this assumption, and allow the country's trade to affect its terms of trade. We revert again to the two-good model, and the 'closed-economy' conditions of Pareto-optimality are still assumed to be fulfilled.[30] Similarly, all other features of the model used thus far will be retained.

We shall first relax the assumption of constant international prices only partly: we shall assume these prices to remain constant in trade with the rest of the world (country C), but to be variable in trade with the country's union partner (country B).[31] For simplicity—this changes nothing in the analysis and its conclusions—we will assume that before the establishment of the union no trade with country B took place: all imports of M were purchased from country C.[32] The analysis is presented with the aid of figure 29, which again should be understood to incorporate the information of figure 27 (which will not be reconstructed to avoid cluttering).

As before, pre-union production is at E, and trade with C takes place to the left along $c'c'$. The slope of the line bb represents now not the price ratio in trade with partner-union B but the prevailing home price at B *without* any trade of A with B—before, that is, the effect of the union takes place. Had this been a constant price, the post-union trade of A and B would have taken place at this price ratio, and bb would have been A's budget-restraint line, with home production at G and consumption to its left on bb. It is now assumed, however, that with the opening of trade with B and the purchase of M from it, following the union, the price of M in trade with B rises. The new price, in the post-union equilibrium position, will be represented by the slope of b^*b^*. Home production is then at G^*, home consumption at H, and the trade vector is G^*H. The line b^*b^*, it should be noted, is *not* a budget restraint: not *any* amount of trade could be conducted at the price designated by it—just the amount represented by the move from G^* to H.

Consumption locus H is manifestly inferior to the consumption basket which would have been selected had trade been possible along line bb: as is intuitively obvious, the home country is less well off as a result of the rise in price of its import good than it would have been without this rise. In terms of the classification used earlier, both the positive trade-creation effect and consumption effect are weaker; whereas the negative trade-diversion effect is stronger. The likelihood of a welfare gain, from the creation of the union, is thus smaller. Yet, in the general case and without additional information it will still be concluded that the outcome could be either way: welfare could either improve or deteriorate.

We shall now proceed to relax also the assumption that trade with the rest of the world—country C—is conducted at constant prices; and make these prices too depend on home-country A's trade—the more A demands import good M from country C the higher will M's price be, and vice versa. With the union, and the lowering of the price of M (as seen by consumers in the home country) in trade with B, imports of M will turn from C to B; this, just as it tends to raise the price of M in purchases from B, will tend to lower its price in trade with C. Two possibilities have to be distinguished now. First, the range of possible price variations in C may be such that at the price ratio established by

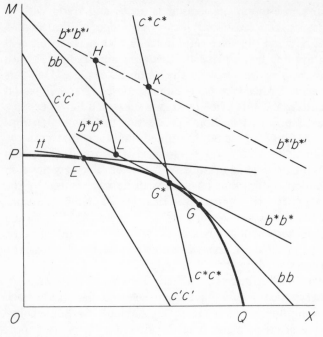

Figure 30

A's trade with B alone, supply of import good M from C will be zero; this, of course, was the situation when C's price ratio was assumed to be constant. In this case, the potential change in the terms of trade with country C is irrelevant. Trade will be conducted with B alone, and we simply revert to the analysis which has just been presented by means of figure 29.

The more interesting possibility is where a price is established at which home country A buys some positive amounts of imports from *both* B, the union partner, and C, the rest of the world. The price faced by home consumers and producers will, of course, be uniform. But the country's trade will be conducted at two international prices: one, with union partner B, equal to the home price; and the other, with country C, where the price of import good M is lower by the rate of duty than the home price or B's price. This situation is presented in figure 30.

As before, E is the pre-union production position. Trade takes place to its left along $c'c'$ (which is, however, no longer a budget-restraint line for the economy); and bb is the pre-union price ratio in B. With the union and the turning of trade from C to B, the price of M rises in trade with B, and the new price is represented by the slope of b^*b^*. It should be noticed, however, that the price rise is *smaller* than in the case of constant prices in trade with C: by assumption, at the price which would have been established without trade with C some supply of M would be forthcoming from C, so that the price would have to fall. The line b^*b^* in figure 30 is thus steeper—representing a lower price of M—than the equivalent line in the case analyzed by figure 29.

The price of M in trade with C will be now lower than before the union:[33] this price is represented by the slope of c^*c^*, which is steeper than $c'c'$, the pre-union price line. The relation between this price ratio and the price in trade with B (equivalent to the home price) will be exactly the relation between the pre-union price in C and A's home price—the discrepancy between each pair of prices being equal to the tariff rate, which remained unchanged on purchases of imports from C. The new equilibrium production point will now be G^*. The price ratio in trade with B, as well as the home price, is b^*b^*; and the price ratio in trade with C is c^*c^*, the slope of which differs from that of b^*b^* exactly as the slope of $c'c'$ differs from that of tt.

Trade with B, in the new equilibrium, is designated by the vector G^*L; and trade with C by the vector G^*K. To find the consumption locus, construct through K a parallel, $b^{*\prime}b^{*\prime}$, to b^*b^*; and from L, a parallel to c^*c^*, intersecting $b^{*\prime}b^{*\prime}$ at point H. Since the vector LH is equivalent to G^*K, H will thus be the consumption locus in the new equilibrium.

We can now make a few welfare comparisons. Since the home price facing consumers is represented by the slope of $b^{*\prime}b^{*\prime}$ (it being parallel to b^*b^*), H must be superior to (strictly, at least as good as) any point on $b^{*\prime}b^{*\prime}$. Since the latter is parallel to b^*b^* and above it, H thus represents a superior position to any point on b^*b^*. And, in turn, any such point selected on b^*b^* would have been superior to the point H selected on b^*b^* in figure 29, for reasons which by now should be obvious: both the positive trade-creation and consumption effects are stronger and the

negative trade diversion is weaker in the case represented by
b^*b^* in figure 30 than in that represented in figure 29, the former
indicating a steeper line (a lower price of import M) than the
latter. Thus, consumption basket H in figure 30 must be superior
to the consumption basket H in figure 29; that is, the admission
of variable prices in trade with the non-union world increases
the likelihood of a welfare gain resulting from the union.

It may be seen, moreover, that consumption basket H (in
figure 30) may be superior or inferior, to the potential consumption which would have been selected on line bb, had the latter
been the economy's budget restraint. Line bb is, we recall, the
budget restraint which would have been established, after the
union, had all international prices been constant. Thus, given a
set of pre-union international prices, it is generally impossible to
rank the consumption positions which would be established
under (a), the situation in which all these prices are constant;
and (b) when all these prices are variable, increasing with increased purchases of imports by A and vice versa. In other
words, it is impossible to determine whether, as a general rule,
the admission of the possibility of changes in the country's terms
of trade as a result of the union makes the union more or less
likely to raise the economy's welfare. All that could be said is
that the more elastic the supply of imports from partner union B
is (the closer the slope of b^*b^* is to that of bb), and the less
elastic the supply of the rest of the world (the *larger* the
difference of the slope of c^*c^* from that of $c'c'$), the more likely
is this additional terms-of-trade effect to be positive.

Finally, it should be noted—although this is not demonstrated
directly in figure 30—that the post-union position H could conceivably be superior to the *free trade* position (not shown in the
diagram). This result—impossible in the cases analyzed hitherto—is, of course, due to the fact that with variable prices
abroad, free trade no longer leads to an optimum position and is
no longer an optimum policy. This will be amplified in the
following section. But before that, a few words may be added on
the effect of the union on welfare outside the home country—an
aspect we have disregarded until now, and will go on ignoring
after this brief attention.

As long as international prices are assumed to be unaffected
by trade of the home country, the act of the union could have no

welfare impact on the world outside the home country. When prices are variable in trade with the union partner, but not with the rest of the world, the partner's welfare will change—this will be discussed briefly in the following section; but welfare of the rest of the world will be unaffected. Once the terms of trade with the rest of the world (country C) too are assumed to be variable, welfare in that area will change in an unambiguous manner: the terms of trade of this area with the home country, and with the union as a whole, will deteriorate, and with no offsetting factor this must mean a welfare loss. As for the welfare of the world as a whole—the home country, its union partners, and the rest of the world all combined—no general conclusion about the direction of its change can be reached. But then, it should be recalled that with the existence of tariffs in foreign countries, even the complete non-discriminatory removal of tariffs by the home country and the following by it of a free-trade policy do not necessarily increase welfare in the world as a whole.

5 Economic rationale of geographic discrimination

Most of our analysis has assumed a setting in which free trade is optimum, yet tariffs are found in the home country, and we have enquired whether, under these circumstances, a customs union will raise the community's welfare. But even if a customs union were found to not just raise welfare but be a second best, an explanation for the establishment of the union would still be missing. Since, if a change from the pre-union, non-optimal position is contemplated, rational behaviour should lead, in this setting, to the first-best policy of completely free trade, and not just to a geographically discriminating removal of tariffs.

The rationale of a customs union may be purely 'political'; that is, the union may well be motivated by considerations other than those of welfare derived from consumption of goods and services. To the explanation and examination of these considerations, the 'economic' theory of customs unions cannot, by definition, make any contribution. The union may also be economically motivated, and seized upon as a political device. Protection of various industries has been established in the past—whether due to 'just' or 'unjust' considerations at that time would be immaterial. An optimal policy would require the complete removal of protection, but this may not prove feasible under existing political circumstances. A customs union, which may be expected or presented to confer other blessings, may then make feasible a partial removal of protection, involving a geographic discrimination.

While both these types of consideration are probably very real, they imply the pursuance of a non-optimal policy on 'economic' grounds. It may be inquired, however, whether a purely economic rationale may be found for the establishment of the union; that is, whether a customs union—or another form of trade preferences—may be an optimum policy. Naturally, the posing of this question rules out the existence of circumstances in which free trade is an optimum policy. In terms of our earlier classification, trade preferences may conceivably be an optimum policy if under free trade either one or more of the closed-economy conditions for the maintenance of Pareto optimum is not fulfilled, or the open-economy conditions are violated. In most of the following we shall still retain the assumption that the closed-economy conditions are met, but consider the possibility that the open-economy conditions are not maintained under free trade. This, we recall, implies that the country is assumed to be not 'small' but 'large'—its trade is assumed to have an effect on international prices. In other words, we shall look for possible terms-of-trade effects as economic rationale for geographic discrimination. The following considerations are then suggested.

(i) With variable international prices, we recall, not a zero tariff (free trade) but some positive tariff rate is an optimal policy. The nature of this optimum tariff has been discussed earlier[34] in a setting in which the outside world consisted of one country. With the outside world separated into many units, however, and assuming that prices in these units are not necessarily identical (due to transportation costs or interferences in trade flows), there is no longer a *single* optimum tariff. Just as for any monopolist-monopsonist facing separated markets, an optimum policy for the home country will be to practice price discrimination; with a uniform home price, this obviously implies a discriminatory tariff system (taking, as we do all along, tariffs to be the device through which the government interferes in trade flows). The less elastic a foreign country's supply of imports to the home country and demand for its exports—the less elastic, that is, the foreign offer (reciprocal-demand) curve—the higher would be the optimum level of the tariff imposed on imports from that country.

While this demonstrates a system of tariffs involving geographic discrimination to be superior to any system of uniform tariffs (including zero tariffs—the free trade policy), it does *not* establish the case for a custom *union*, as a particular form of tariff discrimination. It will be only an accident if a customs union, involving the complete removal of tariffs on imports from the partners, is found to be an optimum policy. A necessary condition for such an occurrence is that the offer curves to the country of its union partners should be infinitely elastic. Yet, if for institutional (legal, political, or other) reasons only free trade, a uniform tariff system, or a full-fledged customs union are the possible alternatives, the customs union—though not a first best—may be superior to both other alternatives. This is essentially the point made towards the end of the last section. It should be obvious that a *necessary* condition for such a superiority is that the union-partner's (or partners') offer curve should be more elastic than the offer curve of the rest of the world. That is, if this is the motivation of the union, countries with relatively constant prices (in trade with the home country) should be its candidates for union partnership.

(ii) We have, until now, abstracted altogether from possible changes, as a result of the union, in the tariff on imports from the non-union world. In terms of the classification at the beginning of this discussion, we have analyzed a free-trade area rather than a customs union, by assuming that each partner's tariff on imports from third countries is not affected by the union. We may now introduce, in the present context, the possibility of a joint, uniform tariff of the union partners on imports from the outside world.[35]

Assume that before the union, each of its (two, for simplicity) partners maintained a set of optimum tariffs. When cooperation between the two countries is admitted, this set will be recognized as being non-optimal—*sub*-optimal, to be precise. In their separate policy decisions, each of the countries ignored, before the union, the effect of its trade on the terms of trade of the partner's country with the rest of the world; when these effects are taken into account, the tariff of each of the union partners on imports from the rest of the world would have to be raised. This is, again, equivalent to the difference between the firms acting separately and, alternatively, joining in a monopolistic organization, in which both firms' profits would rise by selling less and raising their selling prices.[36]

This argument too does not necessarily indicate the supremacy of a customs union: the two countries could have reached an agreement to raise their tariffs on trade with third countries, somehow allocating the added gains between them, without necessarily removing tariffs in trade between the two partners. But, again, a full-fledged union might be the only institutionally feasible form of cooperation and geographic discrimination. Alternatively, this argument may point out not the single rationale of establishing the union, but simply an added aspect.

(iii) We have seen that, with variable international prices, the price paid for imports from the union partner rises due to the establishment of the union: the home country's terms of trade (with the partner) deteriorate, and the partner's terms of trade improve. This, we recall, diminishes the welfare gain (or increases the welfare loss) of the home country from the union. At the same time, however, it creates a welfare gain for the partner: if the abolition of tariffs in the home country is the only act of the union, the partner country will certainly benefit from the establishment of the union. Since, in general, positive tariffs exist before the union and are abolished by the union in all the countries joining it, each of them is thus both in the position of the 'home country' and of the 'partner' in our analysis; and the 'partner's' aspect is a source of potential benefit which would *not* be realized by a unilateral removal of tariffs in the home country. In terms of the two-good model employed before, suppose that before the union, not only does the home country A have a tariff duty on imports of M, but partner-country B has a duty on its imports of X. The abolition of both tariffs, and the turning of both countries' trade towards each other, now diminish, or even reverse, the tendency noted before of A's terms of trade with B to deteriorate: the price of M in the two countries' trade with each other will rise less, and may even fall. In a multiple-good context assume, for simplicity, that the net result involves no change in the terms of trade between the two partners. It may be shown that the outcome of the union must be then an improvement of both partners' terms of trade with the rest of the world.[37] And the gain from this improvement may conceivably outweigh the welfare loss suffered from the fact that tariffs have not been abolished altogether but retained, in a geographically discriminating manner, on part of each country's trade.

All of these potential gains from the establishment of the union have been concerned, we recall, with variable international prices leading to terms-of-trade effects; but the closed-economy optimum conditions have still been assumed to be fulfilled. We shall now add another possible argument, involving a situation in which a deviation from the closed-economy optimum too is assumed to have prevailed.

(iv) Take an industry in the home country, which has—or, what is more relevant, is believed to have—a relatively strong positive degree of external economies. For an optimum to be achieved, policy measures should be taken to encourage this industry to expand beyond what it would in a market free of government interference.[38]

Suppose the industry in question expands enough, by a prohibitive tariff, to provide fully the consumption in the home market, and is judged still to have relatively strong (additional) external-economy effects at this stage. By an appropriate subsidy, home consumption and production could still be made to grow; but, of course, with an increasing discrepancy between consumer and producer prices, this would involve a continuously (and probably rapidly) rising welfare loss—for each additional unit of production—to be set against the benefit expected from the external effects. If recourse can be had to the foreign market, this further expansion could be made at lower welfare costs.

At the point at which home production just replaces all imports, the home price is equal to the foreign price (as seen by home producers and consumers). With an outside world which presents an infinitely elastic supply and demand schedule to the home country, any additional production of the industry under consideration created by a production subsidy will be sold abroad at the given, fixed price. This would still involve an increasing marginal cost of production, and an increasing discrepancy between this cost and the price received for the product; but the discrepancy will widen less than in sales to the home market, since the selling price will not decline. Even when foreign demand is not perfectly elastic, it is sufficient for it to be more elastic than home demand—a situation which may normally be expected—for this superiority of expansion for exports over expansion for the home market to be maintained.

Assume now, however, that such a policy is ruled out. One possible reason is that a subsidy cannot be granted, for one institutional constraint or another.[39] Another reason would be that all (relevant) foreign markets are protected by high tariffs, and we shall assume that, in any case, at least some foreign markets are protected by tariffs. The removal of such a tariff by a foreign country would, in this situation, enable the home country to realize the gain under consideration from sales abroad. Naturally, the removal of all tariffs by all foreign countries would be best for the home country, enabling it to reach a true optimum position; but it may be assumed that any such removal of a foreign tariff would have to be 'bought', the 'price' paid by the home country involving some geographic discrimination—which is our 'customs union'. The benefit from such union to the home country will be larger the higher is the tariff duty on the good in question in the potential union partner, and the more elastic the demand in that market, and, on the other hand, the weaker are the (positive) externalities of the goods whose home production will contract as a result of the removal of tariffs on imports from the potential union partner. Even if all of the removed tariffs apply to goods whose external effects are as strong as those which are realized in industries whose exports and production expand, a benefit will still be reaped as the result of specialization in production among the two union partners.[40] Hence, the customs union will be superior both to the pre-union position of protection and, due to the existence of externalities, to free trade. This is thus another potential economic rationale for the establishment of a customs union.[41]

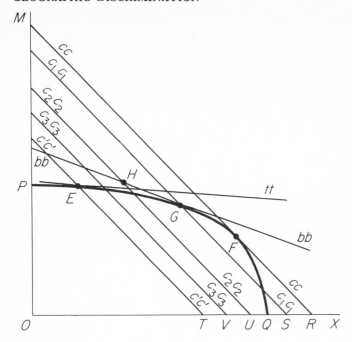

Figure 31

6 Measurement of gains and losses

In this last section, we shall translate the analysis of welfare gains and losses due to the union into a measurement of the magnitudes involved by units of a given good. We shall apply the method and techniques used for that purpose in the last chapter, and only recall that conceptual problems are involved in this shift to measurement, which should be constantly borne in mind.[42] The measurement will fall back on the two-good model, in which all Pareto-optimum conditions are assumed to be fulfilled in the home country, and international prices are constant (the home country is 'small'). The transormation from analysis to measurement is performed by means of figure 31.

In figure 31, the pre-union home price (with a tariff t) is represented by the slope of tt; home production is at E; and trade with country C takes place to its left along $c'c'$. Following the union, home production shifts to G and trade with country B takes place to its left, with home consumption somewhere on bb. Since we have already developed, in the last chapter, the measurement of the consequences of a shift from restricted trade to free trade, or vice versa, it will be convenient now to view the act of the union as if it consisted of two separate steps. First, the tariff t is abolished altogether, leading to free trade, and second, the tariff is re-imposed on imports from country C, leading (assuming, of course, an effective union) to the shift of trade from C to B. The first step having been analyzed before, we only have now to measure the consequence of the second.

Under free trade, home production is at F, and consumption somewhere to its left on budget-restraint line cc. With the shift from free trade to the union (the imposition of a tariff on imports from C), home production moves to G. With free-trade international prices, this is equivalent to a loss of RS units of X: had this amount been added to the country's product, the economy would be again on its free-trade budget-restraint line cc. Distance RS thus measures the production loss, in units of X, of moving from free trade to the union.

With the union, however, the economy's budget restraint is *not* c_1c_1, but rather bb, since trade now takes place with B. Suppose home consumption is now at H, with GH being the trade vector. Had the country been still trading with C, at the latter's prices, a quantity OU of X would have been just sufficient to allow the country—with a budget-restraint line c_2c_2—to secure the consumption basket H. The distance SU is thus an added loss—a trade-shift loss—due to the move from free trade to the union. It is easily seen that this loss is equal to the amount of imports represented by the trade vector GH times the excess of country B's price of imports M, in units of X, over the price in country C.

But, finally, had the economy been indeed on budget-restraint line c_2c_2, the consumption basket selected would have been not H but another basket (to its left). Since H would still be a possibility, it must be inferior (or, at the limit, just equal to) the alternative basket. To make consumers just as well off as at H, with free-trade prices, the amount OV of X would be sufficient: the best location on c_3c_3 would just yield the same welfare as consumption basket H. The distance UV is hence this added

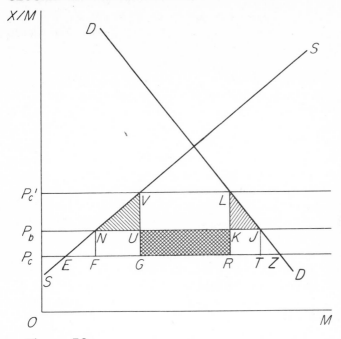

Figure 32

loss—the consumption loss from the shift from free trade to the union. The combined loss of this shift—the production, trade shift, and consumption losses added together—thus amounts to RV. When this is set against the gain of the first step—the movement from trade restricted by universal tariff t to free trade—the net gain or loss of the union will be found.[43] The combination of all these elements will now be done by the use of Marshallian supply and demand curves, the supply curve being derived from the transformation curve.[44] This is done using figure 32.

The supply and (compensated) demand curves are, respectively, SS and DD. P_c is the price of M, in units of X, in trade with country C, and P_b the price in trade with B. The size of the tariff per unit of M is t, and the pre-union home price, P_c', is equal to $P_c + t$. Home consumption of M before the union is $P_c'L$, home production is $P_c'V$, and the difference VL is provided by imports (from C).

We now consider, as before, the act of the union as if it consisted of two separate steps. First, the tariff is abolished altogether, and free trade is introduced. Home price will become P_c, home production P_cE, home consumption P_cZ, and imports (from country C) EZ.

As we recall from the analysis of the last chapter, the gain from this step, measured in units of X, is the combination of the two triangles EGV and ZRL. The second step involves a reimposition of a tariff on imports from C (whether at the size t or any other size which would make the union effective). This will shift the source of imports to country B. The new home price will become P_b, home production will be P_bN, home consumption P_bJ, and imports (now from country B) NJ. This will involve losses of two kinds. First, like the imposition of a tariff at the rate equal to the excess of P_b over P_c, production and consumption losses equal to the triangles EFN and ZTJ, respectively, will be incurred; these are equal, respectively, to the production loss RS and the consumption loss UV in figure 31. Second, the fact that the amount of imports NJ is now bought at the price P_b rather than P_c (as it would had a uniform tariff equal to $P_b - P_c$ been indeed imposed) involves an additional loss equal to the amount of imports times the price differential; that is, to the rectangle $NJTF$. This area is the equivalent of the trade-shift loss SU in figure 31. The combined loss from the shift from free trade to a union thus amounts to the area $EZJN$. When this loss is set against the gain of the first step—the move to free trade—the net result appears as follows: triangles NUV and JKL represent gains from the union. These are, respectively, in terms of our earlier classification, the (positive) trade-creation and consumption effects of the union. The rectangle $GRKU$, on the other hand, represents a loss: this is the (negative) trade-diversion effect, equal to the amount of pre-union imports (VL, or UK) times the excess price ($P_b - P_c$, or UG) borne now by each unit of these imports. In terms of the quantities and elasticities involved, these sums may be written as:[45]

(1) $NUV = \frac{1}{2}(P'_c - P_b)^2 \, \varepsilon Q_0$

(2) $JKL = \frac{1}{2}(P'_c - P_b)^2 \, \eta C_0$

(3) $GRKU = (P_b - P_c) M_0$

where ε is the elasticity of supply, η is the elasticity of (compensated) demand, Q_0 is pre-union production, C_0 pre-union consumption, and M_0 pre-union import of good M. The combined area of these three sums, measuring the net gain and designated by W, is thus:

(4) $\qquad W = \tfrac{1}{2}(P_c' - P_b)^2 (\varepsilon Q_0 + \eta C_0) - (P_b - P_c) M_0$

or, since $P_c' = P_c + t$

(5) $\qquad W = \tfrac{1}{2}[t - (P_b - P_c)]^2 (\varepsilon Q_0 + \eta C_0) - (P_b - P_c) M_0$

This net change could obviously be either positive or negative. We may easily verify, by use of (5), some of our former propositions regarding the likelihood of the union resulting in a gain or a loss. Thus, we may first see immediately that the higher is t, the pre-union tariff, the higher is the gain component and the more likely the result of a net gain. Second, the lower is M_0 in relation to Q_0 or C_0—the lower, that is, the pre-union relative size of imports—the lower is the loss component and the more likely a net gain. Third, the closer P_b is to P_c—the less the excess price of imports in the union partner over the price in the rest of the world—the higher will be the positive component, the lower the negative component, and the more likely a net gain. Fourth, the higher the elasticities of home supply and home demand of the import good, ε and η (in a two-good world, this also implies high elasticities for the other good), the higher the positive element and the more likely a net gain from the union. Finally, the fuller the tariff elimination in the union is, the more likely is a net gain: if the tariff were not removed completely but only partially, t in (5) would have to be replaced by $t\,[1 - (1 - r)P_b]$, where r is the proportion of the tariff removed; the positive component of (5) would then be lowered, whereas the negative element would be unaffected—provided, of course, that this partial reduction of the tariff still makes the union effective and the analysis relevant.

The measurement of welfare change by the union which appears in (5) could be extended to a many-good world, in the manner developed in the last chapter.[46] The use of this method for actual estimation of gains and losses would certainly present overwhelming difficulties, of the nature pointed out in that discussion.[47] But in the absence of a better indication, it could be cautiously adopted for a very rough evaluation of the range of gains and losses which may be expected from the union, or at least for a judgement of whether the union is more likely to result in a gain or a loss to the country.

Notes

1 An import tariff combined with an equal export subsidy would leave unaffected the *relative* price of the two goods (as well as absolute prices in a monetary economy, when the exchange-rate adjustment is carried out).

2 In principle, an opposite act, of levying particularly high duties on imports from a specific country or a group of countries, is entirely equivalent to the granting of favourable preferences: it favours one country in relation to the other. In practice, however, the imposition of extra duties (above the 'regular' scale) on imports from small sub-units of the outside world is very infrequent.

3 J. Viner (1950, p. 5).

4 If each of the foreign supply schedules is assumed to be perfectly elastic, trade in effect will take place with only one of the foreign countries unless two or more foreign prices happen to be identical.

5 Assuming that any such trade does indeed take place, following the elimination of the tariff.

6 Chapter 2, p. 37.

7 This development is due primarily to J. E. Meade (1955b, Chapter VII), and R. G. Lipsey and K. Lancaster (1956–57).

8 Lipsey and Lancaster, *ibid.*, pp. 11–12.

9 J. Viner (1950, Chapter IV, particularly pp. 41–44). Viner had made the same argument, but without resort to these terms, in a much earlier contribution (in Swedish, 1931).

10 See the discussion in Chapter 2, pp. 20–22.

11 The nature of Viner's model is discussed extensively in M. Michaely (1976). See also M. B. Krauss (1972); J. Bhagwati (1971) and the ensuing exchange between A. P. Kirman and Bhagwati (1973); and H. G. Johnson (1974).

12 Obviously, had country B—the union partner—been a cheaper source of M than country C, only trade creation would have been possible: either the pre-union position would have been that of trading with B, so that the union would have no effect (abstracting from the consumption side); or it would have been that of autarky, in which

case trade creation would take place. In this case, the welfare effects are unambiguous, since the union leads to (or does not disturb) a free-trade position.

13 Viner presented his analysis as dealing with 'the consequences of the removal, as the result of customs union, of duties which previously had operated effectively as a barrier, *partial or complete*, to import' (1950, p. 43; italics added). As has been seen, however, Viner's model is necessarily confined to the analysis of situations in which before the union either the tariff is ineffective (once more, disregarding consumption), or it acts as a *complete*, rather than partial, barrier. In fact, this is the way Viner does conduct his analysis.

14 Pointing this out, and extending the analysis to cover the consumption effect, has been a major contribution of J. E. Meade's work (1955a) to the theory of customs unions. This has been later presented in a more formal manner in the analyses of F. Gehrels (1956–7) and R. G. Lipsey (1957, 1960 and 1970).

15 See Chapter 2, section 4.

16 This is basically similar to the procedure followed in section 1 of the last chapter. But note that the method of 'equivalent variation' is used here, whereas the 'compensating variation' was looked for there (see note 1 in that section). This will help to tie in the quantitative expressions offered here, of the various factors of work, with the measurement of the welfare impact which will be developed in the last section of the present chapter.

17 The introduction of increasing marginal costs into the analysis of customs unions was another major contribution of Meade's (1955a) study. The formal analysis of a customs union with increasing costs, in the conventional three-country two-good model, is apparently found first in M. Michaely (1965).

18 This is, of course, Viner's 'partial barrier' to imports, which could not be handled in his own model. See note 13 above.

19 Once more: if imports are cheaper in B, the union partner, than in C, the union is simply a move from restricted trade to free trade.

20 Most of the following propositions are listed and discussed in J. E. Meade (1955a, Chapter VIII).

21 In the limit, when the tariff is high enough to become prohibitive, only trade creation takes place—trade diversion being impossible in the absence of imports. The net production effect must then be positive (as is, always, the consumption effect). This is the (trivial) case in which the union could only lead to a welfare gain.

In the constant costs, straight-line transformation curve model of

Viner, the demonstration would be slightly different. Here, only one component of the net production effect is possible—either it is trade creation or trade diversion. The higher the pre-union tariff rate, the more likely it is that the tariff will be prohibitive, thus leading to trade creation rather than to trade diversion following the union.

22 'Smallness' by itself is, of course, devoid of meaning. One trade flow is compared here with another assuming the transformation curve—the economy's potential—and the economy's production to be given. In general, the 'smallness' of trade must be related to the size of the economy.

23 This proposition is found in R. G. Lipsey (1960, p. 508).

24 'Similarly' in the sense that the former condition related the welfare gain to the elasticity of supply, while the present one associates it with the elasticity of demand.

25 This convention is due primarily to the contributions of J. E. Meade and R. G. Lipsey. In one place, Lipsey argues categorically that this conclusion 'is an absolutely general proposition in the theory of second best; it applies to all suboptimal positions, and customs-union theory only provides a particular example of its application' (1960, p. 506). This is supposed to be proven in the Lipsey–Lancaster analysis of the general theory of the second best. But there the contention is properly hedged: '. . . a partial preferential reduction of tariffs is more likely to raise welfare than is a complete preferential elimination of tariffs. Of course, this conclusion depends upon the specific assumptions made . . .' (R. G. Lipsey and K. Lancaster, 1956–57. p. 21).

Meade's rule is stated similarly: '. . . A partial all-round reduction by the partner countries of their duties on each other's trade is more likely to do good and less likely to do harm than is the subsequent total elimination of those duties.' (J. E. Meade, 1955a, p. 110). His discussion is based on intuitive reasoning and is presented in a rather cautious manner.

It should be noted that explicitly or implicitly, both Meade and Lipsey (despite the latter's claim of 'an absolutely general proposition') assume a *multi-good* framework of analysis.

26 This may easily be realized by the use of a diagrammatic analysis such as that of figure 24 in the last chapter, or from the formula for estimating the welfare impact of the tariff in which, we recall, the tariff rate appears in the second power. See section 1 of the last chapter.

27 Lipsey's definite conclusion seems to depend on his framework of analysis. Instead of the three groups of 'B goods', 'C goods' and 'potential B goods' introduced here, Lipsey employs just two goods—a 'B good' and a 'C good' (in addition to an 'A good'). In such

a model, Lipsey's proposition would indeed emerge unequivocally.

28 Like many other topics in the theory, this debate starts with Viner, who argued that a customs union is more likely to increase welfare 'the *less* the degree of complementarity—or the *greater* the degree of rivalry—of the member countries with respect to *protected* industries, prior to customs union.' (J. Viner, 1950, p. 51; italics in source). From an attached footnote (*ibid.*, note 11), it appears that Viner probably thought the accepted convention, 'that rivalry is a disadvantage and complementarity is an advantage in the formation of customs unions' should be reversed. H. Makower and G. Morton, in an article devoted primarily to this issue, have not addressed themselves directly to the likelihood of success, but to its extent. Their findings may be summarized by the statement that when all tariffs are prohibitive, 'Union between complementary economies is unambiguously more advantageous'; otherwise, '*if* two Unions both offer a loss, the one offering the smaller loss is the Union between the more complementary pair of countries.' (1953, pp. 40–41). Meade's proposition is that 'the formation of a customs union is more likely to lead to a net increase in economic welfare if the economies of the partner countries are actually very competitive or similar but potentially very complementary or dissimilar' (1955, p. 107). Lipsey's contention, similar to Viner's, is 'that customs unions are likely to cause losses when the countries involved are complementary *in the range of commodities that are protected by tariffs*' (1960, p. 498; italics in source). Meade's proposition seems to have become the accepted convention in the literature.

29 This interpretation probably applies to Meade's definition of the countries being 'actually very competitive'. He illustrates by the following example: 'Consider two countries, one specially suited to produce primary products and the other to produce manufactured goods. The primary producer has by protection developed some high-cost manufactures and the manufacturing country has by protection developed some high-cost domestic agriculture. As a result their actual structures are rather similar—both are producing wheat and both clothing'. In this example, the two countries could hardly be considered 'very competitive' in any reasonable sense of this term: relative prices must differ considerably between the two countries. Nor, it should be noted, are the economies 'rather similar' in structure: even if both impose prohibitive tariffs, and production is carried out in both at their respective autarky positions, the weights of the two industries (manufacturing and agriculture) should be very different in the two economies if demand conditions are roughly the same, or at least do not offset the differences in production possibilities. All we can infer from this example is that the home country does not specialize as it

would under free trade but diversifies its production by the imposition of high tariffs.

Lipsey's interpretation of Viner's 'competitiveness' or 'rivalry' is that of having great 'degree of overlapping between the class of commodities produced under tariff protection' (1960, p. 498). This notion is most probably framed in the constant-cost model, with which Lipsey (like Viner) works. It implies a situation in which the tariff system has led to the existence of domestic production (hence, in the constant-cost framework, to the complete absence of imports) in many industries. Since in each such industry trade creation is the only possible production effect—trade diversion being ruled out by the absence of imports—the likelihood of gain from the union is indeed higher when the number of such industries is large. But to refer to the home country in this situation as being 'actually competitive' with the partner country would be a confusing application of this term.

30 The introduction of variable international prices may raise additional questions, require rather elaborate models, and often result in long taxonomical exercises. Most of these will be avoided here, and only a few simple qualifications of the former analysis will be presented. Much of the theory of customs unions under variable prices has been developed in recent years, primarily in the treatises of J. Vanek (1965) and M. C. Kemp (1969) and the papers of R. Mundell (1964), S. W. Arndt (1968, 1969) and J. R. Melvin (1969).

31 Note that here free trade is still an optimum position!

32 In the constant prices analysis, this assumption was not required. Trade with both countries (B and C) could take place only in the exceptional event of both foreign countries having precisely the same (constant) price—in which the (pre-union) distribution of A's trade between B and C would be a matter of accident.

33 This is inevitable because the situation analyzed here, we recall, is that of a 'free-trade area', in which tariffs of the members on imports from non-members remain *unchanged*. In a full-fledged customs union, where tariffs of members on imports from non-union countries are changed (presumably some of them upward but others downward), the result could be different.

34 See Chapter 2, section 2.

35 For a discussion devoted primarily to this issue, see J. Spraos (1964).

36 This has long been recognized as a possible motivation of, and benefit from, the establishment of a union. It is discussed extensively by Viner (1950, particularly pp. 55–58).

37 See R. Mundell (1964). This proposition applies, it should be

noticed, to the 'free-trade area' we have been analyzing most of the time; that is, to a situation in which external tariffs (on imports from non-member countries) remain unchanged. And the terms-of-trade gain discussed here is separate from the effects of a cooperative change in the union's external tariffs, which has been discussed in the earlier point.

38 This situation is assumed, and the emerging benefit of a customs union demonstrated, in separate but basically similar analyses by H. G. Johnson (1965d), C. A. Cooper and B. R. Massell (1965), and J. Bhagwati (1969, Ch. 15, particularly pp. 351–355). Johnson (p. 258) refers to what is simply termed here external effects as a 'collective preference for industrial production, in the sense that the electorate is willing to spend real resources through government action in order to make the volume of industrial production and employment larger than it would be under free international competition'. Similarly, Cooper and Massell assumed (p. 402) 'a social preference for particular types of economic activity—which we shall call 'industry'—compared with other forms of activity;' whereas Bhagwati terms the preference for industry a 'modified utility function' (p. 351).

39 Johnson (*op. cit.*, p. 263) assumes that these institutional constraints prevent the introduction of an *export* subsidy. In the circumstances analyzed, however, a *production* subsidy will have an identical effect with that of an export subsidy. Hence, the constraint has to be interpreted more widely, to cover the exclusion of production as well as export subsidies.

40 This is probably the main point emerging from the analysis of Cooper and Massell (*op. cit.*). In today's major meaningul customs union—the European Economic Community—this must be a minor aspect. It probably was much more significant in many trade and payments agreements conducted after World War II, in which trade preferences were granted not by removal of tariffs but by discriminatory relaxation of import quotas and exchange allocations.

41 In the literature of customs unions, and probably even more in public debates of the issue, much attention is paid to the impact of the union on efficiency, technology, and the like—sometimes termed (see B. Balassa, 1962, p. 14) as 'dynamic' factors. These refer either to factors classified here as 'external' effects; or to the possible impact of production and specialization on the production process (i.e., on the transformation curve itself). In either case, nothing specific to the customs-union issue may be added to the general discussion of these effects (see, respectively, Chapter 2, section 5 and Chapter 3, section 2). It should be recalled, again, that whenever such factors are present, free trade is no longer an optimal policy.

42 See Chapter 5, section 1.

43 When c_3c_3 is to the right of $c'c'$, as it is shown here, the net result of the union is certainly a gain. When c_3c_3 is to the left of $c'c'$, there could still be a gain: home prices before the union are those represented by tt, rather than by $c'c'$; whereas with the union, the home price is equal to the international price (bb). Hence, a budget-restraint line *left* of $c'c'$ within a certain range would be sufficient to secure the welfare level reached under the restricted trade (this reflects, of course, the consumption loss of the tariff).

44 See, again, the analysis in section 1 of the last chapter, where this is discussed in the shift from figure 23 to figure 24. A measurement of the losses and gains of a customs union in a way basically similar to that of figure 32 has first been provided by D. D. Humphrey and C. E. Ferguson (1960). See also M. O. Clement, R. L. Pfister, and K. J. Rothwell (1967).

45 See again Chapter 5, section 1.

46 See Chapter 5, sections 2 and 3.

47 Besides these difficulties, we have of course to recall that the measurement is based on highly simplifying assumptions. One of these is that the country is small—international prices are given and un-changed. The use of principally the same method for the measurement of welfare gains and losses for an economy whose trade does effect its import price is presented in H. G. Johnson (1962, pp. 63–74); the resulting measurement formulation is, of course, more complicated than the one developed here. Johnson discusses also the measurement of welfare changes in the union as a whole, as well as in the whole world. The latter issue—measurement of the effect of the union on the world's welfare—occupies a considerable part of J. E. Meade's treatise (1955a). Meade's measure, based on a cardinal-utility approach, amounts to summing up as positive changes the new trade flows created (anywhere in the world) by the union, and as negative changes reductions in pre-union trade flows, each flow multiplied by the rate of tariff duty applying to it before the union; the net outcome then measures the union's effect on world welfare. As either an *ex-ante* or *ex-post* measure, Meade's method would probably face at least as much difficulty in actual application as the 'welfare triangles' method.

References

This list consists mostly, but not exclusively, of works cited in the text.

Anderson, J. A. (1970), 'General equilibrium and the effective rate of protection', *Journal of Political Economy*, Vol. 78.

Arndt, S. W. (1968), 'On discriminatory vs. non-preferential tariff policies', *Economic Journal*, Vol. 78.

Arndt, S. W. (1969). 'Customs union and the theory of tariffs', *American Economic Review*, Vol. 59.

Arrow, K. J. (1962), 'The economic implications of learning by doing', *Review of Economic Studies*, Vol. 29.

Balassa, B. (1962), *The Theory of Economic Integration*, George Allen & Unwin.

Balassa, B. (1965), 'Tariff protection in industrial countries: an evaluation', *Journal of Political Economy*, Vol. 73.

Balassa, B. (1967), *Trade Liberalization among Industrial Countries: Objectives and Alternatives*, McGraw-Hill.

Balassa, B. and associates (1971), *The Structure of Protection in Developing Countries*, Johns Hopkins Press.

Balassa, B. and Kreinin, M. E. (1967), 'Trade liberalization under the "Kennedy Round": the static effects', *Review of Economics and Statistics*, Vol. 49.

Balassa, B. and Schydlowsky, D. M. (1968), 'Effective tariffs, domestic cost of foreign exchange, and the equilibrium exchange rate', *Journal of Political Economy*, Vol. 76.

Balassa, B. and Schydlowsky, D. M. (1972), 'Domestic resource costs and effective protection once again', *Journal of Political Economy*, Vol. 80.

Baldwin, R. E. (1948), 'Equilibrium in international trade: a diagrammatic analysis', *Quarterly Journal of Economics*, Vol. 62.

Baldwin, R. E. (1952), 'The new welfare economics and gains in international trade', *Quarterly Journal of Economics*, Vol. 66.

Baldwin, R. E. (1970), *Non-Tariff Distortions in International Trade*, George Allen & Unwin.

Barber, C. L. (1955), 'Canadian tariff policy', *Canadian Journal of Economics and Political Science*, Vol. 21.

Bardhan, P. K. (1965), 'Optimum accumulation and international trade', *Review of Economic Studies*, Vol. 32.

Bardhan, P. K. (1966), 'Equilibrium growth in the international economy', *Quarterly Journal of Economics*, Vol. 79.

Barker, T. S. and Han, S. S. (1971), 'Effective rates of protection for United Kingdom production", *Economic Journal*, Vol. 81.

Basevi, G. (1966), 'The United States tariff structure: estimates of effective rates of protection of United States industries and industrial labor', *Review of Economics and Statistics*, Vol. 48.

Basevi, G. (1968), 'The restrictive effect of the US tariff and its welfare value', *American Economic Review*, Vol. 58.

Batra, R. and Pattanaik, P. K. (1970), 'Domestic distortions and the gains from trade', *Economic Journal*, Vol. 80.

Bhagwati, J. N. (1958), 'Immiserizing growth: a geometrical note', *Review of Economic Studies*, Vol. 25.

Bhagwati, J. N. (1965), 'On the equivalence of tariffs and quotas', in R. E. Baldwin et al., *Trade, Growth and the Balance of Payments*, Rand McNally and North-Holland.

Bhagwati, J. (1968a), *The Theory and Practice of Commercial Policy: Departures from Unified Exchange Rates*, Princeton University, International Finance Section Special Papers in International Economics No. 8.

Bhagwati, J. N. (1968b), 'Distortions and immiserizing growth: a generalization', *Review of Economic Studies*, Vol. 35.

Bhagwati, J. (1969), *Trade, Tariffs and Growth*, MIT Press.

Bhagwati, J. N. (1971a), 'The generalized theory of distortions and welfare', in J. N. Bhagwati, R. W. Jones, R. A. Mundell, and J. Vanek (eds), *Trade, Balance of Payments and Growth*, North-Holland.

Bhagwati, J. (1971b), 'Trade-diverting customs unions and welfare-improvement: a clarification', *Economic Journal*, Vol. 81.

Bhagwati, J. N. and Desai, P. (1970), *India: Planning for Industrialization*, Oxford University Press.

Bhagwati, J. and Johnson, H. G. (1960), 'Notes on some controversies in the theory of international trade', *Economic Journal*, Vol. 70.

Bhagwati, J. N. and Johnson, H. G. (1961), 'A generalized theory of the effects of tariffs on the terms of trade', *Oxford Economic Papers*, Vol. 13.

Bhagwati, J. N. and Kemp, M. C. (1969), 'Ranking of tariffs under monopoly power in trade', *Quarterly Journal of Economics*, Vol. 83.

Bhagwati, J. N. and Ramaswami, V. K. (1963), 'Domestic distortions, tariffs and the theory of optimum subsidy', *Journal of Political Economy*, Vol. 71.

Bhagwati, J. N., Ramaswami, V. K. and Srinivasan, T. N. (1969), 'Domestic distortions, tariffs, and the theory of optimum subsidy: some further results', *Journal of Political Economy*, Vol. 77.

Bhagwati, J. N. and Srinivasan, T. N. (1971), 'The theory of wage differentials: production response and factor price equalization', *Journal of International Economics*, Vol. 1.

Bhagwati, J. N. and Srinivasan, T. N. (1973), 'The general equilibrium theory of effective protection and resource allocation', *Journal of International Economics*, Vol. 3.

Bickerdike, C. F. (1906), 'The theory of incipient taxes', *Economic Journal*, Vol. 16.

Bruno, M. (1963), *Interdependence, Resource Use and Structural Change in Israel*, Bank of Israel.

Bruno, M. (1972), 'Domestic resource costs and effective protection: clarification and synthesis', *Journal of Political Economy*, Vol. 80.

Bruno, M. (1973), 'Protection and tariff change under general equilibrium', *Journal of International Economics*, Vol. 3.

Clements, M. O., Pfister, R. L., and Rothwell, K. J. (1967), *Theoretical Issues in International Economics*, Houghton Mifflin.

Cooper, C. A. and Massell, B. F. (1965a), 'Toward a general theory of customs unions for developing countries', *Journal of Political Economy*, Vol. 73.

Cooper, C. A. and Massell, B. F. (1965b), 'A new look at customs union theory', *Economic Journal*, Vol. 75.

Corden, W. M. (1957a), 'The calculation of the cost of protection', *Economic Record*, Vol. 33.

Corden, W. M. (1957b) 'Tariffs, subsidies and the terms of trade', *Economica*, Vol. 24.

Corden, W. M. (1966a), 'The structure of a tariff system and the effective protective rate', *Journal of Political Economy*, Vol. 74.

Corden, W. M., (1966b), 'The effective protective rate, the uniform tariff equivalent and the average tariff', *Economic Record*, Vol. 42.

Corden, W. M. (1967a), 'Monopoly, tariffs and subsidies', *Economica*, Vol. 34.

Corden, W. M. (1967b), 'Protection and foreign investment', *Economic Record*, Vol. 43.

Corden, W. M. (1971a), *The Theory of Protection*, Oxford University Press.

Corden, W. M. (1971b), 'The effects of trade on the rate of growth', in J. N. Bhagwati, R. W. Jones, R. A. Mundell, and J. Vanek, (eds), *Trade, Balance of Payments and Growth*, North-Holland.

Dardis, R. (1967), 'Intermediate goods and the gain from trade', *Review of Economics and Statistics*, Vol. 49.

Ethier, W., (1972), 'Input substitution and the concept of the effective rate of protection', *Journal of Political Economy*, Vol. 80.

Evans, H. D. (1971), 'Effects of protection in a general equilibrium framework', *Review of Economics and Statistics*, Vol. 53.

Findlay, R. F. (1970), *Trade and Specialization*, Penguin Modern Economics.

Findlay, R. and Grubert, H. (1959), 'Factor intensities, technological progress and the terms of trade', *Oxford Economic Papers*, Vol. 11.

Finger, J. M. (1969), 'Substitution and the effective rate of protection', *Journal of Political Economy*, Vol. 77.

Flanders, M. J. (1964), 'Prebisch on protectionism: an evaluation', *Economic Journal*, Vol. 74.

Flanders, M. J. (1965), 'Measuring protection and predicting trade diversion', *Journal of Political Economy*, Vol. 73.

Fleming, M. (1956), 'The optimal tariff from an international standpoint', *Review of Economics and Statistics*, Vol. 38.

Gehrels, F. (1956–57), 'Customs unions from a single country viewpoint', *Review of Economic Studies*, Vol. 24.

Graaff, J.de V., (1949–50), 'On optimum tariff structures', *Review of Economic Studies*, Vol. 17.

Grubel, H. G. and Johnson, H. G., (eds) (1971), *Effective Tariff Protection*, GATT and the Graduate Institute of International Studies.

Guisinger, S. E. (1969), 'Negative value added and the theory of effective protection', *Quarterly Journal of Economics*, Vol. 83.

Haberler, G. (1936), *The Theory of International Trade*, William Hodge & Company.

Haberler, G. (1950), 'Some problems in the pure theory of international trade', *Economic Journal*, Vol. 60.

Hagen, E. E. (1958), 'An economic justification of protectionism', *Quarterly Journal of Economics*, Vol. 72.

Halevi N. (1969), 'Economic policy discussion and research in Israel', *American Economic Review*, Vol. 59.

Hause, J. C. (1966), 'The welfare costs of disequilibrium exchange rates', *Journal of Political Economy*, Vol. 74.

Holzman, F. D. (1969), 'Comparison of different forms of trade barriers', *Review of Economics and Statistics*, Vol. 51.

Humphrey, D. D. (1969), 'Measuring the effective rate of protection: direct and indirect effects', *Journal of Political Economy*, Vol. 77.

Humphrey, D. D. and C. E. Ferguson (1960), 'The domestic and world benefits of a customs union', *Economia Internazionale*, Vol. 13.

Johnson, H. G. (1958), 'The gain from freer trade with Europe: an estimate', *Manchester School*, Vol. 26.

Johnson, H. G. (1960), 'The cost of protection and the scientific tariff', *Journal of Political Economy*, Vol. 68.

Johnson, H. G. (1962), *Money, Trade and Economic Growth*, George Allen & Unwin.

Johnson, H. G. (1965a), 'The theory of tariff structure, with special reference to world trade and development', in H. G. Johnson and P. B. Kenen, *Trade and Development*, Librairie Droz.

Johnson, H. G. (1965b), 'The costs of protection and self-sufficiency', *Quarterly Journal of Economics*, Vol. 79.

Johnson, H. G. (1965c), 'Optimal trade intervention in the presence of domestic distortions', in R. E. Baldwin et al. *Trade, Growth and the Balance of Payments*, Rand McNally and North-Holland.

Johnson, H. G. (1965d), 'An economic theory of protectionism, tariff bargaining, and the formation of customs unions', *Journal of Political Economy*, Vol. 73.

Johnson, H. G. (1966a), 'The neo-classical one-sector growth model: a geometrical exposition and extension to a monetary economy', *Economica*, Vol. 33.

Johnson, H. G. (1966b), 'The welfare costs of exchange-rate stabilization', *Journal of Political Economy*, Vol. 74.

Johnson, H. G. (1967), 'The possibility of income losses from increased efficiency or factor accumulation in the presence of tariffs', *Economic Journal*, Vol. 77.

Johnson, H. G. (1968), 'The gain from exploiting monopoly or monopsony power in international trade', *Economica*, Vol. 35.

Johnson, H. G. (1969), 'The theory of effective protection and preferences', *Economica*, Vol. 36.

Johnson, H. G. (1970), 'A new view of the infant industry argument', in I. A. McDougall and R. H. Snape, (eds), *Studies in International Economics*, North-Holland.

Johnson, H. G. (1971), 'Effective protection and general equilibrium theory', Ch. 15 in *Aspects of the Theory of Tariffs*, George Allen & Unwin.

Johnson, H. G. (1974), 'Trade-diverting customs union: a comment', *Economic Journal*, Vol. 84.

Johnson, H. G. and Grubel, H. G. (1967), 'Nominal tariffs, indirect taxes and effective rates of protection: the Common Market countries 1959', *Economic Journal*, Vol. 77.

Jones, R. W. (1971), 'Effective protection and substitution', *Journal of International Economics*, Vol. 1.

Kaldor, N. (1940), 'A note on tariffs and the terms of trade', *Economica*, Vol. 7.

Kemp, M. C. (1962), 'The gain from international trade', *Economic Journal*, Vol. 72.

Kemp, M. C. (1969), *A Contribution to the General Equilibrium Theory of Preferential Trading*, North-Holland.

Khang, C. (1973), 'Factor substitution in the theory of effective protection: a general equilibrium analysis', *Journal of International Economics*, Vol. 3.

Kirman, A. P. and Bhagwati, J. N. (1973), 'Trade diverting customs unions and welfare improvement: an interchange', *Economic Journal*, Vol. 83.

Kleiman, E. and Michaely, M. (1973), 'The measurement of welfare loss from tariffs: some further explorations', Institute for International Economic Studies (University of Stockholm) Seminar Paper No. 36.

Krauss, M. B. (1972), 'Recent developments in customs union theory: an interpretive survey', *Journal of Economic Literature*, Vol. 10.

Krueger, A. O. (1966), 'Some economic costs of exchange control: the Turkish case', *Journal of Political Economy*, Vol. 74.

Leamer, E. E. and Stern, R. M. (1970), *Quantitative International Economics*, Allyn & Bacon.

Leith, J. C. (1968), 'Substitution and supply elasticities in calculating the effective protective rate', *Quarterly Journal of Economics*, Vol. 82.

Lerner, A. P. (1936), 'The symmetry between import and export taxes', *Economica*, Vol. 3.

Lipsey, R. G. (1957), 'The theory of customs unions: trade diversion and welfare', *Economica*, Vol. 24.

Lipsey, R. G. (1960), 'The theory of customs unions: a general survey', *Economic Journal*, Vol. 70.

Lipsey, R. G. (1970), *The Theory of Customs Unions: A General Equilibrium Analysis*, Weidenfeld and Nicolson.

Lipsey, R. G. and Lancaster, K. (1956–57), 'The general theory of second best', *Review of Economic Studies*, Vol. 24.

Magee, S. P. (1973), 'Factor market distortions, production, and trade: a survey', *Oxford Economic Papers*, Vol. 25.

Makower, H. and Morton, G. (1953), 'A contribution towards a theory of customs unions', *Economic Journal*, Vol. 63.

Meade, J. E. (1955a), *The Theory of Customs Unions*, North-Holland Publishing Company.

Meade, J. E. (1955b), *Trade and Welfare*, Oxford University Press.

Melvin, J. R. (1969), 'Comments on the theory of customs unions', *Manchester School of Economic and Social Studies*, Vol. 37.

Michaely, M. (1965), 'On customs unions and the gains from trade', *Economic Journal*, Vol. 75.

Michaely, M. (1967), 'A note on tariffs and subsidies', *American Economic Review*, Vol. 57.

Michaely, M. (1971), *Israel's Foreign Exchange Rate System*, Maurice Falk Institute for Economic Research in Israel.

Michaely, M. (1975), 'The welfare loss of negative value added', *Journal of International Economics*, Vol. 5.

Michaely, M. (1976), 'The assumptions of Jacob Viner's theory of customs unions', *Journal of International Economics*, Vol. 6.

Mundell, R. A. (1957), 'International trade and factor mobility', *American Economic Review*, Vol. 47

Naya, S. and Anderson, J. (1969), 'Substitution and two concepts of effective rate of protection', *American Economic Review*, Vol. 59.

Nurkse, R. (1953), *Some Problems of Capital Formation in Underdeveloped Countries*, Oxford University Press.

Ohlin, B. (1931), 'Protection and non-competing groups', *Weltwirtschaftliches Archiv*, Vol. 33.

Ohlin B. (1933), *Inter-regional and International Trade*, Harvard University Press.

Ohlin. B. (1943), *Utrikeshandel och handelspolitik* (3rd edition), Bokförlaget Natur och Kultur.

Oniki, H. and Uzawa, H. (1965), 'Patterns of trade and investment in a dynamic model of international trade', *Review of Economic Studies*, Vol. 32.

Patinkin, D. (1963), 'Demand curves and consumer's surplus', in C. F. Christ et al., *Measurement in Economics*, Stanford University.

Posner, M. V. (1961), 'International trade and technical changes', *Oxford Economic Papers*, Vol. 13.

Ramaswami, V. K. and Srinivasan, T. N. (1971), 'Tariff structure and resource allocation in the presence of factor substitution', in J. N. Bhagwati, R. W. Jones, R. A. Mundell, and J. Vanek (eds), *Trade, Balance of Payments, and Growth*, North-Holland.

Ray, A. (1973), 'Non-traded inputs and effective protection: a general equilibrium analysis', *Journal of International Economics*, Vol. 3.

Rybczynski, T. M. (1955), 'Factor endowment and relative commodity prices', *Economica*, Vol. 22.

Samuelson, P. A. (1938), 'Welfare economics and international trade', *American Economic Review*, Vol. 28.

Samuelson, P. A. (1939), 'The gains from international trade', *Canadian Journal of Economics and Political Science*, Vol. 5.

Samuelson, P. A. (1962), 'The gains from international trade once again', *Economic Journal*, Vol. 72.

Scitovsky, T. de (1942), 'A reconsideration of the theory of tariffs', *Review of Economic Studies*, Vol. 10.

Snape, R. H. (1969), 'Sugar: costs of protection and taxation', *Economica*, Vol. 36.

Soligo, R. and Stern, J. J. (1965), 'Tariff protection, import substitution, and investment efficiency', *Pakistan Development Review*, Vol. 5.

Spraos, J. (1964), 'The condition for a trade-creating customs union', *Economic Journal*, Vol. 74.

Stolper, W. F. and Samuelson, P. A. (1941), 'Protection and real wages', *Review of Economic Studies*, Vol. 9.

Tan, A. H. H. (1970), 'Differential tariffs, negative value-added and the theory of effective protection', *American Economic Review*, Vol. 60.

Travis, W. P. (1964), *The Theory of Trade and Protection*, Harvard University Press.

Vanek, J. (1965), *General Equilibrium of International Discrimination*, Harvard University Press.

Viner, J. (1931), 'The most-favoured-nation clause', *Index*, Vol. 6 (in Swedish).

Viner, J. (1950), *The Customs Union Issue*, Carnegie Endowment for International Peace.

Viner, J. (1951), *International Economics*, The Free Press.

Wemelsfelder, J. (1960), 'The short-term effect of the lowering of import duties in Germany', *Economic Journal*, Vol. 70.

Index